Conducting Interviews
Child Victims of Abuse
Witnesses of Crime

This book is a practical and thoughtful guide for the forensic interview of children, presenting a synthesis of the empirical and theoretical knowledge necessary to understand the account of child victims of abuse or witnesses of crime.

It is a complex task to interview children who are suspected of being abused in order to gather their stories, requiring the mastery of many skills and knowledge. This book is a practical one in that constant links are made between the results of the research and their relevance for the interventions made when interviewing child victims of abuse or witnesses of crime and in understanding their maltreatment. This book also presents in a detailed and concrete way the revised version of the National Institute of Child Health and Human Development (NICHD-R) Protocol, a forensic structured interview guide empirically supported by numerous studies carried out in different countries. The step-by-step explanations are illustrated with a verbatim interview with a child, as well as other tools to help the interviewer to prepare and handle an efficient and supportive interview.

Conducting Interviews with Child Victims of Abuse and Witnesses of Crime is essential reading for stakeholders in the justice, social and health systems as well as anyone likely to receive allegations from children such as educators or daycare staff. Although the NICHD-R Protocol is intended for forensic interviewers, the science behind its development and application is relevant to all professionals working with children.

Mireille Cyr is a licensed psychologist and a professor in the Department of Psychology at the Université de Montréal. Among other research in child sexual abuse, she has conducted studies on the French version of the National Institute of Child Health and Human Development Protocol that is now taught in Québec, Canada and in many French-speaking countries in Europe. She is the scientific director of CRIPCAS, a research center dedicated to sexual abuses and marital problems and co-holder of the Marie-Vincent Foundation Chair on Sexual Abuse Against Children. In the last 20 years, she has trained police officers and other psychosocial and judicial professionals, mostly in Europe and Canada. She is the author of numerous books, chapters and articles and the impact of her work has been recognized by numerous awards. She is a member of the Royal Society of Canada.

Conducting Interviews with Child Victims of Abuse and Witnesses of Crime

A Practical Guide

Mireille Cyr

Routledge
Taylor & Francis Group

LONDON AND NEW YORK

Cover image: © Thanasis Zovoilis / Getty Images

First published 2022
by Routledge
4 Park Square, Milton Park, Abingdon, Oxon OX14 4RN

and by Routledge
605 Third Avenue, New York, NY 10158

Routledge is an imprint of the Taylor & Francis Group, an informa business

British Library Cataloguing-in-Publication Data
A catalogue record for this book is available from the British Library

Library of Congress Cataloging-in-Publication Data
Names: Cyr, Mireille, 1955– author.
Title: Conducting interviews with child victims of abuse and witnesses of crime : a practical guide / Mireille Cyr.
Description: Abingdon, Oxon ; New York, NY : Routledge, 2022. | Includes bibliographical references and index.
Identifiers: LCCN 2021043338 (print) | LCCN 2021043339 (ebook) | ISBN 9781032208152 (hbk) | ISBN 9781032208039 (pbk) | ISBN 9781003265351 (ebk)
Subjects: LCSH: Child abuse. | Interviewing in child abuse. | Child witnesses.
Classification: LCC HV6626.5 .C95 2022 (print) | LCC HV6626.5 (ebook) | DDC 362.76—dc23/eng/20211103
LC record available at https://lccn.loc.gov/2021043338
LC ebook record available at https://lccn.loc.gov/2021043339

ISBN: 978-1-032-20815-2 (hbk)
ISBN: 978-1-032-20803-9 (pbk)
ISBN: 978-1-003-26535-1 (ebk)

DOI: 10.4324/9781003265351

Typeset in Sabon
by Apex CoVantage, LLC

Originally published in France as:
Recueillir la parole de l'enfant témoin ou victime. De la théorie à la pratique
By Mireille Cyr
© Dunod 2019, Malakoff
© English Translation, Mireille Cyr
This English language edition is an adaptation of the original French language edition

To all professionals dedicated to the protection of abused children

Contents

Foreword

When Kathy Sternberg first mooted the value of a structured investigative interview protocol in the mid-1990s, she was motivated by frustration regarding the failure of training focused on the communication of basic principles to forensic interviewers, but her suggestion was initially greeted skeptically by the other members of our team – Yael Orbach, Irit Hershkowitz, Phillip Esplin, and me. However, we had no better idea and were so set about creating the guidance – first for the pre-substantive phase of the forensic interview (Sternberg et al., 1997) and then for the entire interview (Orbach et al., 2000). The value of what became the NICHD (National Institute of Child Health and Human Development) Protocol was quickly apparent: Interviewers trained to use the NICHD Protocol began to elicit more freely recalled information from alleged victims (Orbach et al., 2000) and began to feel more confident assessing the validity of the allegations or suspicions under investigation. So clear were the changes in practice that the Israeli Department of Youth Investigation, which had been a crucial and valued collaborator in our research on child witnesses for many years, mandated use of the NICHD Protocol in all investigative interviews of alleged abuse victims in 1996, prompting attempts by our team to study its utility in other cultural and legal contexts. Indeed, since the end of the twentieth century, published research on investigative interviews of children has overwhelmingly focused on the value of structured protocols, principally the NICHD Protocol (Lamb et al., 2008) and later the Revised NICHD Protocol (Lamb et al., 2018), and the number of teams undertaking such research has increased, with Mireille Cyr's group at the University of Montreal and the National Police School of Quebec prominent among them. From the time of their first publication in 2009 (Cyr & Lamb, 2009), Cyr and her colleagues have published innovative and original research on the factors affecting interview quality and children's informativeness that have greatly enriched the literature.

As more agencies have sought to take advantage of that research and implement the use of the NICHD Protocol (La Rooy et al., 2015), however, we have collectively become aware of the difficulties associated with training interviewers to conduct effective investigative interviews. Successfully adopting evidence-based practice requires extensive and intensive training, without which changes in practice tend to be short-lived (Lamb, 2016). For the last two decades, Mireille Cyr has trained interviewers in many French-speaking countries, developing in the process a unique and invaluable understanding of the techniques most likely to effect lasting change. Her insights were distilled into a book titled *Recueillir la parole de l'enfant témoin ou victime: De la théorie à la pratique* (2014; second edition in 2019), which complemented her training courses and specialized supervisory activities, and I am delighted that she has now updated and expanded that book for English-speaking readers. The present book provides a succinct explanation of the rationale underlying the structure and components of the NICHD Protocol and details the exercises and techniques that are critically important for those who are striving to acquire expertise or assist others in doing so. As such, the book is an essential adjunct to and a component of any intensive training program designed to assist interviewers in adapting their practices. It is a unique resource and will fill an important gap in the literature. I am delighted to see it made available for a wide audience.

Michael E. Lamb
University of Cambridge

References

Cyr M. (2014). *Recueillir la parole de l'enfant témoin ou victime: De la théorie à la pratique*, Paris, France, Dunod éditeurs.

Cyr M. (2019). *Recueillir la parole de l'enfant témoin ou victime: De la théorie à la pratique* (2e ed.), Paris, France, Dunod éditeurs.

Cyr M., Lamb M. E. (2009). "Assessing the effectiveness of the NICHD investigative interview protocol when interviewing French-speaking alleged victims of child sexual abuse in Quebec", *Child Abuse & Neglect*, 33(5), 257–268.

Lamb M. E. (2016). "Difficulties translating research on forensic interview practices to practitioners: Finding water, leading horses, but can we get them to drink?" *American Psychologist*, 71, 710–718.

Lamb M. E., Hershkowitz I., Orbach Y., Esplin P. W. (2008). *Tell me what happened: Structured investigative interviews of child victims and witnesses*, Chichester and Hoboken, NJ, Wiley.

Lamb M. E., Brown D. A., Hershkowitz I., Orbach Y., Esplin P. W. (2018). *Tell me what happened: Questioning children about abuse* (2nd ed.), Hoboken, NJ, John Wiley & Sons Inc.

La Rooy D., Brubacher S. P., Aromäki-Stratos A., Cyr M., Hershkowitz I., Korkman J., Myklebust T., Naka M., Peixoto K.E., Roberts K.P., Steward H., Lamb M.E. (2015). "The NICHD Protocol: A review of an internationally-used evidence-based tool for training child forensic interviewers", *Journal of Criminological Research, Policy and Practice*, 1(2), 76–89.

Orbach Y., Hershkowitz I., Lamb M. E., Sternberg K. J., Esplin P. W., Horowitz D. (2000). "Assessing the value of structured protocols for forensic interviews of alleged child abuse victims", *Child Abuse & Neglect*, 24, 733–752.

Sternberg K. J., Lamb M. E., Hershkowitz I., Yudilevitch L., Orbach Y., Esplin P. W., Hovav M. (1997). "Effects of introductory style on children's abilities to describe experiences of sexual abuse", *Child Abuse & Neglect*, 21(11), 1133–1146.

Acknowledgments

I didn't know when in 1999, I attended a training session in Salt Lake City organized by Michael E. Lamb and his colleagues that this meeting would greatly influence my future research and training activities.

I would like to sincerely thank Michael E. Lamb for his generous support over the years, as well as his encouragement and help in editing this book.

I thank both Michael E. Lamb and Irit Hershkowitz for our regular discussions and for all the rigor and hard work they and their colleagues put into developing the NICHD Protocol and its revised version. Thank you also for giving my first research team (Jacinthe Dion, Nancy Richard, Roxane Perreault, and Pierre McDuff) access to your colleagues, knowledge, and resources to guide our first steps in applying the NICHD Protocol. We have inherited your passion for the development of empirically supported investigative techniques for working with children.

In the last twenty years, my journey was also facilitated by many people who paved the way for research projects but also for the application of the NICHD Protocol in the field. My continued and sustained collaboration with the École nationale de police du Québec (National Police School of Quebec) and the many police organizations in Quebec has made it possible to pursue research projects and disseminate this knowledge. My collaboration with many investigators and trainers in Quebec and in Europe, as well as forensic experts, child psychiatrists and psychologists, lawyers, and other professionals, has enriched my comprehension of the difficulties encountered when conducting investigative interviews with children and nourished both my research and training activities. They are all exceptional people, really concerned about the well-being of children. I would like to thank the Marie-Vincent Foundation, which subsidizes the Research Chair on Child Sexual Abuse, as well as all the granting organizations that have funded my research projects (CIHR, SSHRC, FRQSC, Quebec Ministry of Justice). This research could not have been carried out without the active participation of many master's and doctoral students, research assistants, police officers, social workers, and of course, parents and their children. Thanks also to Routledge and Éditions Dunod for their efficiency in the production of the book. Thanks to my family for their support and love.

Introduction

This book presents a synthesis of the empirical and theoretical knowledge necessary to understand the accounts of child victims of abuse or witnesses of crime. It presents in a detailed and concrete way the revised version of the National Institute of Child Health and Human Development (NICHD) Protocol, a protocol empirically supported by numerous studies carried out in different countries. This book is intended for stakeholders in the justice, social, and health systems, as well as anyone likely to receive allegations from children (e.g., educators, daycare staff). Thus, it is aimed at investigators from police services, social workers who work in child protection organizations, and child psychiatrists, doctors, and psychologists who receive disclosures from children as part of their professional practice and who may be called upon to provide psycho-legal expertise or to assess the credibility of these children's accounts. This book will also be useful to prosecutors and judges who will have to deal with these children when legal proceedings are initiated. In fact, all university students of criminology, law, psychology, social work, or psychoeducation who are interested in the question of abused children will benefit from this book. This book is innovative by the constant links that are made between the results of the research and their relevance for the interventions made to the field. This book is intended to be a practical and thoughtful guide for children's testimony.

Seeking the truth in cases of allegedly abused children is always a delicate task, and the line between good and bad practice is very narrow. Most of the time, in the case of an investigative interview, the investigator must, during a single meeting, gain the trust of a child who is most often suspicious of adults, given the child's relationship with abusive or untrustworthy adults. In addition to having to deal with the child's reluctance, the investigator must collect as much information as possible about the events that have occurred without influencing the child on the nature of the details that should be reported. The interviewer is quickly confronted with the limited capacity of the children to understand the goals of the interview and to give detailed accounts, accounts having a logical structure and including all the information, allowing a good grasp of the alleged event.

Children's abilities to accurately report events that may have happened to them vary with their age. It is, therefore, important to have a good knowledge of these variations in order to be able to adapt both the questions and the content sought. Thus, it is not enough for the interviewer to have very good interpersonal skills; s/he must also have knowledge of children's memory and the questions and interactions that make them more suggestible. In addition, the interviewer must be able to assess the capacities of children according to their stage of development. Based on this knowledge, the interviewer will be able to adapt more flexibly to each child since each meeting is unique and brings specific challenges.

This work is intended above all to be a practical guide on the conduct of interviews or assessments with children presumed victims of maltreatment. As the majority of research on interviews with children has focused on cases of sexual or physical abuse, several elements concern this theme. However, the information in this book also applies to any child who has been the victim of other forms of abuse or who has witnessed the abuse of other children and scenes of domestic violence, murder, or any other crime. Of the eight chapters that make up this work, one chapter addresses the process of disclosure, and three allow us to review fundamental dimensions related to memory, suggestibility, and children's cognitive and language development. Three other chapters focus on conducting the interviews, discussing the existing protocols and tools, and detailing the revised version of the NICHD Protocol and on the knowledge acquired with this protocol, which is, at present, the most studied. The conclusion allows us to understand the challenges that remain to be met.

Chapter 1 presents the incidence rates and prevalence of known sexual abuse cases and other forms of maltreatment. It then discusses what is currently known about the disclosure process and the factors that prevent or delay disclosure in children. False allegations are defined along with the factors associated with them.

Chapter 2, on children's memory, provides a comprehensive review of the knowledge acquired to date. Thus, through the various stages of the encoding of the event, its retention, and its retrieval during interviews, the reader will be made aware of the fragility of children's memory. Factors likely to influence the child's memory are also discussed. After reading this chapter, the reader should better understand the functioning of children's memory and know that information based on recall memory is most likely to give a true account.

Children, like adults, can be influenced during an interview and even tend to adjust their statements to the interviewer's perceived expectations or as a result of the influence of the interviewer. Chapter 3 deals with the suggestibility of children. Factors related to the characteristics of children are reviewed in order to bring out the practical implications. Second, we will discuss the factors related to the questions and the context of the interview. All the studies conducted to date have clearly shown that the first factor responsible for the quality of the information obtained is the quality of the questions asked to the child. The factors related to the interviewer are also presented in order to identify the best attitudes to adopt. This chapter also helps to highlight how any interview with children is likely, when conducted without respecting the principles underlying memory and suggestibility, to contaminate their account. Children's understanding and expectations regarding the interview are likely to increase their suggestibility and, therefore, the quality of the information obtained. Finally, the effects of suggestive interviews on elements that the child could incorporate in his/her account are discussed.

One of the major challenges faced by anyone who meets a child for evaluation or interview purposes stems from the great variability observed in children's capacities for the same age level. Chapter 4 does not address the development of children as a whole as this would be an endeavor that goes beyond the objectives of this book. It is limited to notions related to cognitive development and language – notions that prove to be the most relevant to the practice of expert interviews. Reading this chapter should enable professionals to better detect, from the beginning of the interviews, the children's level of development in order to adjust their expectations accordingly as well as to the quantity and variety of content that the child will be able to offer.

Chapter 5 deals with the main guidelines made following the extensive research carried out on the interview with a child. The interview protocols that have been widely disseminated are briefly reviewed. This will allow readers to situate the model that currently influences their practice and its strengths and limitations. This chapter presents aids and tools, such as drawing, dolls, and dog-assisted interviewing, to help the child in the delicate task of giving the most comprehensive account. He also discusses the potential benefits and risks of using these aids.

Chapter 6 provides a detailed description of the revised version of the NICHD Protocol. It offers a concrete illustration of several of the main principles set out in the previous chapters. The phases of this protocol are defined, as well as their objectives. The questions to use and the note-taking required to work with open-ended questions are illustrated. The pre-interview information to properly plan the meeting and the context in which it should take place are also discussed. Finally, training procedures recommended to fully master this protocol are presented. For those who have been trained in this protocol, this chapter will be a very useful reminder.

One of the strengths of the NICHD Protocol is the large amount of empirical knowledge accumulated about it. Chapter 7 presents the results concerning the capacities of this protocol to increase the number of open-ended questions, to reduce the use of questions that are too precise, and to obtain as much detail as possible from the children from their recall memory. The revised version of the NICHD Protocol increases the non-suggestive support offered to the child. The effectiveness of this protocol in supporting children with cognitive developmental delays, including children with autism spectrum disorder or attention deficit disorder, will be described, as well as the effect of using this protocol on the judicial process. The need for adequate training and the usefulness of post-training supervision have also been documented and will be presented in detail. New knowledge about children's testimony in court and, in particular, those related to questions will be developed.

The conclusion highlights the achievements in terms of knowledge and intervention with children presumed to be victims or witnesses of maltreatment and discusses the challenges that await researchers and professionals in the coming years. After reading this book, any professionals who meet a child will know not only the attitudes, behaviors, and questions that they must put into practice but also, if they do not do so, the risks they run in the search for the truth.

Chapter 1

Factors influencing disclosure

- Who are the children who disclose their abuse?
- Do children try to protect the perpetrator by not disclosing their abuse?
- How many children lie and make false allegations?
- Are false allegations more numerous when parents are divorced or going through a divorce?

In this chapter, we will address the issue of disclosing abuse and, more specifically, sexual abuse. The incidence and prevalence rates will first be presented in order to better understand the extent of child maltreatment. We will then examine, based on the available empirical data, the factors that facilitate their disclosure and those that are likely to hinder it. Finally, the issue of false allegations will be discussed as well as the factors associated with them, in order to draw the most comprehensive possible picture of the situations likely to arise when a child is heard during an investigative interview or an assessment to determine if he/she is a victim of maltreatment.

1 Prevalence and incidence

Prevalence refers to the number of people in a given population who have experienced child abuse. As prevalence covers the whole life, rates are generally assessed by so-called retrospective studies using self-reported questionnaires in which the participant is asked to report his/her experience for the period covering childhood and adolescence. The prevalence of abuse has been documented particularly for sexual abuse, physical abuse, and emotional abuse. To determine the international prevalence of child maltreatment, Stoltenborgh and colleagues conducted three meta-analyses. For sexual abuse, they reviewed 217 articles published between 1980 and 2008, including 331 independent samples for a total of 9,911,748 participants (Stoltenborgh, Van IJzendoorn, Euser, & Bakermans-Kranenburg, 2011). Their results indicate that the prevalence for girls is between 16.4%, the lowest level, and 19.7%, the highest level, for an average rate of 18%. Among boys, the prevalence oscillates between 4.1% and 19.3% for an average of 7.6%. The prevalence estimated from self-reported data is higher (12.7%) than that from official sources (4%). Creighton (2002) indicates that the number of cases that reach the attention of the authorities, child welfare, or the police is always lower than the actual number of cases of abuse.

In their review of the literature on emotional abuse, Stoltenborgh and colleagues (Stoltenborgh, Bakermans-Kranenburg, Alink, Van Ijzendoorn, 2012) identified 29

DOI: 10.4324/9781003265351-1

studies involving 7,082,279 participants. They report that the rates vary considerably depending on whether they are obtained from professionals (0.3%) or they come from questionnaires self-reported by participants (36.3%) for a combined rate of 26.7%. No gender difference is noted, indicating that boys and girls are at the same risk of experiencing emotional abuse.

The meta-analysis concerning the prevalence rates of physical abuse was made from 111 studies grouping 168 independent samples, for a total of 9,698,801 participants (Stoltenborgh, Bakermans-Kranenburg, Van IJzendoorn, & Alink, 2013). According to professionals, the prevalence rates of physical abuse are 0.3%, while they reach 22% when they are established from self-reported questionnaires. This study also shows that the broader the definition of physical abuse and the longer the period of time covered (0 to 18 years), the higher the observed rates. A study conducted on a representative sample of the Canadian population indicates that 32% of people over the age of 18 reported at least one form of maltreatment suffered before the age of 15 (Afifi et al., 2014). Physical abuse (26.1%) is the most frequently reported form of violence, followed by sexual violence (10.1%) and parental exposure to domestic violence (7.9%). Women are more often victims of sexual abuse (14.4%) than men (5.8%) and also more often witnesses of partner violence (8.9% versus 6.9%). Men are more frequently victims of physical abuse (31.0%) than women (21.3%). It is important to note that few of these incidents of maltreatment had been reported or dealt with by the authorities since only 7.6% of those who have suffered maltreatment have been in contact with child protective services. Cases of physical abuse are the most frequently reported (16.8%) (Afifi et al., 2015).

Incidence indicates the number of new cases reported or detected over a specific and restricted period of time. Most often, relevant data is obtained in the context of child protection. Incidence studies underestimate the extent of maltreatment, as the data used is based only on cases reported to child welfare services or other authorities. These data, therefore, only represent a proportion of actual cases. In addition, incidence studies observe fewer cases of sexual abuse than prevalence studies because the former cover a much more limited period than the latter, which cover the whole of life before adulthood. Incidence rates are also likely to vary by country and by child protection law or system.

The most recent data on child abuse in Canada show that there were 39.2 investigations for maltreatment per 1,000 children in 2008 (Public Health Agency of Canada, 2010). For 36% of the investigations carried out, the suspicions of abuse or neglect were corroborated, while for 8% of them, the evidence was not sufficient and doubt remained. In 30% of the cases, the suspicions did not seem to be founded. Exposure to domestic violence and neglect are the most frequently corroborated forms of maltreatment, comprising 34% each of the cases investigated, followed by physical (20%), psychological (9%), and sexual (3%) violence. It is rare to find sexual abuse combined with other forms of maltreatment, as it comprises around 1% of the cases investigated. On the other hand, in investigations where sexual abuse was the main form of maltreatment, physical abuse was noted in 11% of the cases investigated, and 8% of the children concerned required medical care. Psychological violence was also noted in 47% of cases in which sexual abuse was the main form of maltreatment (e.g., threats, verbal abuse or denigration, exploitation). As for the frequency of sexual abuse, they constitute an isolated incident in 49% of cases and repeated incidents in 51% of investigations. As for the combinations of maltreatment observed, we note that neglect is frequently associated with exposure to domestic violence or psychological violence, that emotional abuse is combined with exposure to domestic violence, and that physical violence is often associated with emotional abuse or exposure to domestic violence.

In the United States, the last incidence study in 2019 reported a small decrease from previous years (in 2018, it was 9.2 / 1,000) with 656,000 children (8.9 / 1,000). A total of 84.5% of victims suffer a single type of maltreatment. In order of frequency, the more frequent maltreatment reported involves 61% of neglect, 10.3% of physical abuse, 7.2% of sexual abuse, and 6.8% of other types of maltreatment (threat of abuse, parental alcohol/drug use, lack of supervision, abandonment of newborn safety). In addition, a national estimate of 1,840 children died from abuse and neglect at a rate of 2.50 per 100,000 children in the population (U.S. Department of Health and Human Services, 2021).

2   The difficulty of disclosing maltreatment

Of all forms of child maltreatment, sexual violence is probably the most underreported and the most difficult to detect. Indeed, domestic violence, physical abuse, and neglect give signs that can be identified by different people around the child and family. Childhood sexual abuse usually occurs in a closed world where only the perpetrator and the child are present. In addition, when physical sequelae are present, they are usually located in little exposed areas of the child's body. The data suggests that a significant number of children will not disclose their sexual abuse when it occurs. In fact, in their review of available studies, London and her colleagues (London, Bruck, Ceci, & Shuman, 2005) examined two sources of data, namely (1) retrospective data on adults concerning their disclosure as a child and (2) current data from children assessed for sexual abuse allegations. The average disclosure rate observed in six of the eleven retrospective studies was 33%. This means that two-thirds of the adults questioned did not disclose the sexual abuse they had suffered during their childhood. In cases where the assault was exposed, only between 10% and 18% remember that their assault was reported to authorities.

In addition, in their review of sixteen studies of children in treatment for sexual abuse, referred for evaluation in child protection centers or even to specialized medical teams, London and her colleagues reported an average disclosure rate of 64% with a range from 24% to 96%. These highly variable rates are explained by the heterogeneity of the groups of children examined and the conditions under which these disclosures were obtained. The results of the studies are quite consistent that when the child revealed a sexual abuse to a professional or another person, the child is more likely to reveal it again when questioned in a formal setting (Leach, Powell, Sharman, & Anglim, 2017).

Two Canadian surveys carried out on representative samples of adults also show that 31% of men have never disclosed the sexual abuse of which they were victims in childhood, while this rate varies between 16% and 26% for women (Hébert, Tourigny, Cyr, McDuff, & Joly, 2009; Tourigny, Hébert, Joly, Cyr, & Baril, 2008). In total, 21.2% of victims reportedly disclosed their assault within a month, while nearly half (48.8%) waited 5 years or more before disclosing the assault. Significantly more people who have delayed disclosure for a long time or who have not disclosed it show clinical symptoms of psychological distress and post-traumatic stress disorder. Finally, another Canadian survey of a large population sample showed that less than 9% of victims of sexual abuse had reported the event to child protective services (MacMillan, Jamieson, & Walsh, 2003).

The theory proposed by the psychiatrist Summit (Summit, 1983) to take into account the process of revealing sexual abuse is fairly widely known and is used in the courts, although the empirical data at our disposal does not seem to support this proposition. Summit's theory suggests that the disclosure process has five stages: (1) secrecy, (2) helplessness, (3) entrapment and accommodation, (4) delayed, confrontational, and unconvincing disclosure, and (5) retraction of the disclosure. Summit, therefore, suggests that children who are sexually assaulted often blame themselves for the assaults and doubt themselves. As they fear the perpetrator's reactions and the impact a disclosure might have on their family and environment, these children try to remain silent and adjust to the situation. However, when the child decides to reveal what happened, it will be done gradually over time and in a process that will involve outright rejection or retraction of previous disclosures. The data presented above confirm that a large proportion of children will delay the disclosure of their aggression or even never disclose it, which corresponds to the stage of secrecy. However, the available data do not confirm that, for the majority of children, disclosure occurs gradually or that it is accompanied by retraction.

We have little data on recantation rates, but those observed to date vary between 4% and 23% (see Katz, 2014). The analysis of these data requires an ecological perspective (see below) since different factors influence this phenomenon. Malloy and Lyon (2006) observe that among children who recanted, 23% were more likely to have been assaulted by a family member and to be under the age of 10. In addition, in these cases, the non-abusive parent provided little support and was reluctant to believe the child's disclosures. These observations are confirmed by the study of Katz (2014), which indicates that other factors have a role to play, in particular cultural and religious factors, the placement of the child outside the family after the disclosure, the incarceration of the perpetrator (particularly if it is the father), and the threats or blame received by the child from other members of his/her family (e.g., mother, grandparents). Maintaining contact with the perpetrator also increases the probability of recantation (Malloy, Mugno, Rivard, Lyon, & Quas, 2016).

3   Factors that influence disclosure

Recent research is shedding light on the factors that may delay or prevent children from disclosing their abuse. Collin-Vézina and his colleagues (Collin-Vézina, De La Sablonnière-Griffin, Palmer, & Milne, 2015) grouped the factors preventing disclosure according to an ecosystemic model. Three levels are identified: (1) intrapersonal, (2) relational, and (3) sociocultural.

1   So at the first level, namely that of the idiosyncratic factors that belong to the person, we note

   - the internalization of blame (feelings of shame and responsibility, fear of disappointing others, and feeling of being damaged);

- self-protection mechanisms (minimization of abusive experience, loss of trust in others, repressed memories); and
- immaturity of development (insufficient understanding of sexuality, confusion about the abusive situation, lack of means to disclose).

2   At the second level, namely that of relational factors, we find

- violence and dysfunction in the family (feeling of not being safe, fear of reprisals, protection of others, self-sacrifice);
- power dynamics (manipulation, threat, law of silence, multiple facets of the relationship with the perpetrator);
- awareness of repercussions (change in the perception of others, fear of consequences, avoidance of the involvement of authorities); and
- a fragile social network (person to whom to reveal or able to support, absence of support in the school network).

3   At the last level, namely that of sociocultural factors, we see

- social stigma (fear of being judged crazy, homosexuality);
- the taboo of sexuality (lack of knowledge);
- nonexistent services (awareness programs, access to services, help lines); and
- culture or historical period (invisibility of sexual abuse in society), the latter factor being more present for older people in the sample.

All of these factors are likely to prevent children or adolescents and even adults from disclosing their situation. This model thus makes it possible to organize in a coherent picture the many obstacles that can prevent disclosure, in addition to underlining the important role that the family environment and society can represent as an obstacle to disclosure. Several of these factors were examined, including the age and the gender of the child, the type of abuse, and internal factors, such as fear of consequences, perception of responsibility, and the effect on the confidant and those around him/her.

Several studies have observed a linear relationship between disclosure and the child's age (Hershkowitz, Horowitz, & Lamb, 2005; Hershkowitz, Lamb, & Katz, 2014; Lippert, Cross, Jones, & Walsh, 2009). Among 26,446 children, Hershkowitz and colleagues (2005) note that 47.5% of children aged 3 to 6, 66.7% of those aged 7 to 10, and 74.1% of children aged 11 to 14 made a disclosure about sexual abuse or physical abuse. In a sample aged 3 to 16 years, an Australian study (Leach et al., 2017) observes that the disclosure rate increased until the age of 11 years and that it then decreased until the age of 16. The low rate of disclosure in very young children can be explained, among other things, by their cognitive limitations and their lack of knowledge about sexuality. These two factors can influence their ability to report sexual behaviors directed toward them since they do not understand that these acts are inappropriate and prohibited. The results of a few studies (Hershkowitz, Horowitz, & Lamb, 2007; Malloy, Brubacher, & Lamb, 2011; Schönbucher, Maier, Mohler-Kuo, Schnyder, & Landolt, 2012) also indicate that older children, even if they have made disclosures, are more likely to postpone the timing, particularly in cases of intra-family sexual abuse. These children tend to feel more responsible and anticipate more negative consequences for themselves and for others. Data reported by Leach and colleagues (Leach et al., 2017) also indicate that adolescents are less likely to disclose when the suspect has a history of abuse, echoing fears seen in older children of "being hurt" if they disclosed the assault (see Malloy et al., 2011).

As for the gender of the child, the results obtained are not always consistent. Based on large samples, several studies observe that girls are more likely to reveal than boys (Hershkowitz, Horowitz, & Lamb, 2007; Hershkowitz et al., 2014; Lippert et al., 2009). In the national study of Hershkowitz, Horowitz and Lamb (2007), this significant difference only applies to situations of sexual abuse, and this is particularly true for boys aged 11 to 14, whose disclosure rate is lower. Other studies do not observe this gender-related difference (Goodman-Brown, Edelstein, Goodman, Jones, & Gordon, 2003; Leach et al., 2017).

The relationship between the perpetrator and the child also influences the child's desire to disclose the abuse; when the perpetrator is the parent, the child is more likely not to disclose (Hershkowitz, Horowitz & Lamb, 2007; Leach et al., 2017; Lippert et al., 2009). Hershkowitz and her colleagues also observe that the rate of nondisclosure is higher in cases of sexual abuse than in those of physical abuse.

The results for the severity or frequency of the abuse are inconsistent. For the severity of the actions taken, three studies observe that children who have undergone vaginal or anal penetrations (Leach et al., 2017; Lippert et al., 2009) or even been touched over clothing (Pipe et al., 2007) are more likely to disclose, while other studies do not observe such a relationship (Hershkowitz et al., 2014). For frequency, Malloy et al. (2011) indicate that children who report multiple incidents are eight times more likely to disclose than children who report a single incident when other studies do not find a link (Leach et al., 2017).

Regarding the internalization of blame and self-protection mechanisms, several studies have examined the barriers to disclosure. A qualitative study based on transcripts of investigative interviews indicates that adolescents (62.5%) identify internal obstacles, such as shame, fear, and ambivalence, as obstacles to their disclosure, whereas children (69.2%) more often report external obstacles, such as blackmail, manipulation, and gifts (Alain, Dion, & Cyr, 2018). Schaeffer and colleagues (Schaeffer, Leventhal, & Asnes, 2011), following an analysis of 191 investigative interviews with children aged 3 to 18 years old, report that the main reasons given by children for not having spoken about their victimization are threats received from the perpetrator, fear that something bad will happen, lack of opportunity to disclose, lack of understanding that it is an abuse, and whether it is a friend or lover who committed the gestures. Among adolescent girls, Schönbucher and colleagues (2012) note that fear of parental sanctions or fear of parents reporting the sexual abuse to the police prevents children from disclosing their assault. In their study of the consequences expected by children aged 5 to 13 years old, Malloy et al. (2011) indicate that they expect significantly more consequences for them (70%) than for the suspect (21%) or for other people around them (9%). When the assaults have been committed by other children, that is, by minors, the children have less expectation of consequences for the suspect than if the assault was made by an adult. As the children get older, the more they report expecting consequences for themselves. Children who report consequences for themselves are more likely to have delayed disclosure than those who disclose immediately. As for the nature of the consequences expected, the most frequent are negative emotions (17.2%), physical injuries or death (14.7%), and legal consequences such as imprisonment (13.2%) for the suspect. Expectations of physical injury or death are more often reported by boys than girls and also by older children who have been severely assaulted by a family member. Not surprisingly, children who have received threats are more likely to expect negative consequences than those who have not. These researchers conclude that the self-protective function of not disclosing the abuse appears obvious since most of the expected consequences are for the child himself/herself and that the fear of these consequences is associated with longer delays before disclosure. This also appears compatible with the social function of secrecy – that is, the desire to protect others.

The bond with the confidant and his/her early reaction are other factors that influence the disclosure. The results tell us that young children tend to disclose their abuse to their parents or to a trusted adult, while older children, especially adolescents, confide more in their friends (Alain et al., 2018; Hershkowitz, Horowitz & Lamb, 2007; London et al., 2005; Schaeffer et al., 2011). In order not to reveal their abuse, adolescents and young adults cite not wanting to annoy the people to whom this information would be revealed, seeing these people as emotionally too unstable to deal with the disclosure or as being is not sufficiently close or reliable. Several victims were not sure their parents would be on their side. Feelings of shame, fear of stigma, and fear of not being believed or having parental sanctions are among the most frequently reported concerns (Schönbucher et al., 2012). In children aged 7 to 12 years old, the perception of the expected parental reaction also influences behavior (Hershkowitz, Lanes & Lamb, 2007). The fact that parents usually react anxiously to stress is associated with delaying disclosure for 88% of children. The results of this study, although it relates to a small number of cases (30), indicate that school-age children have a good perception of the stress that the disclosure of their abuse on their parents will provoke. Thus, children often choose not to reveal abuse so as not to undermine a parent they perceive as anxious. During the investigative interview, when questioned about the disclosure, 36% of the children report a strong reaction (e.g., crying, confrontation of the perpetrator) by the person to whom they confided their abuse, and 32% experienced a non-supportive reaction (e.g., anger toward the child, not being believed) (Ahern & Lamb, 2017).

In addition, parental support is an important factor that influences disclosure; the fear of not being believed or supported by parents has been observed in several studies (Hershkowitz, Lanes & Lamb, 2007; Schönbucher et al., 2012). In addition, in families where parents were less supportive of their children, the rate of serious crimes was higher (92% versus 44%), and incidents were more often multiple (93% versus 37%).

Among adolescents, the results of a qualitative study (McElvaney, Greene, & Hogan, 2012) conducted in Ireland indicate that the disclosure process is a planned choice. Thus, three dynamics emerged: active withholding of information (e.g., not wanting people to know his/her experience, having denied when asked, forcing the confidant to keep the secret), the experience of a "pressure cooker" effect (e.g., ambivalence and feeling distress, emotional cost of keeping the secret, unplanned disclosure), and confiding (e.g., choice of a trusted person, sharing in confidence, need for confidentiality). These results agree with those of Staller and Nelson-Gardell (2005), who indicate that disclosure is not a one-way process. These authors observe three stages in the disclosure process in thirty-four adolescent girls. The first stage is living with oneself (e.g., feelings of shame and blame, confusion concerning the attitude to have vis-à-vis the perpetrator with whom the teens wish to maintain a non-abusive relationship). In the second, the choice of a confidant and the expected response are evaluated, and the third step allows the child to evaluate on the basis of the effect of the disclosure and the consequences of repeating it to other people or in other situations. Thus, children receive, analyze, and assess how adults react to them. For these authors, disclosure should be seen in the context of communication and relationship with others. The person likely to receive the confidence plays an important role in this dialogue and influences the future decisions of the abused child to confide or not. This hypothesis is supported by research highlighting the importance of the responses of others, especially those of the mother, which can encourage disclosure (Hershkowitz, Lanes & Lamb, 2007; Mathews, Hendricks, & Abraham, 2016), and the mediating effect of psychological distress in disclosure. In addition, Alain et al. (2018) report that 82% of adolescents in their study (compared with 45% of the children) had to disclose their sexual abuse more than once before these allegations were taken seriously.

IMPLICATIONS FOR PRACTICE

These studies indicate to us that the barriers to disclosure are numerous and concern both the beliefs and attributes of the person who suffers the abuse and the familial, social, and religious environments in which they operate. For the professional who meets an adult, it may be easier to ask questions about the presence or absence of child abuse. With children, in the absence of external signs that could indicate the presence of maltreatment, it is always risky to approach the subject without becoming suggestive; this subject will be dealt with in a future chapter. However, it should be remembered that many preschool children who have been assaulted and who do not reveal it do not understand what the interviewer is talking about or do not understand that the actions taken against them are unacceptable in our societies. For school-age children and older children, the intimate bond with the perpetrator, the feeling of responsibility ("to have accepted" that the acts were committed), and the fear of the consequences for them and those around them seem to be important barriers in addition to social isolation. This highlights the importance of taking the time to build a trusting relationship with the child before addressing the main topic of the interview. Trying to assure or reassure these children that they are not responsible (see Chapter 6) could also be an important lever that allows the child to take the risk of revealing maltreatment. However, here too, the interventions should be made in a non-suggestive manner to preserve the child's speech.

4 False allegations

Anyone who meets with a child to find out if he/she is or has been a victim of abuse must work with multiple assumptions, including that the child may make a false allegation. By definition, a false allegation happens when a child explicitly claims to be the victim of maltreatment when this abuse has not happened (Poole & Lamb, 1998). Some authors suggest that we should also include cases where, following suspicion, parents or other persons have made a report or have lodged a complaint; cases investigated that turn out to be unfounded; allegations that result from intentional or unintentional coaching; misinterpretations given to events; and even allegations resulting from inadequate interviewing techniques (Ceci & Bruck, 1995). Studies suggest that between 23% and 43% of the cases investigated turn out to be unfounded (Jones & McGraw, 1987; Anthony & Watkeys, 1991; Oates et al., 2000; Trocmé & Bala, 2005). However, it is important to note that these figures include investigations that were carried out when the child himself/herself had not made an allegation. In a pan-Canadian study, Trocmé and Bala (2005) indicate that out of the 35% of cases unfounded after investigation, the rate of false allegations made intentionally would be only 4%. The corresponding rate was slightly higher for sexual abuse (6%) than for physical abuse (4%), neglect (4%), or emotional abuse (2%). However, in the cases of sexual abuse, none of the false allegations identified were made by the children.

Certain factors or contexts are more likely to be associated with false allegations. Thus, there are more cases of false allegations reported when parents are in the process of divorce or in disputes surrounding child custody. Several authors (Faller, 1991; Bala, Mitnick, Trocmé, & Houston, 2007) indicate that often these false allegations are based on a part of the reality, in particular that of anxious parents who misinterpret certain signs (e.g., rashes, anxiety by the child in the presence of the other parent, physical manifestations of affection) and too quickly conclude that sexual abuse has happened. In such circumstances, the allegations would most often come from the parents and not from the children (Elterman & Ehrenberg, 1991). With the disappointment and disenchantment of marital breakdown, divorced parents can become convinced that their partner is capable of just about anything, including sexual abuse.

It is also important to stress that separation or divorce can become an opportunity to reveal that an assault has actually taken place. Indeed, the fact that the child no longer lives under the same roof as the perpetrator may make him/her feel more secure in disclosing victimization. It is also more difficult for the perpetrator to prevent the child from speaking (Thoennes & Tjaden, 1990). In addition, the child may perceive that the non-abusive parent is more willing to hear and believe his/her disclosures (Faller, 1991).

On the other hand, separation can promote the appearance of opportunities to commit sexual acts toward the child that did not exist in united families (Bala, Lee, & McNamara, 2001; Faller, 1991). Alleged perpetrators may be overwhelmed by loneliness and may exhibit regressive behavior in many areas of their lives. Faller (1991) stresses the importance in these cases of checking to what extent indications of a sexual attraction toward the children could have been noted before the divorce.

Another situation where false allegations are likely to occur is the phenomenon of rumor. Rumor is news that is created and spread to explain an event of which little is known about the real facts; it, therefore, stems from generalized uncertainty (Rosnow, 1991). In addition, it arises in situations that are important or worrying to people. When the rumor is associated with a feeling of personal anxiety related to the situation, it is transmitted more quickly since it serves to legitimize this feeling of anxiety. The speed with which it spreads depends on whether it appears plausible or reliable. Thus, in all situations where a child is assaulted in an environment where other children live, such as daycare services, nurseries, schools, and sports clubs, a rumor could contribute to spreading false allegations. Children can then integrate an erroneous rumor into their memory, whether it is spread by adults or by children. They then report that they saw the facts spread by the rumor when they only heard about it. A study (Principe, Kanaya, Ceci, & Singh, 2006) of 175 preschool children aged 3 to 5 years old indicates that when children freely recall events, the elements that come from the rumor are more present in their story only when specific questions or suggestions are used. For the authors, this demonstrates the ability of a rumor to confuse the minds of young children as to the source of the information stored in their memory (see Chapter 2). Other studies of children aged 3 to 5 years old have also observed the influence that conversations between witness and non-witness children can have on the production of details, with non-witnesses tending to give more information than witnesses (Principe & Schindewolf, 2012).

Having preconceived ideas, such as an interviewer's prejudices or tunnel vision or narrow vision of things, is another phenomenon that can lead to false allegations (St-Yves, 2014). We will see in the next chapters that memory is influenced by the questions asked of children. When the interviewer comes to the interview already having preconceived ideas about the facts, he/she shapes the interview – without always being aware of it – so that the disclosure conforms to the preconceptions. In addition to looking only for information that confirms interviewer's hypotheses, he/she avoids questioning certain aspects that could produce contradictory information.

When the statement comes from the parent, it is quite common for the investigation to find false allegations. This is especially true when the child is not the person who made the allegation. For example, Jones and McGraw (1987) observed that out of 575 cases of sexual abuse, 6% were fictitious allegations: 5% of cases emanate from adults, which leaves a rate of child allegations of only 1%. In another study, Anthony and Watkeys (1991) find that 8.5% of allegations were false and intentionally fabricated; however, they observed that 6% of cases came from adults and 2.5% from children. These results are also consistent with those of Trocmé and Bala (2005), who noted, in cases of sexual abuse, that no false allegation came from children and that all false allegations were made by adults. For other forms of maltreatment, false allegation rates could range from 1% to 5%. Obviously, this does not imply that any statement of abuse by a parent about their child will prove to be false, but there is a greater chance that this will happen than if it is the child who discloses abuse by a parent. In addition, we have also seen previously that when the child thinks that a parent will not believe him/her, s/he tends not to reveal the incident or to postpone the moment to do it. Research suggests that in these situations, it is also possible that children who have made first disclosure and are not believed by their parents tend to retract later (Elliott & Briere, 1994). Malloy, Lyon, and Quas (2007) observed, between 257 substantiated cases files, a rate of 23.1% of recantation. These were more frequent among younger victims, those abused by a parent figure and children who lacked the support of a non-offending caregiver. In another study where 58 children who recanted were matched with 58 who did not recant, researchers observe that children who were removed from home after their initial disclosure and those separated from their siblings were less likely to recant. Being believed or not by their siblings and visitations with the alleged perpetrator were important factors related to recantation (Malloy et al., 2016). Recantation often has an influence on the perception of the child's credibility and on the resulting legal procedures.

Age is usually a good indicator of a child's developmental abilities, and there appears to be a link between this and false allegations. From the age of 3.5 years, children are able to lie, especially when they have done something forbidden, but before the age of 7, they have little capacity to become effective liars (Henderson & Andrews, 2018). After this age and with the development of their cognitive ability, they learn to control their nonverbal behavior, conceal their knowledge or fake their ignorance, and maintain consistency in their lie (Talwar & Crossman, 2012). Few studies can give us definitive insight into false allegations, but social workers report that they obtain more false allegations from adolescents (Everson & Boat, 1989). Obviously, adolescents have more cognitive strategies that allow them to use lying to achieve the ends they want. However, these same cognitive abilities can also be used to delay or deny any allegation in order to protect some people around them.

IMPLICATIONS FOR PRACTICE

Although the figures available to us seem to indicate that false allegations represent only about 6% of alleged cases of maltreatment, it is nonetheless important to detect them. Indeed, the consequences of these false allegations for the alleged perpetrator are serious and can often ruin the life of an innocent person. In cases involving divorces, separations, or disputes over custody rights, the costs of unfounded allegations are high. Rigorous analysis of all available evidence, very high-quality interviews, and investigative work based on multiple hypotheses are always required to disentangle the true from the false.

References

Afifi T. O., MacMillan H. L., Boyle M. P., Taillieu T. M., Cheung K. B. A., Sareen J. M. D. (2014). "Child abuse and mental disorders in Canada", *Canadian Medical Association Journal*, 186(9), 324–332.

Afifi T. O., MacMillan H. L., Taillieu T., Cheung K., Turner S., Tonmyr L., Hovdestad W. (2015). "Relationship between child abuse exposure and reported contact with child protection organizations: Results from the Canadian Community Health Survey", *Child Abuse & Neglect*, 46, 198–206.

Ahern E., Lamb M. E. (2017). "Children's reports of disclosure recipient reactions in forensic interviews: Comparing the NICHD and MoGP protocols", *Journal of Police and Criminal Psychology*, 32(2), 85–93.

Alain S., Dion J., Cyr M. (2018). "Examen des caractéristiques du dévoilement de l'agression sexuelle chez les enfants [Examination of the characteristics of disclosure of sexual assault in children]", *Revue Internationale de Criminologie et de Police Technique et Scientifique*, LXXI, 88–109.

Anthony G., Watkeys J. (1991). "False allegations in child sexual abuse: The pattern of referral in an area where reporting is not mandatory", *Children & Society*, 5, 111–122.

Bala N., Lee J., McNamara E. (2001). "Children as witnesses: Understanding their capacities, needs, and experiences", *Journal of Social Distress & the Homeless*, 10, 41–68.

Bala N., Mitnick M., Trocmé N., Houston C. (2007). "Sexual abuse allegations and parental separation: Smokescreen or fire?" *Journal of Family Studies*, 13(1), 26–56.

Ceci S. J., Bruck M. (1995). *Jeopardy in the courtroom: A scientific analysis of children's testimony*, Washington, DC, American Psychological Association.

Collin-Vézina D., De La Sablonnière-Griffin M., Palmer A., Milne, L. (2015). "A preliminary mapping of individual, relational, and social factors that impede disclosure of childhood sexual abuse", *Child Abuse & Neglect*, 43, 123–134.

Creighton S. J. (2002). "Recognising changes in incidence and prevalence", in Browne K. D., Hanks H., Stratton P., Hamilton C. (Eds.), *Early prediction and prevention of child abuse: A handbook*, Chichester, Wiley, 5–22.

Elliott D. M., Briere J. (1994). "Forensic sexual abuse evaluations of older children: Disclosure and symptomatology", *Behavioral Sciences and the Law*, 12(3), 261–277.

Elterman M. F., Ehrenberg M. F. (1991). "Sexual abuse allegations in child custody disputes", *International Journal of Law and Psychiatry*, 14, 269–286.

Everson M. D., Boat B. W. (1989). "False allegations of sexual abuse by children and adolescents", *Journal of the American Academy of Child & Adolescent Psychiatry*, 28, 230–235.

Faller K. C. (1991). "Possible explanations for child sexual abuse allegations in divorce", *American Journal of Orthopsychiatry*, 61(1), 86–91.

Goodman-Brown T. B., Edelstein R. S., Goodman G. S., Jones D. P. H., Gordon D. S. (2003). "Why children tell: A model of children's disclosure of sexual abuse", *Child Abuse & Neglect*, 27, 525–540.

Hébert M., Tourigny M., Cyr M., McDuff P., Joly J. (2009). "Prevalence of childhood sexual abuse and timing of disclosure in a representative sample of adults from Quebec", *The Canadian Journal of Psychiatry*, 54(9), 631–636.

Henderson H. M., Andrews S. J. (2018). "Assessing the veracity of children's forensic interviews", in Otgaar H., Howe M. L. (Eds.), *Finding the truth in the courtroom: Dealing with deception, lies and memories*, New York, Oxford University Press, 103–135.

Hershkowitz I., Horowitz D., Lamb M. E. (2005). "Trends in children's disclosure of abuse in Israel: A national study", *Child Abuse & Neglect*, 29(11), 1203–1214.

Hershkowitz I., Horowitz D., Lamb M. E. (2007). "Individual and family variables associated with disclosure and nondisclosure of child abused in Israel", in Pipe M.-E., Lamb M. E., Orbach Y., Cederborg A.-C. (Eds.), *Child sexual abuse: Disclosure, delay, and denial*, Mahwah, Lawrence Erlbaum Associates Publishers, 65–75.

Hershkowitz I., Lamb M. E., Katz C. (2014). "Allegation rates in forensic child abuse investigations: Comparing the revised and standard NICHD protocols", *Psychology, Public Policy, and Law*, 20(3), 336–344.

Hershkowitz I., Lanes O., Lamb M. E. (2007). "Exploring the disclosure of child sexual abuse with alleged victims and their parents", *Child Abuse & Neglect*, 31(2), 111–123.

Jones D., McGraw E. M. (1987). "Reliable and fictitious accounts of sexual abuse to children", *Journal of Interpersonal Violence*, 2(1), 27–46.

Katz C. (2014). "'Please believe me; I am the biggest liar that exists': Characterising children's recantations during forensic investigations", *Children and Youth Services Review*, 43, 160–166.

Leach C., Powell M. B., Sharman S. J., Anglim J. (2017). "The relationship between children's age and disclosures of sexual abuse during forensic interviews", *Child Maltreatment*, 22(1), 79–88.

Lippert T., Cross T. P., Jones L. M., Walsh W. (2009). "Telling interviewers about sexual abuse: Predictors of child disclosure at forensic interviews", *Child Maltreatment*, 14(1), 100–113.

London K., Bruck M., Ceci S. J., Shuman D. W. (2005). "Disclosure of child sexual abuse: What does the research tell us about the ways that children tell?" *Psychology, Public Policy, and Law*, 11(1), 194–226.

MacMillan H. L., Jamieson E., Walsh C. A. (2003). "Reported contact with child protection services among those reporting child physical and sexual abuse: Results from a community survey", *Child Abuse & Neglect*, 27(12), 1397–1408.

Malloy L. C., Brubacher S. P., Lamb M. E. (2011). "Expected consequences of disclosure revealed in investigative interviews with suspected victims of child sexual abuse", *Applied Developmental Science*, 15(1), 8–19.

Malloy L. C., Lyon T. D. (2006). "Caregiver support and child sexual abuse: Why does it matter?" *Journal of Child Sexual Abuse: Research, Treatment, & Program Innovations for Victims, Survivors, & Offenders*, 15(4), 97–103.

Malloy L. C., Lyon T. D., Quas J. (2007). "Filial dependency and recantation of child sexual abuse allegations", *Journal of the American Academy of Child & Adolescent Psychiatry*, 46(2), 162–170.

Malloy L. C., Mugno A. P., Rivard R. A., Lyon T. D., Quas J. (2016). "Familial influences on recantation in substantiated child sexual abuse cases", *Child Maltreatment*, 21(3), 256–261.

Mathews S., Hendricks N., Abrahams N. (2016). "A psychosocial understanding of child sexual abuse disclosure among female children in South Africa", *Journal of Child Sexual Abuse*, 25(6), 636–654.

McElvaney R., Greene S., Hogan D. (2012). "Containing the secret of child sexual abuse", *Journal of Interpersonal Violence*, 27(6), 1155–1175.

Oates R. K., Jones D. P. H., Denson D., Sirotnak A., Gary N., Krugman R. D. (2000). "Erroneous concerns about child sexual abuse", *Child Abuse & Neglect*, 24(1), 149–157.

Pipe M.-E., Lamb M. E., Orbach Y., Sternberg K. J., Stewart H. L., Esplin P. W. (2007). "Factors associated with nondisclosure of suspected abuse during forensic interviews", in Pipe M.-E., Lamb M. E., Orbach Y., Cederborg A.-C. (Eds.), *Child sexual abuse: Disclosure, delay, and denial*, Mahwah, Lawrence Erlbaum Associates Publishers, 77–96.

Poole D. A., Lamb M. E. (1998). *Investigative interviews of children: A guide for helping professionals*, Washington, DC, American Psychological Association.

Principe G. F., Kanaya T., Ceci S. J., Singh M. (2006). "Believing is seeing: How rumors can engender false memories in preschoolers", *Psychological Science*, mars, 17(3), 243–248.

Principe G. F., Schindewolf E. (2012). "Natural conversations as a source of false memories in children: Implications for the testimony of young witnesses", *Developmental Review*, 32, 205–223.

Public Health Agency of Canada. (2010). *Canadian incidence study of reported child abuse and neglect 2008 (CIS-2008): Major findings*, Ottawa, ON, 122 pages.

Rosnow R. L. (1991). "Inside rumor: A personal journey", *American Psychologist*, 46(5), 484–496.

Schaeffer P., Leventhal J. M., Asnes A. G. (2011). "Children's disclosures of sexual abuse: Learning from direct inquiry", *Child Abuse & Neglect*, 35(5), 343–352.

Schönbucher V., Maier T., Mohler-Kuo M., Schnyder U., Landolt M. A. (2012). "Disclosure of child sexual abuse by adolescents: A qualitative in-depth study", *Journal of Interpersonal Violence*, 27(17), 3486–3513.

Staller K. M., Nelson-Gardell D. (2005). "'A burden in your heart': Lessons of disclosure from female preadolescent and adolescent survivors of sexual abuse", *Child Abuse & Neglect*, 29(12), 1415–1432.

Stoltenborgh M., Bakermans-Kranenburg M. J., Alink L. R. A., Van IJzendoorn M. H. (2012). "The universality of childhood emotional abuse: A meta-analysis of worldwide prevalence", *Journal of Aggression, Maltreatment & Trauma*, 21(8), 870–890.

Stoltenborgh M., Bakermans-Kranenburg M. J., Van IJzendoorn M. H., Alink L. R. A. (2013). "Cultural-geographical differences in the occurrence of child physical abuse? A meta-analysis of global prevalence", *International Journal of Psychology*, 42(2), 82–94.

Stoltenborgh M., Van IJzendoorn M. H., Euser E. M., Bakermans-Kranenburg M. J. (2011). "A global perspective on child sexual abuse: Meta-analysis of prevalence around the world", *Child Maltreatment*, 16(2), 79–101.

St-Yves M. (2014). "Rapport in investigative interviews five fundamental rules to achieve it", in St-Yves M. (Ed.), *Investigative interviewing: The essentials*, Toronto, CA, Thomson Reuters, 1–28.

Summit RC. (1983). "The child sexual abuse accommodation syndrome", *Child Abuse & Neglect*, 7, 177–193.

Talwar V., Crossman A. M. (2012). "Children's lies and their detection: Implications for child witness testimony", *Developmental Review*, 32(4), 337–359.

Thoennes N., Tjaden P. G. (1990). "The extent, nature, and validity of sexual abuse allegations in custody/visitation disputes", *Child Abuse & Neglect*, 14, 151–163.

Tourigny M., Hébert M., Joly J., Cyr M., Baril K. (2008). "Prevalence and co-occurrence of violence against children in the Quebec population", *Australian and New Zealand Journal of Public Health*, 32(4), 331–335.

Trocmé N., Bala N. (2005). "False allegations of abuse and neglect when parents separate", *Child Abuse & Neglect*, 29(12), 1333–1345.

U.S. Department of Health and Human Services, Administration for Children, Youth and Families, Children's Bureau. (2021). *Child maltreatment 2019*, Washington, DC, US Department of Health and Human Services.

Chapter 2

Memory in children

- From what age can a child have accurate memories of past events?
- What type of memory is most likely to be accurate?
- What is the effect of time on children's memories?
- Are traumatic events better preserved in memory?

The memory of children, particularly that of the very young and that of school-age children, has been the subject of a considerable amount of research since the end of the 1970s. This accumulation of knowledge allows us to better understand the capacities and children's mnemonic boundaries (Howe, Toth, & Cicchetti, 2015; La Rooy, Malloy, & Lamb, 2011). Thus, it becomes easier to anticipate the performance of a child during an interview aimed at obtaining his/her memories about a given event. The objective pursued in this chapter is not to provide an overview of the knowledge concerning the development and functioning of memory in children but rather to identify the dimensions that are relevant to the collection of memories of children who were maltreated or who witnessed events. Thus, in this chapter, after having defined what memory is, we will examine the various factors that may influence the quality of memories during encoding, during the retention period, or during recovery. Other factors that influence memory, such as the child's age, involvement or participation in the event, the nature of the traumatic event, and the memory of the abused child, will be detailed below.

1   Definition of memory

Memory is a large and complex field. In the case of child witnesses or victims, the authors were especially concerned with one particular aspect of declarative memory, namely episodic memory, as opposed to semantic memory (Bauer, 2009, 2015). As the name suggests, episodic memories are about specific events or episodes, as opposed to the timeless or placeless memories that make up our repertoire of knowledge about the world (semantic memory). In addition, all of the authors have focused their attention on a particular subtype of episodic memory, either autobiographical memory or personal memory. Autobiographical memories are memories of episodes that are self-relevant or self-defined. This is what the word auto refers to in "autobiographical." In this book, autobiographical memory is the one that interests us the most. It can be defined as the memory of life events (Bauer, 2015; Howe, Courage, & Rooksby, 2009) and, therefore, includes all memories related to our personal history such as the

DOI: 10.4324/9781003265351-2

who, when, and where of personal events which, when grouped together, allow us to have the knowledge of who we are. Even before birth, the child has the neurological mechanisms to encode information or events from different sensory modalities (Howe et al., 2009). However, it is only around the age of two, when the cognitive self, a structure that helps organize information and experiences, appears, that memories become accessible. The cognitive self facilitates the grouping and personalization of the memory of events in what will become autobiographical memory. The development of autobiographical memory depends mainly on maturation factors and not on environmental factors. For example, children with developmental delay (Down syndrome, autism, intellectual disability) see the cognitive self appearing later (Howe et al., 2015).

When adults remember an event, they often have the impression that they have recorded all the information and that the memory of this event scrolls through their head like a film replaying the reality exactly. However, memory is never a true copy of an event. Indeed, memory is a process rather than a static event; it is "reconstruction, not reproduction" (Yapko, 1994; Howe et al., 2015). This means that the events are not recorded passively and that they are not recovered mechanically. This definition of memory is part of a constructivist perspective that is central to research carried out in the field of cognitive development. This perspective, therefore, emphasizes the active involvement of the person in his/her search to understand the experiences that occur to him/her (Baker-Ward, Ornstein, & Starnes, 2009). Therefore, since memory is reconstructive, it can be corrupted during the initial encoding of the event, during its retention, or during its retrieval. In the next few paragraphs, the factors that influence each of these stages of memorization will be discussed in more detail.

2   The initial encoding

Encoding or recording the event is the first step in creating a memory. However, not everything is stored in memory (Ornstein & Haden, 2002). Given the fundamental limitations of the human cognitive system, only certain information from the event is selected for further processing, while others are excluded. Among the factors that influence this selection, the degree of attention paid by the child to the event plays an important role. For sexual abuse, the encoding of the event is done accidentally rather than deliberately. In other words, when an event of sexual abuse occurs, the children do not know that they will one day have to give a detailed account of it. Children can, therefore, pay less attention and not make a conscious effort to retain as much information as possible as they might do during a visit to the botanical garden, knowing that they will have to submit a written report of this visit upon return to school. In addition, in very young children, the attention span is limited so that they cannot retain a large number of details. Since this attention span increases with age, school-age children and adolescents are able to provide much more detail than very young children. However, it is important to remember that, even in adults, not all of the information about the course of an event is recorded.

Another important factor that influences the selection of the encoded elements is the interest in or attention paid to various dimensions (Roediger & Gallo, 2002). Thus, when several people participate in the same event, certain elements will be memorized by all the people, while certain precise details will be recorded only by a single individual. For example, if several children participate in a party, all will remember the clown who came to entertain them and make small animals with inflatable balloons, while only some of them will remember in detail some of the other aspects of the event, such as what they ate, the games they played, or the physical appearance of the place where the party was celebrated. Here, it is our predispositions, our interests, and our previous knowledge that determine the attention paid to specific details.

Our previous experiences and knowledge are also important dimensions that influence the encoding of events as they help us give meaning to the experience that is taking place (Ornstein & Haden, 2002). This often unconscious interpretive process uses both semantic (general knowledge) and episodic (specific knowledge linked to a specific event) mnemonic representations. For example, studies have shown that when children are told in detail about a medical examination they will have to undergo, they retain that in much more vivid detail than children who have undergone the same examination without any prior information (Peterson, 2012). However, having very strong basic knowledge can also hinder the retention of information by leading the child to pay attention selectively – that is to say, to monitor certain characteristics of the event to the detriment of others. In addition, this general knowledge of the event to be memorized can be used when the memory weakens over time to make up for forgotten information (Baker-Ward et al., 2009). This is what adults do when they recall a specific event. We use our knowledge and past experiences (e.g., going to the grocery store) to be able to report in detail everything we did on Friday two weeks ago when we went to the grocery store. In other words, we use our past experiences to fill in the elements that were not recorded in our memory during a recent event. Finally, sometimes children use their knowledge to describe something unfamiliar to them, thus introducing confusion as to what may have happened.

2.1 Post-event encoding

The encoding of an event can be done in a prolonged manner – that is to say, beyond the moment experienced as such (Baker-Ward et al., 2009). Paz-Alonso and his colleagues (Paz-Alonso, Larson, Castelli, Alley, & Goodman, 2009) refer to this phenomenon as a post-event elaboration. Endogenous (e.g., thinking and rumination) and exogenous (e.g., conversations and exposure to correct or erroneous information) factors can influence the first encoding made in memory. Thus, personal reflections on recent events can come to alter our own perspective, just like the rumination of these events or the efforts made to give them meaning; thus, these representations are modified. Conversation with others during or after the event also helps to better inscribe the information in memory. However, these conversations about the lived event, especially if the event is not fully understood, can bring about a change in the interpretation of this representation (Principe & Schindewolf, 2012; Salmon & Reese, 2015). This is particularly likely to happen with major events that are reported by the media (e.g., hurricane or September 11 attacks) or events for which family photo albums or auditory or visual encodings are available. In addition, memory distortions can occur as a result of the presentation of contradictory information that can particularly influence children or suggestible people (Principe & Schindewolf, 2012). Although knowledge about the influence of conversations on children's memory is still scarce, it can be argued that certain factors are more likely to be influential, including talking about an event with someone familiar rather than with a stranger or chatting with a mother who has a high capacity for elaboration and is able to communicate contextual (place, time) or perceptual (color, sound) information (Principe & Schindewolf, 2012; Salmon & Reese, 2015).

Events with a negative connotation are likely to arouse in children the same type of evaluation as in adults by way of cognitive elaboration, rumination, or personal reflections. However, these mechanisms are likely to be less spontaneous in children and most often involve the participation of an adult in their development. For example, mothers are more likely to ask open-ended questions and provide causal explanations when discussing negative events with their child than when addressing positive events; thus, they influence the child's memory by encouraging him/her to take the event into account and to elaborate on it (Paz-Alonso et al., 2009). It should be noted that these endogenous and exogenous factors can also play a role in maintaining and strengthening memories, and therefore, they can slow down the normal course of forgetting but also contribute to the decrease in the accuracy of personal memories. Under some conditions, the decrease in memory over time can be significantly reduced when the information stored in the memory is reactivated during the retention period by repeated exposures to some aspect of the original event (e.g., watching television images of the hurricane again). This allows reintegration of the memory.

IMPLICATIONS FOR PRACTICE

Several implications for practice arise from the knowledge acquired about memory encoding. First, it is important to remember that not everything is stored in memory. Encoding is selective with elements chosen based on prior knowledge, interests, and motivations. The events that will be best recorded are those that are unique, distinct, and personally meaningful. Thus, it is possible that information that would be crucial in identifying the perpetrator, the place or time of the sexual abuse, or the event being investigated may not have been recorded in the memory of a child at the time the event took place. The conceptualization of encoding as a cognitive process, which is not fixed and which extends beyond the event, indicates to us that it is important to verify what experiences could have helped to maintain or increase memory or even disrupt or distort its recall (Baker-Ward et al., 2009). For example, one should carefully assess (1) the extent to which the child has been subjected to suggestive questioning by the parents or the first person who heard the disclosure or (2) whether a therapeutic intervention may have transformed the child's perspective on his/her experience and, therefore, its representation in his/her underlying memory.

3   Retention period

Following the initial encoding of information about an event, the information will be stored for safekeeping. Different factors can influence the quality of memory during this retention period. Among these are the length of detention, prior knowledge, the child's metacognitive abilities, the degree of exposure to the event, and contamination after the event.

The adage "Memory is a faculty that forgets" is a truth known to all. It has been consistently shown, for different situations and for different types of material

(Rubin & Wenzel, 1996), that the relationship between time and retention follows a logarithmic function – that is to say, a curve that descends rapidly to stabilize after a certain time. In other words, the loss of information recorded in the minutes and hours following an activity or a given event is very rapid, and it stabilizes thereafter.

We have previously stressed that prior knowledge about an event has an effect on children's attention span and, therefore, on the amount of information they can retain. This knowledge also plays a role in the retention of events. This is because it is easier to remember things that we know or events that we can give meaning to. Thus, each new information will be grouped around schema. These are like general themes that include interconnected items; these themes are remembered by the links that are established between them. In other words, past experiences can increase the retention of new information since it is attached to an existing schema.

Another important factor, especially in children, is their cognitive ability to process information about an event they have just experienced. Indeed, before the age of about 7 years (see Peterson, 2012, for a review of the literature), children do not have a cognitive mental structure that enables them to organize the recorded information effectively. They, therefore, do not have an efficient system for classifying their event to remember, and this hinders their storage and recall since the information is difficult to locate (Roediger & Gallo, 2002; Ornstein, 1995). For example, children will more easily remember certain actions performed during a medical visit, such as hearing tests or vaccinations, while they will hardly remember checking reflexes because they have little prior knowledge to categorize this information (Ornstein, 1995). This ability to organize and store information related to lived events increases gradually with age.

The degree of exposure to an event that one wishes to remember plays a crucial role in the amount of information that can be memorized. Thus, the more often an event is repeated (e.g., taking a bath, brushing your teeth), the easier it will be to store in memory all the details relating to that event. With the repetition of the event, the strength of the memory also increases. Research indicates that the amount of detail reported by children increases if the event (magic show, reading a book) has occurred one, four, or eight times (Connolly, Gordon, Woiwod, & Price, 2016; Brubacher, Roberts, & Powell, 2012). In addition, the first (primacy effect) or the last (recency effect) event, depending on the time between the event and interview, is usually better remembered than other instances of the event (Connolly et al., 2016).

However, repetition does not only have advantages when it comes to autobiographical memory and the maltreatment that children may experience repeatedly. Indeed, when an event recurs in a very similar way from one time to another, as in the case of intrafamily sexual abuse or physical abuse, this information tends to group together under a memory called "script." Script memory is a schema that groups and organizes familiar and routine events. When retrieving information grouped together in this way, both children and adults tend to report events in a condensed way and only give details that are common from one event to another (Roediger & Gallo, 2002). Therefore, this gives rise to a poorer and more skeletal account of the events experienced. This is why, during an interview with a child or an adult, it is preferable to work from a specific episode in order to obtain as much detail as possible.

IMPLICATIONS FOR PRACTICE

Several implications flow from this knowledge. The delay between the moment where the information is stored and when it is retrieved, for example, during a disclosure or an investigative interview, is an important factor. The shorter the deadline, the greater the chances of obtaining several details. Lack of knowledge about sexuality and intercourse means that children may have observed or experienced gestures (e.g., seeing ejaculation) that they are not able to give meaning to. In such a situation, this information may not be stored or memorized. At best, the children may be able to use other knowledge or concepts they already have to describe what has been seen, such as reporting that "yogurt" has come out of the penis. In addition, in order to remedy the fact that children do not have metacognitive abilities to organize information, it may be useful to focus on specific details provided by the child to help him/her remember as much as possible of the information regarding these details. This technique will be described in more detail in the chapter on the NICHD Protocol, which includes a section on invitation questions using clues. Finally, when a child talks about situations that have been repeated several times, it is useful to work from memory relating to a specific episode and not from script memory (Brubacher, Powell, & Roberts, 2014). Such a strategy will increase the amount of information the child can remember.

4   Retrieval and recall memory

Retrieval is when information about a memory is recovered from storage. Obviously, in order to extract memories, they must first have been recorded and then kept. Several factors can influence the quality of the retrieval, including the type of memory requested, the source of the information being recorded, and the level of activation/emotion aroused during this recovery.

A determining factor in the accuracy of the information that will be obtained during retrieving is how memory will be used. In fact, in the context of hearing children, as in the case of any type of interview conducted with them, the types of questions that are asked greatly influence the recovery strategies used. Researchers have made a distinction between recall memory, recognition memory, and memory from cues (La Rooy et al., 2011; Roediger & Gallo, 2002). Recall memory is that which is used when one freely remembers a past event. It is that memory that is called upon when children or adults are invited to describe to us everything they remember about a specific event. It is also this type of memory that is used when the child produces a free story. The events may be reported chronologically, although the starting point may not be the start of the event; this is particularly common in very young children.

Recognition-based memory, on the other hand, uses strategies that lead us to check whether the information we are asked for matches what has been encoded in memory. For example, it is this type of memory that is used when answering exams with multiple-choice answers. It is also the type of memory that is used when the child answers questions like "Did he have a beard?"

Another strategy aimed at retrieving information from memory is by using clues based on what the child had said. This strategy aims to provide specific clues that can come from or are provided to the person's story. It is, therefore, a variant of recall memory, but instead of offering the person a choice, it offers a clue (as in recognition memory) to lead the person to search his/her memory for more information using this precise clue. An example of this strategy is asking, "Tell me more about his hand rubbing your stomach." A considerable body of research has shown that information from free recall memory is more likely to be accurate than information from recognition memory, in both children and adults (Pipe & Salmon, 2009). This is especially true in young children who have fewer cognitive strategies to retrieve information. However, research also indicates that free recall produces stories that are accurate but may be limited in relation to the total information that may have been recorded. It is for this reason that the use of cues, particularly of self-generated cues (i.e., from the person's story), is recommended in order to maximize the amount of information that can be obtained with a child or an adult. The efficiency of these cues is based on the principle of the specificity of the encoding (Tulving & Thomson, 1973). This principle states that the more the cue aiming for retrieval resembles, overlaps, or replicates the way an experience is first encoded, the more effective the cue will be in obtaining details of that episode.

Another important aspect to consider at the time of retrieving is the source of encoding memories (Thierry, Lamb, & Orbach, 2003). This notion refers to our ability to identify the origin of the memory that has been memorized. This makes it possible, for example, to distinguish whether the reported event was actually experienced, only imagined, read in a book, or watched on television. This confusion between the sources of encoding memories can lead to the illusion of memories. When events are brought together in time or are similar in their presentation, location, or other ways, they are more easily confused (Roediger & Gallo, 2002). Thus, difficulties in recognizing the source of encoding memories can lead young children to report that they have experienced events or seen objects when they have only heard an adult talk about it or simply seen the event at home television (Principe & Schindewolf, 2012). In the context of the investigative interview, children who are able to identify the source of their memory are also those who give the most details about multiple experiences of sexual abuse (Thierry et al., 2003). Older children find it easier to distinguish details belonging to specific episodes in multiple instances of abuse (Brubacher, Malloy, Lamb, & Roberts, 2013), although laboratory studies suggest that accuracy is not always high (Brubacher et al., 2012). This phenomenon is particularly important when children are subject to many questions from their parents or professionals who, in some cases, may suggest erroneous details (Blandon-Gitlin & Pezdek, 2009; Principe & Schindewolf, 2012). The information that is requested is liable to interfere with the encoding of information already contained in the memory and, therefore, to contaminate it.

The emotions or the level of activation involved in this retrieval of memories can also influence the number of details that will be obtained during the retrieval. For example, Quas and Lench (2007) observe in their study that children who had a higher state of arousal when they watched a fear-inducing film and who were interviewed by a supportive (warm and friendly) interviewer made fewer errors in response to suggestive questioning. On the other hand, children who showed a high state of arousal at the time of questioning and who faced a non-supportive (cold and detached) person produced more errors in response to suggestive questions. This result has implications, including during children's interviews and their testimony in court. Malloy and her colleagues (Malloy, Mitchell, Block, Quas, & Goodman, 2007) suggest that the inability of a child to communicate effectively when experiencing intense emotion is due to the fact that a child must use his/her attention to try to regulate residual stress from the original event instead of focusing that attention on finding important things in memory.

IMPLICATIONS FOR PRACTICE

During an interview, the questions asked of the child will be crucial for retrieving the information sought. These will be reviewed in detail in chapters 3 and 6. However, it can be remembered that in order to preserve the accuracy of the memories collected, retrieving should target memory use based on free recall and on self-generated cues. In addition, we must not forget that the time elapsed since the event is another important factor that influences the quality of memory traces and, therefore, retrieving; the more peripheral details (e.g., the clothes worn, the time of day, the words exchanged) are forgotten more quickly than the central details (e.g., the actions taken). The same is true for the number of details and the accuracy of the information collected, which decreases over time (Ceci & Bruck, 1995; Poole & Lamb, 1998; Ornstein, 1995). It may also be useful, depending on the context in which the interview with the child takes place, to remind the child that it is important to report things that have really happened. However, Poole and Lamb (1998) indicate that in very young children, information from the parent is often taken to be the real thing. They relate an example of a real-life story where a little girl, to whom the interviewer asked if what she reported had really happened, answered "yes" and, after a short pause, added, "Mom told me." However, during an interview with children aged 5 and over, one could, at the end of the interview, ask the child whether certain elements, about which the interviewer has doubts, are things that they have experienced or felt or if this information comes from another source, such as the parent or another interviewer in a previous interview. Instructions suggesting ignoring sources of information other than what the child has experienced may also contribute to more accurate accounts (Schaaf, Bederian-Gardner, & Goodman, 2015).

5   Other factors that may influence children's memory

5.1   Age

The age of children when events occur is very important in determining the number of memories they will be able to memorize (Peterson & Warren, 2009). In fact, children under the age of 2 at the time of the events usually remember nothing or, at best, very fragmentary elements, even for stressful events. This phenomenon is probably due to the fact that the memories could not then be verbalized since the child had not yet acquired the language (Howe et al., 2009). Likewise, older children seem to have retained only fragmentary elements of events if they occurred when they were very young. Some of these fragments may be thought to be associated with other memories related to later events that have come together to produce a coherent narrative (Peterson & Warren, 2009).

Thus, preschool-age children will usually give less detailed, less comprehensive, and less consistent accounts of stressful or emotional events than school-age children. This is also true for events without emotional components. However, very young children, such as 2- or 3-year-olds, are able to recall stressful events accurately under certain conditions (Paz-Alonso et al., 2009). However, it is only around the age of 3.5 years that the children are able to report details in sufficient numbers to allow us to understand the event in question (Fivush, Haden, & Adam, 1995). Children may retain memories of events that occurred a few months or years earlier (Fivush, Peterson, & Schwarzmueller, 2002). For example, 8-year-olds are able to recall events they would have experienced 5 years earlier (Bauer, 2015). Based on research findings, Howe (2011) indicates that children can retain memories of events from a very young age over a period of 2 to 5 years. However, we know that adults have very poor memories of their early childhood. This phenomenon, called infantile amnesia, was first used by Freud (1905–1953) to describe the fact that adults seem unable to remember events that happened to them during their childhood (i.e., before the age of 5 or 6 years), with an almost total absence of memories of the first 3 years of life (Howe et al., 2009; Peterson, 2012). So while it is not surprising that a 5-year-old can remember a sexual abuse experienced at age 3, it is unlikely that an adult will have retained such a memory unless post-event encoding conditions were at work. Usually, these accounts are reconstructions of what likely happened, reconstructions based on information from conversations with others (parents or siblings), suggestions from the interviewer, or a vague memory that has been reinterpreted in relation to the current knowledge (Malloy & Quas, 2009; Principe & Schindewolf, 2012).

These differences in memory performance with age may reflect developmental changes in cognitive functioning, such as improvements in the speed of information processing, language acquisition, and the development of an increased capacity to use complex mental strategies and accumulate knowledge about previous events. With age, children forget less, and this explains why as they age, they retain more detailed memories than toddlers (Bauer, 2015).

Whether the emotional impact of an event is positive or negative, the events that are remembered best are those that are distinct, unique, and have personal consequences (Howe, 2011). In this way, events that occurred in childhood that are particularly important to oneself and that have personal significance could be retained even in adulthood. However, it is difficult to predict which autobiographical elements will be remembered in the long term as our personal history is constantly evolving. Thus, the new events added to our autobiographical knowledge base can also be used to modify the memories that are already stored there.

IMPLICATIONS FOR PRACTICE

The age of the child, both at the time of the event and at the time of the interview, is a determining factor in the amount of detail that can be obtained. For the interviewer, it is, therefore, not only important but essential to respect the developmental capacities of children. So if a 3-year-old boy can accurately report actions committed against him during the past year, that account will probably be in two or three sentences (e.g., "He showed me his pee, said to touch it. I said no and I ran away").

5.2   Participation versus observation

An event is better memorized if the person is involved or participates in it than if the person is a simple observer (Paz-Alonso et al., 2009) or is told about an event (Connolly & Gordon, 2014). However, it appears that children who observe a highly stressful or traumatic event (e.g., physical, sexual, or emotional abuse by another family member) may encode and retain memories of that event similar to those related to lived events (Howe, 2011).

IMPLICATIONS FOR PRACTICE

The account given by a child victim and that of another child who may have been a witness will, therefore, be likely to contain certain overlaps, but the amount of detail and the nature of these details could vary due to, among other things, the active role played by the child. In addition, previously named factors, such as knowledge, interests, and attention spans, are likely to influence the recording and retention of information as well.

5.3   The memory of stressful or traumatic events

A few questions concerning the relationship between stress and memory in children have been clarified. All research (Howe et al., 2015; Peterson, 2012) demonstrates the robust nature of children's memory for a single stressful event. These studies, including painful medical procedures or natural disasters like hurricanes, have repeatedly observed that children have increased memory of these stressful and salient events. For example, Peterson and Whalen (2001) demonstrate, for different age groups, that children, when interviewed one week after an accident, remembered 75% of the information related to their injuries and, five years later, 73%. Their recollection of treatment received in hospital was lower – 57% after one week and 50% five years later. As for the accuracy of these details, it was very high with 94% of details correct one week after the incident and 86% and 77% five years later for the information respectively concerning the injury and the treatment in hospital. Research also suggests better retention for events that are emotionally charged (Paz-Alonso et al., 2009; Peterson, 2012). This would be explained by the usual mechanisms of memory (i.e., these emotionally charged events are also more significant, distinct, and salient). Research shows that distinct negative events are particularly well recalled and retained over time by children as young as 3 years old (Howe et al., 2015).

In the case of memories of a stressful event, it has been established that the relationship between stress and memory is not direct (Bauer, 2009; Deffenbacher, Bornstein, Penrod, & McGorty, 2004). Experienced stress increases or decreases memory performance. This relationship is an inverted "U" relationship, where too much or too little stress produces poor memory, while an intermediate level of stress could produce optimal memory. This model explicitly recognizes that stressful events are associated with physiological responses and distress behaviors (e.g., crying, pain, distress reports) that affect memory performance. In addition, other moderators may be at work, such as characteristics of the child (e.g., the child's temperament, parent-child attachment style, emotional regulation) (Salmon & Reese, 2015) or of the interview or interviewer (e.g., cold versus warm interviewer, emotional tone, openness). These will be detailed in the chapter dealing with children's development.

Another explanation for the link between memory and stressful events concerns the relation between the degree of stress caused by the event and the level of attention elicited. Deffenbacher and colleagues (2004) suggest that the type of attention elicited would be different depending on the nature of the stressful event. These authors distinguish two modes of attention control, namely the arousal mode and the activation mode. Arousal mode directs the response to a high level of attention, while activation mode provides a defensive fight or flight response. This defensive response is elicited by events that threaten the integrity of the body or self-esteem that can create a considerable level of distress. In their theoretical model, these authors suggest that as stress increases, memory for the details on which attention is focused will also increase. However, when the stress reaches very high levels, there will be a dramatic drop in memory performance. This model accounts for research results obtained from adults (Peterson & Warren, 2009), and therefore, further studies are needed to confirm its relevance for children since some studies have not observed this relationship (Peterson, 2012).

IMPLICATIONS FOR PRACTICE

The degree of fear, stress, or anxiety experienced by children at the time of the events is likely to affect the quality of their memory; these traumatic events are better recorded and retained in memory. However, it is difficult to make a direct link between the severity of the event and the quality of the memory since this relationship is influenced by many factors. Thus, when the acts committed include touching, which may have been presented to the child as a game, it is possible that the amount of information recorded is poorer than if the event caused a certain degree of stress or even captured the attention of the child by the novelty that it represented. Research conducted to date suggests that the same memory mechanisms are at play during traumatic events (Howe et al., 2015). As the stress experienced by the children during the interview is also likely to influence the quality of their story, it is important to take time to develop a bond of trust with the child. The meeting place should also be quiet and devoid of distraction (Poole, 2016).

6   Memories of child abuse

An important question without a definitive answer is whether traumatic events of a more chronic nature, such as child abuse, are more easily remembered than neutral or positive events. As pointed out by Greenhoot and Bunnel (2009), a widespread idea in the clinical literature is that the memory of particularly stressful events would be pushed outside of consciousness and forgotten through defense mechanisms specific to the psychology of traumas, such as dissociation and repression, mentioned for the first time by Freud. These explanations and the theories that flow from them come from the many clinical observations of adults who had traumatic stories during their childhood and who seem to have difficulty recalling specific elements of these experiences. Although research on this topic is still in its early stages, some answers are available.

A first explanation for the disturbances in autobiographical memory suggests that they are attributable to stress-related damage to the hippocampus. This is because high levels of stress produce a hormone, cortisol, and prolonged exposure to a high level of this hormone can cause atrophy of the hippocampus. This would result in permanent memorization problems since the hippocampus is responsible for a wide variety of memory processes, including the consolidation and recall of declarative representations of verbal memory, as well as implicit and spatial memory. This hypothesis comes mainly from research done on animals. In humans, the neuroanatomical evidence is less clear, and according to other hypotheses, the decrease in the hippocampus is associated with states of post-traumatic stress and depression and not with the trauma itself. A few studies in children suggest that children's brains are susceptible to the same damage from the hippocampus due to stress (Howe et al., 2015).

To explain memory problems associated with trauma, the hypothesis formulated by Williams in 1996 on affective regulation is often cited (Greenhoot & Bunnel, 2009). This model suggests that aversive childhood experiences lead to the development of a persistent avoidant cognitive style that involves avoiding thinking and speaking about past traumatic events in order to block potential negative affect. This model revised by Williams and colleagues in 2007 emphasizes the role of current conditions of trauma and depression related to autobiographical memory. The model indicates that this functional avoidance pattern can be intensified by different conditions that are typical of people with a traumatic history, such as depression, rumination, a high number of negative self-representations, intrusive memories, and deficits in executive resources. Since the majority of research has focused on adults, it is difficult to decide whether these disturbances in autobiographical memory arise from the trauma itself or whether they are an adult response to conditions of recall of memories or of the functioning of thought.

However, three studies of longitudinal data by Greenhoot and colleagues (Greenhoot, Johnson, Legerski, & McCloskey, 2009) support this theory. They observed that adolescents who were exposed to abuse in their family context during their childhood produce shorter and more general memories but also produce fewer memories in response to neutral cues. In addition, the weak responses they give following the interviewer's requests are compatible with functional avoidance and suggest that, even if these young people may have memorized specific events, they are less motivated or able to report them. This research also found that non-abused adolescents use more emotional language in response to questions about negative events that they have experienced; this observation converges with other studies that indicate that children express more emotions and refer more to internal states when recalling negative events rather than positive or neutral events. Adolescents with a history of aggression do not show such an increase in emotional expression when discussing conflicting childhood memories. Although their language is more emotional, they use fewer words and emotions in response to these cues than non-abused adolescents.

In addition to the hypothesis of affective regulation of negative effects by avoidance, two other hypotheses can be formulated to explain that people who have experienced trauma have poorer memories (Greenhoot & Bunnel, 2009). One of these hypotheses suggests that people with a history of abuse encode very few emotional details from the start. These conflicting events can be particularly confusing for children living in violent contexts, making it difficult for them to fully assess or label their own emotions and those of others related to these events. The other hypothesis suggests that these children have become, in a certain way, desensitized in the face of the conflicts to which they are repeatedly exposed. In other words, even though traumatic events often have a distinctive character, which should make them better remembered, in children who experience such abusive events repeatedly, this distinctiveness may no longer be perceived over time. This makes these conflicting events less emotionally charged for them than they would be for individuals without a history of abuse. It should be noted, however, that research on the psychophysiology of desensitization or hypersensitization in children has produced mixed results that do not allow one or the other of the hypotheses to be confirmed.

IMPLICATIONS FOR PRACTICE

The current state of research concerning the memory of traumatized children does not allow us to suggest concrete avenues for intervention. However, results to date suggest that children who have experienced repeated abuse would have more difficulty producing a detailed narrative.

7   Conclusion

Children from the age of 3.5 years are able to produce short, accurate accounts of particular events they have experienced. As the child grows, not only will their memory be better organized, but the amount of information that can be recalled will increase considerably.

It is important to remember that not all aspects of an event are stored in memory and that the child's knowledge and interests are important factors that influence the details that will be preserved. Thus, if important elements are not mentioned in the child's free story, which is more likely to be accurate, the interviewer should consider the hypothesis that these details are likely to be missing because they were not retained at the time the events took place. It is, therefore, prudent, before questioning children about elements that they have not mentioned, to remind them that if they do not remember this information, they should say so. The shorter the time between the event and the interview with the child, the better the recollection should be. Several factors – such as the fact of having actively participated in the event, that it was stressful, that this event occurred frequently, or even that the child was subjected to repeated maltreatment – can also influence the quality of the memory. Although the direction of these effects cannot always be determined, some improving memory and others weakening it, these factors must be considered by the interviewers who must adjust their need for information to the child's capacity to provide this information.

References

Baker-Ward L., Ornstein P. A., Starnes L. P. (2009). "Children's understanding and remembering of stressful experiences", in Quas J. A., Fivush R. (Eds.), *Emotion and memory in development: Biological, cognitive, and social considerations*, New York, Oxford University Press, 28–59.

Bauer P. J. (2009). "Complications abound, and why that's a good thing", in Quas J. A., Fivush R. (Eds.), *Emotion and Memory in Development: Biological, Cognitive, and Social Considerations*, New York, Oxford University Press, 374–393.

Bauer P. J. (2015). "A complementary processes account of the development of childhood amnesia and a personal past", *Psychological Review*, 122(2), 204–231.

Blandon-Gitlin I., Pezdek K. (2009). "Children memory in forensic contexts: Suggestibility, false memory, and individual differences", in Bottoms B. L., Najdowski C. J., Goodman G. S. (Eds.), *Children as victims, witnesses, and offenders: Psychological science and the law*, New York, Guilford.

Brubacher S. P., Malloy L. C., Lamb M. E., Roberts K. P. (2013). "How do interviewers and children discuss individual occurrences of alleged repeated abuse in forensic interviews?" *Applied Cognitive Psychology*, 27(4), 443–450.

Brubacher S. P., Powell M. B., Roberts K. P. (2014). "Recommendations for interviewing children about repeated experiences", *Psychology, Public Policy, and Law*, 20(3), 325–335.

Brubacher S. P., Roberts K. P., Powell M. (2012). "Retrieval of episodic versus generic information: Does the order of recall affect the amount and accuracy of details reported by children about repeated events?" *Developmental Psychology*, 48(1), 111–122.

Ceci S. J., Bruck M. (1995). *Jeopardy in the courtroom: A scientific analysis of children's testimony*, Washington, DC, American Psychological Association.

Connolly D. A., Gordon H. M. (2014). "Can order of general and specific memory prompts help children to recall an instance of a repeated event that was different from the others?" *Psychology, Crime & Law*, 20(9), 852–864.

Connolly D. A., Gordon H. M., Woiwod D. M., Price H. L. (2016). "What children recall about a repeated event when one instance is different from the others", *Developmental Psychology*, 52(7), 1038–1051.

Deffenbacher K. A., Bornstein B. H., Penrod S. D., McGorty E. (2004). "A meta-analytic review of the effects of high stress on eyewitness memory", *Law and Human Behavior*, 28(6), 687–706.

Fivush R., Haden C., Adam S. (1995). "Structure and coherence of preschooler's personal narratives over time: Implications for childhood amnesia", *Journal of Experimental Child Psychology*, 60, 32–56.

Fivush R., Peterson C., Schwarzmueller A. (2002). "Questions and answers: The credibility of child witness in the context of specific questioning techniques", in Eisen M. L., Quas J. D., Goodman G. S. (Eds.), *Memory and suggestibility in the forensic interview*, Mahwah, NJ, Lawrence Erlbaum Associates, 331–354.

Greenhoot A. F., Bunnel S. L. (2009). "Trauma and memory", in Bottoms B. L., Najdowski C. J., Goodman G. S. (Eds.), *Children as victim, witness and offender: Psychological science and the law*, New York, Guilford Press, 36–56.

Greenhoot A. F., Johnson R. J., Legerski J., McCloskey L. A. (2009). "Stress and autobiographical memory functioning", in Quas J. A., Fivush R. (Eds.), *Emotion and memory in development: Biological, cognitive, and social considerations*, New York, Oxford University Press.

Howe M. L. (2011). *The nature of early memory: An adaptive theory of the genesis and development of memory*, New York, Oxford University Press.

Howe M. L., Courage M. L., Rooksby M. (2009). "The genesis and development of autobiographical memory", in Courage M. L., Cowan N. (Eds.), *The development of memory in infancy and childhood*, 2nd ed., New York, Psychology Press, 177–196.

Howe M. L., Toth S. L., Cicchetti D. (2015). "Memory and developmental psychopathology", in Cicchetti D., Cohen D. J. (Eds.), *Developmental psychopathology*, 2nd ed., Hoboken, John Wiley & Sons, 629–655.

La Rooy D. J., Malloy L. C., Lamb M. E. (2011). "The development of memory in childhood", in Lamb M. E., La Rooy D. J., Malloy L. C., Katz C. (Eds.), *Children's testimony: A handbook of psychological research and forensic practice*, 2nd ed., Malden, John Wiley & Sons, 49–68.

Malloy L. C., Mitchell E., Block S., Quas J. A., Goodman G. S. (2007). "Children's eyewitness memory: Balancing children's needs and defendants' rights when seeking the truth", in Toglia M. P., Read J. D., Ross D. F., Lindsay R. C. (Eds.), *The handbook of eyewitness psychology, vol. I: Memory for events*, Mahwah, Lawrence Erlbaum Associates Publishers, 545–574.

Malloy L. C., Quas J. A. (2009). "Children's suggestibility: Areas of consensus and controversy", in Kuehnle K., Connell M. (Eds.), *The evaluation of child sexual abuse allegations: A comprehensive guide to assessment and testimony*, Hoboken, John Wiley & Sons Inc., 267–297.

Ornstein P. A. (1995). "Children's long term retention of salient personal experiences", *Journal of Traumatic Stress*, 4, 581–605.

Ornstein P. A., Haden C. A. (2002). "The development of memory: Toward an understanding of children's testimony", in Courage M. L., Cowan N. (Eds.), *Memory and suggestibility in the forensic interview*, Mahwah, Lawrence Erlbaum Associates Publishers, 29–61.

Paz-Alonso P. M., Larson R. P., Castelli P., Alley D., Goodman G. S. (2009). "Memory development: Emotion, stress, and trauma", in Courage M. L., Cowan N. (Eds.), *The development of memory in infancy and Childhood*, 2nd ed., New York, Psychology Press, 197–239.

Peterson C. (2012). "Children's autobiographical memories across the years: Forensic implications of childhood amnesia and eyewitness memory for stressful events", *Developmental Review*, 32(3), 287–306.

Peterson C., Warren K. L. (2009). "Injuries, emergency rooms, and children's memory: Factors contributing to individual differences", in Quas J. A., Fivush R. (Eds.), *Emotion and memory in development: Biological, cognitive, and social considerations*, New York, Oxford University Press, 60–85.

Peterson C., Whalen N. (2001). "Five years later: Children's memory for medical emergencies", *Applied Cognitive Psychology*, déc., 15(7), S7–S24.

Pipe M.-E., Salmon K. (2009). "Memory development and forensic context", in Courage M. L., Cowan N. (Eds.), *The development of memory in infancy and childhood*, 2nd ed., New York, Psychology Press, 241–282.

Poole D. A. (2016). *Interviewing children: The science of conversation in forensic contexts*, Washington, DC, American Psychological Association.

Poole D. A., Lamb M. E. (1998). *Investigative interviews of children: A guide for helping professionals*, Washington, DC, American Psychological Association.

Principe G. F., Schindewolf E. (2012). "Natural conversations as a source of false memories in children: Implications for the testimony of young witnesses", *Developmental Review*, 32, 205–223.

Quas J. A., Lench H. C. (2007). "Arousal at encoding, arousal at retrieval, interviewer support, and children's memory for a mild stressor", *Applied Cognitive Psychology*, 21(3), 289–305.

Roediger H. L., Gallo D. A. (2002). "Processes affecting accuracy and distortion in memory: An overview", in Eisen M. L., Quas J. A., Goodman G. S. (Eds.), *Memory and suggestibility in the forensic interview*, Mahwah, Lawrence Erlbaum Associates, 3–28.

Rubin D. C., Wenzel A. E. (1996). "One hundred years of forgetting: A quantitative description of retention", *Psychological Review*, 103(4), 734–760.

Salmon K., Reese E. (2015). "Talking (or not talking) about the past: The influence of parent – child conversation about negative experiences on children's memories", *Applied Cognitive Psychology*, 32, 791–801.

Schaaf J. M., Bederian-Gardner D., Goodman G. S. (2015). "Gating out misinformations: Can young children follow instructions to ignore false information?" *Behavioral Sciences and Law*, 33, 390–406.

Thierry K. L., Lamb M. E., Orbach Y. (2003). "Awareness of the origin of knowledge predicts child witnesses' recall of alleged sexual and physical abuse", *Applied and Preventive Psychology*, 17(8), 953–967.

Tulving E., Thomson D. M. (1973). "Encoding specificity and retrieval processes in episodic memory", *Psychological Review*, 77, 1–15.

Yapko M. (1994). *Suggestions of abuse: True and false memories of childhood sexual trauma*, New York, Simon and Chutser.

Chapter 3

Suggestibility in children

- What factors make children suggestible?
- Are only very young children suggestible?
- Are imagined or invented stories different from stories about real events?
- Can the suggestibility of an investigative interview be determined by the number of leading questions?

The *suggestibility* of children is an important question since it is at the very center of the veracity of children's testimony about maltreatment they may have suffered or events they have witnessed. Major lawsuits in the United States in the late 1980s made it clear that children, under certain conditions, can produce false stories. Suggestibility generally refers to errors that occur when the witness is exposed to information that is false or to social pressure that encourages certain types of responses. In this chapter, after defining suggestibility, we look at the different factors that make children more suggestible or that protect them from the influence of others, especially those related to the characteristics of the child. Then we examine those related to the investigative interview and its context. The implications for the practice of interviewing will guide the reader on the best ways to limit the influence of suggestibility on the child and to determine to what extent an account may have been contaminated.

1 Definition

Ceci and Bruck (1995), in their work on the testimony of children, define suggestibility as the degree to which the encoding, storage, retrieval, and reporting of events can be influenced by a wide range of internal and external factors. This definition makes it possible to take account of different contexts. For example, it includes giving information while being fully aware that this information diverges from the original event, as is the case when we acquiesce to social pressures, when we lie, or when we want to please significant people. Thus, this definition does not imply that the original memory is altered; the child can remember exactly what happened but chooses, for different reasons, not to report this information. This definition account also for the effect produced by information obtained before or after the event. For example, the child may have been made aware of particular expectations before the event occurs (e.g., in the context of divorce, the mother may suggest that the father of the child is a mean man), and these expectations can influence the perception of subsequent behaviors or events. While these expectations can have a beneficial effect in making

DOI: 10.4324/9781003265351-3

the child more aware of certain behaviors, they can also have a negative impact when ambiguous behaviors are misinterpreted (e.g., when attempts at physical closeness to the father are interpreted as attempted sexual abuse). This definition of suggestibility also allows us to consider certain cognitive and social factors. Therefore, it includes subtle suggestions, expectations, stereotypes, and leading questions that may subconsciously alter memories. It also includes explicit bribery attempts, threats, and other forms of social inducement that can cause children to consciously alter their statements without altering the underlying memory. In the following paragraphs, we discuss the factors likely to increase suggestibility by examining those related to the child and then those relating to the characteristics of the interviews.

2   Factors related to children

Bruck and Melnyk (2004) reviewed the results of sixty-nine studies that examined individual differences in suggestibility, focusing on seventeen factors. Among these, six factors seem to be more related to suggestibility: cognitive factors, language skills, creativity, self-concept, attachment style, and parent-child relationship. In addition to detailing these factors, we also look at the effect of age, socioeconomic level, and culture/ethnicity.

2.1   Cognitive and linguistic factors and creativity

Children who are smarter tend to resist false suggestions better than children with low intelligence or intellectual disabilities (Bruck & Melnyk, 2004). Higher intelligence is associated with better mnemonic strategies, better understanding of interviewer questions, greater confidence in one's own memories, and an ability to assess the plausibility of interviewer suggestions (Harris, Goodman, Augusti, Chae, & Alley, 2009). However, Bruck and Melnyk conclude that beyond the difference observed between children with intellectual disabilities and typically developing children, the level of intelligence of typically developing children does not appear to influence their level of suggestibility. Eisen and colleagues (Eisen, Goodman, Qin, Davis, & Crayton, 2007) observe that higher cognitive functioning, assessed by short-term memory, receptive language comprehension, and intelligence scores, predicted fewer errors (providing false information to respond to specific and misleading questions about an anogenital medical exam). Although the results are not consistent across all studies, it appears that verbal intelligence predicts less suggestibility in children who are 7 and older but not in those who are 5. Verbal rather than nonverbal intelligence is more often associated with better resistance to suggestibility in typically developing children. In preschool children, relationships are observed between the level of language development and children's suggestibility: children with more advanced language skills are more resistant to suggestions (Bruck & Melnyk, 2004).

It is important here to emphasize that children who experience abuse, such as sexual abuse, are more likely to have a delay in the development of their cognitive functioning and in their understanding and use of language (Eigsti & Cicchetti, 2004; Goodman, Bottoms, Rudy, Davis, & Schwartz-Kenney, 2001). For example, Daignault and Hébert (2009) explored the different school adaptation profiles of girls who were victims of sexual abuse and observed that half of these girls obtained a score below the 1st quartile (25th percentile) on the verbal and knowledge sub-scales of an intelligence test. In one of our studies (Dion & Cyr, 2008), children who had been sexually abused had a delay of more than a year and a half in their verbal cognitive development.

Additionally, better executive functions are likely related to the ability to resist false suggestions. The term "executive function" is used to describe the integrated cognitive processes that guide intentional or goal-oriented behaviors. Although there is no universal definition of executive functions, these can include cognitive abilities such as control, planning, working memory (temporary recording of information while performing a task), self-regulation, mental flexibility, the use of attention, and the use of feedback. Children with deficits in executive functions (e.g., poor working memory) may be able to compensate for these difficulties in a supportive interview setting (Harris et al., 2009). However, in the studies reviewed by Bruck and Melnyk, the results obtained were not consistent, and this led these authors to conclude that a relationship could not be shown between executive functions and suggestibility.

In addition, children with intellectual disabilities have significant limits in terms of their cognitive functioning and adaptive behavior, and they frequently have language and communication difficulties (Dion, Bouchard, Gaudreault, & Mercier, 2012; Henry, Bettenay, & Carney, 2011). Although these children tend to be more suggestible, this is not always the case. For example, Henry and Gudjonsson (Henry & Gudjonsson, 2003) observe in their experimental research that children with mild to moderate intellectual disabilities are more likely to modify their responses when specific questions are repeated than are children with an equivalent mental age (an estimate of their actual intellectual development). These same authors also noted that these children were more likely to respond in the affirmative when in doubt (positive response bias) (Finlay & Lyons, 2002). The results of several studies suggest that children with mild to moderate intellectual disabilities can, when questioned using open-ended questions, provide judicially useful and accurate information and that they are generally not more suggestible than children without cognitive problems of the same mental age. However, specific closed-ended questions make children with intellectual disabilities more suggestible (Henry & Gudjonsson, 2003; Henry & Gudjonsson, 1999; Jens, Gordon, & Shaddock, 1990; Michel, Gordon, Ornstein, & Simpson, 2000) (see also Chapter 4).

The six studies that examined children's creativity, cognitive flexibility, and imagination all found a link with suggestibility. Among children aged 5 to 8, those who are most creative are also those who are most suggestible; indeed, more imaginative and creative children develop more false narratives in response to leading questions.

Here, it is important to emphasize that from the age of 6, children are able, just like adults, to distinguish between elements that are fantasy and those which are real. Children of 3-year-olds are able to correctly judge that certain elements are fantasy, such as the fact that pretended actions are not real actions or that the imagined objects cannot appear in real life, although they do tend to believe that imagined positive events are real (Carrick & Quas, 2006). The use of tools associated with fantasy, such as dolls, toys, and drawings (see Chapter 5), as well as interviewer questions that ask the child to pretend or imagine, are likely factors to bring children to the imagination and, therefore, to make them more suggestible.

IMPLICATIONS FOR PRACTICE

As the majority of children who are interviewed in the context of an investigative interview or expertise are likely to come from an environment where they have suffered one or more forms of abuse, the interviewer should always remember to adapt his/her questions and especially to use a vocabulary that is within the understanding of a child who is two years younger than the child questioned. In other words, when interacting with an 8-year-old, it is best to tailor the investigative interview as if interviewing a 6-year-old. In the case of people with intellectual disabilities, an investigative interview should be conducted according to the level of development of mental age and not the actual chronological age. Thus, an interview with an 18-year-old who has the mental development of a 6-year-old should be conducted with vocabulary and questions adapted to a 6-year-old. In addition, it is important to avoid, with these children, questions that must be answered with yes or no; in fact, these questions lead them to answer yes more often than they should. It is also necessary to be careful and not to appeal, when eliciting their story, to imaginative aspects such as "If I were a little bird and had been in your bedroom when your father came, what would I have seen?" In addition, it can be helpful to tell children that they should only talk about things that have really happened to them.

2.2 Self-concept

Children with a positive self-concept may feel relatively confident during interviews. Harris and colleagues (Harris et al., 2009) point out that when an interviewer says something that is wrong, these children have more confidence in their memory accuracy and feel less social pressure to approve this interviewer. On the other hand, children who perceive themselves as inadequate may not say everything they remember, and they may be particularly sensitive to interviewer pressure, or they may succumb to the interviewer's suggestions about inaccurate information. For example, Vrij and Bush (2000) observe that young children are more suggestible than older ones, but this difference disappears when one considers the level of self-confidence of children as assessed by teachers. In 9-year-old children, Mazzoni (1998) observes that the feeling of self-efficacy, operationalized by the degree of confidence in one's own memory, was inversely related to suggestibility. However, this result was not observed in 6-year-old children. With a sample of children aged 6 and 7, Davis and Bottom (2002) find that older children who had a greater sense of self-confidence were able to tell the interviewer s/he was wrong. They were also more resistant to misleading questions than younger ones. Bruck and Melnyk (2004) indicate that in six of the nine studies they identified, a more positive self-concept was associated with a lower tendency to be suggestible.

IMPLICATIONS FOR PRACTICE

These results suggest that a children's level of suggestibility is at least partly explained by the degree of confidence that the children have in their memory and in their ability to tell a story. For this reason, it seems important to inform the children that if they do not remember certain information requested, they should simply indicate that they do not remember it. In addition, children must be allowed to give the fullest possible story using open-ended questions for which they can choose the answers and therefore rely on the memories of which they are most certain.

2.3   Attachment and the quality of the parent-child relationship

Stressful or threatening situations are likely to activate a child's attachment systems, and this motivates them to seek comfort and protection from their parents. Also, how the parent will respond to children's distress can be predicted from the parents' attachment status. Of the six studies reviewed by Bruck and Melnyk (2004), five find that the parent's ability to foster secure attachment (e.g., comfortable intimacy, emotional support for the child, a desire to discuss and "soothe" negative emotions) is associated with a better resistance by the child to false suggestions. Melinder and colleagues (Melinder et al., 2010) also observe that children are more resistant to suggestions when their parents have a less anxious attachment style. Goodman and his colleagues (Goodman, Quas, Batterman-Faunce, Riddlesberger, & Kuhn, 1997) have proposed as an explanation for this bond that parents who have a secure attachment – that is to say, a parent who feels safe in intimate relationships – are more open to talking with their child about stressful events the child has experienced. This would, therefore, have an influence on the children's memory for these events since they can more easily describe negative or difficult experiences, thoughts, and emotions, thus strengthening their memory and their ability to express them.

IMPLICATIONS FOR PRACTICE

The quality of the parent-child relationship and the quality of the child's attachment to its primary caregiver are factors that may influence children's suggestibility. Bruck and Melnyk suggest that children raised by parents who are capable of secure relationships and who are supportive help children develop better self-confidence and a more positive self-concept, which makes children more resistant to leading or suggestive questions. However, it may be difficult for the interviewer to assess the type of attachment children have with their parents or the quality of the parent-child relationship, especially in situations where the parents are not present at the time of the interview. Nevertheless, these results support the importance of taking the time to develop a positive relationship with the child and to help him/her feel competent during the investigative interview.

2.4   Age

In their review of studies, Bruck and Melnyk (2004) find few significant differences as a function of age. They explain these results by the fact that the majority of research on suggestibility has been done with preschool children. Malloy and Quas (2009) indicate that, in general, with increasing age, children's memory accuracy improves and suggestibility decreases. This is true for all events and contexts. We have already pointed out in the chapter on memory that age at the time of the event has a direct effect on the amount of information children recorded. As young children record less information, they are also more vulnerable to pressure from interviewers to seek out specific types of detail. Age at the time of the interview is, therefore, a direct predictor of suggestibility. This is because younger children make more mistakes in responding to leading questions than older children. Although adolescents have more cognitive abilities and are, therefore, less easily influenced, they have a high sensitivity to reward (Chein, Albert, O'Brien, Uckert, & Steinberg, 2011) and a significant fear of social rejection (Ansado, Chiasson, & Beauchamp, 2014), which could increase their suggestibility during investigative interviews.

IMPLICATIONS FOR PRACTICE

It is, therefore, important to consider the age of the child during interviews and to have realistic expectations about their ability to report detailed information. In other words, we must accept that young children's accounts are short and that many forensically important details are often missing from their story. Insisting with a young child for more information on a specific detail, such as the exact position of the perpetrator during the gestures and the physical description of a place or a person, or even asking an older child the exact time of the abuse or the number of events is beyond the child's ability (see Chapter 4). Moreover, faced with this insistence, children feel that they must provide an answer; they then become suggestible, responding to the inappropriate request. It may, therefore, be useful to remind children that they can say that if they do not know the answer to the question that will be asked, they should point it out to the interviewer. For the interviewer, this also means giving up certain information that cannot be obtained reliably.

2.5 Socioeconomic level

The results of the studies that have been conducted are incomplete because they seldom consider a large range of socioeconomic status. In addition, the differences observed are sometimes also linked to differences in child's intelligence, or the levels of education or mental health of the parents or children. Recent studies have linked poverty to behavioral problems that could influence children's performance during forensic interviews. Bruck and Melnyk (2004) report that only one study, out of the six that were available, demonstrates an association between socioeconomic level and suggestibility after controlling for other environmental factors. When associations between children's suggestibility and socioeconomic level are assessed, they indicate that children with higher socioeconomic backgrounds are the least suggestible (Harris et al., 2009), but this effect is weak.

IMPLICATIONS FOR PRACTICE

For interviewers, knowing the socioeconomic level of the child can be a useful indicator of children's capacities, namely that children who come from low socioeconomic backgrounds are more likely to have a delay in language development and comprehension of the task requested and to be more suggestible. Using short sentences and simple vocabulary, as well as the specification of goals and expectations for the investigative interview, should make these children less suggestible.

2.6   Culture, race, or ethnicity

Harris and colleagues (Harris et al., 2009) report that members of a cultural community interpret and respond to unwanted sexual behavior based on their cultural norms. These interpretations and responses can affect resistance to suggestion. For example, children who grow up in a culture that maintains the belief that the devil is responsible for bad things are more susceptible to suggestions about satanic rituals. The degree of obedience children owe adults also varies across cultures. For example, Quas and colleagues (Quas et al., 1999) note differences between children in the United States and children in New Zealand when asked leading and misleading questions about a stressful medical procedure. New Zealand children were more suggestible, and this is in keeping with a culture wherein adults are treated with deference. In another study comparing North American children and Brazilian children, Saltzstein, Dias, and Millery (2004) observe that North American children are more suggestible than Brazilian children when questioned by an older, more authoritative interviewer than by a younger examiner.

Harris and colleagues (2009) indicate that it is also possible that the origin of the interviewer could have an influence on the suggestibility of children. It might be more difficult for children to establish a working and trusting relationship with an interviewer whose origin means that they do not share the same social or cultural codes. However, more research is needed to verify this hypothesis.

IMPLICATIONS FOR PRACTICE

The current state of knowledge regarding the influence of culture or ethnicity is not sufficiently advanced to be able to formulate precise recommendations. However, the data at our disposal leads us to be attentive to these elements and to remember that, depending on their cultural background, some children will be more likely to be suggestible, responding with deference to the perceived authority of the interviewer. In addition, it would be possible that the children could also be influenced by the ethnicity of the interviewer if it differs from their own. Suggestibility during interviews may decrease when interviewers establish a good relationship with a child from a culture different from their own.

3   Factors related to the questions and to the context of the interview

3.1   The questions

The effect of the type of question used by the interviewer on the suggestibility of children is certainly one of the factors that have been examined extensively and for which the research results are the most consistent (Ceci & Bruck, 1995; Feltis, Powell, Snow, & Hughes-Scholes, 2010; Malloy & Quas, 2009). The questions can be grouped into various categories: open-ended questions, directive questions (wh-question), option-posing questions, and finally, suggestive questions (see also Chapters 6 and 7). According to the literature, directive questions and option-posing questions are sometimes described as focused, specific, or closed questions. Although the categorization may vary from one article to another, all authors agree that the likelihood of suggestion is lower with open-ended questions and that it gradually increases when moving to directive questions, then to option-posing questions, and finally to clearly suggestive interventions. This degree of suggestibility is a function of the amount of information conveyed by the question that was not first provided by the interviewee.

Open-ended questions are usually defined as utterances that require responses with multiple words (Poole & Lamb, 1998). They provide minimal information or direction and ask for an account of the event; an example is "Tell me everything that happened from beginning to the end." Because these open-ended questions do not provide any details about the event, they are not suggestive. Open-ended questions can also be more specific and focus on a detail that the child has already revealed, such as "Tell me all about the things you saw around the house." Studies have shown that even young children responding to open-ended questions usually provide accurate information (Brown et al., 2013; Malloy & Quas, 2009). It is important to note, however, that the studies of Ceci and his colleagues (Ceci & Bruck, 1995; Bruck, Ceci, & Hembrooke, 2002) have shown that when one asks children about events that did not occur, very young children (3–4 years) can give false information, even in response to open-ended questions. This happens when the context of the investigative

Table 3.1 Categories of interviewer utterances.

General invitation	Tell me everything that happened from the beginning to end. And then what happened?
Time-segmenting invitation	Tell me everything that happened when he walked into your bedroom (previously described by the child) until he touched you (described by the child)?
	Tell me everything that happened before he lowered your pants (previously described by the child).
Cued invitation	Tell me more about her hand when she touched you (previously described by the child).
	Tell me more about yourself and him in the room (previously described by the child).
	You said that she touched you. Tell me more about that.
Directive	Where were you? When did that happen? What was his name?
Option-posing	Did he tell you not to talk about it? Did this happen a few days ago, or has it been longer?
Suggestive	He told you not to talk about it, didn't he?
	Surely you were in great pain?
Summary	If I understand correctly, it happened last Saturday, you were alone at home, he asked you to follow him to your room, he started to undress you, he touched your private parts, and then someone came into the house, and at that time he told you to get dressed and not to talk about it.
Facilitator	Hum-hum.
	Yes.
	OK.

interview is very suggestive and the child has been exposed to false information before the questioning.

Conversely, specific questions ask for information about a particular detail or concept and are often answered with one or a few words. These can be directive questions like who, what, when, and where or questions offering a limited choice. Option-posing questions are formulated by a "does . . ." and they offer a yes-or-no answer ("Did he hurt you?") or a multiple-choice answer ("Did you touch it over or under your clothes?"; "Did it happen in the living room, bedroom, or kitchen?"). Directive questions are less leading than option-posing questions. Often, they invite the children to give more details about something they have already revealed, such as specifying where the abuse took place. The questions offering a choice are suggestive because they introduce information that has not been disclosed by the child, such as "Did he touch your butt?" or encourage the child to choose one of the options provided, even when it is not really accurate. These specific questions, in addition to eliciting very short answers, are more likely to introduce errors or even contradictions in the information provided by the child (Brown et al., 2013; Lamb & Fauchier, 2001; Orbach & Lamb, 2001).

Several factors help explain why specific questions may increase children's suggestibility and thus elicit inaccurate answers (Lamb, Brown, Hershkowitz, Orbach, & Esplin, 2018). First, in response to open-ended questions, the children themselves decide which information to report. With specific questions that focus on precise details, which may not have been encoded or which children cannot remember, children tend to answer the question anyway. Second, children also tend to answer specific questions that are known to be inaccurate. Moreover, adults, as much as children, often try to answer bizarre questions (e.g., "Is a cup sadder than an orange?"; Walker, 2013). Third, although studies have shown that children's responses are more accurate when the interviewer warns them that it may be appropriate to answer "I don't know," children do not use this option very frequently. In addition, interviewers often tend to ignore this type of response from the child and continue with even more specific questions (e.g., I: "Do you remember when it happened?" C: "No." I: "Was it before or after Christmas?"; Earhart, La Rooy, Brubacher, & Lamb, 2014). For all these reasons, children make more mistakes when specific questions are asked than with open-ended questions. In addition, research has shown that specific questions elicit much less information than open-ended questions, with answers to specific questions shorter.

Suggestive questions can take many different forms. Usually, these questions strongly suggest the expected answer or even take for granted details that have not been revealed by the child. Thus, these utterances may include

- false information or hypotheses that we are trying to get the child to confirm ("He told you not to talk about it, is that right?" or "What did he say?" when the child has not mentioned that he had spoken or said something);
- information not communicated by the child ("I heard that John had touched your private parts");
- inaccurate summaries of information given by the child; and
- multiple options that are not exhaustive ("When you were on the couch, was he on you or were you on him?" or "Did it happen in the morning, at noon, or at night?").

All of these questions are very suggestive and are, therefore, risk eliciting false information, with children feeling compelled to answer even if they do not have the required information rather than saying that they do not know or asking for clarification. Studies have also shown that children tend to acquiesce to suggestive questions despite their memory of the targeted event being accurate. Orbach, Lamb, Abbott, Hershkowitz, and Pipe (2016) observe that 52% of the time, children respond by acquiescing to suggestions. They are more likely to resist (41%) when the suggestion includes a confrontation that questions the veracity or plausibility of the child's statements. Contradictions with information previously given in the investigative interview are more likely to occur (96%) when the children nod than when they resist suggestions.

In addition, understanding the words used in questions is a developmental problem that affects children's suggestibility (Malloy & Quas, 2009; Poole & Lamb, 1998; Walker, 2013). This point will be discussed in more detail in the next chapter. For example, legal terms, the use of pronouns instead of nouns in sentences, and abstract words are all elements that can increase an utterance's suggestibility. Thus, when questions are not worded in a simple and concrete way, and they do not use vocabulary appropriate to the age of the children, the level of inaccuracy and suggestibility increases. When children have often been exposed to suggestions or pressure from non-professional interviewers before being interviewed formally, it is possible that they may provide false information even in response to open-ended questions (Lyon, Malloy, Quas, & Talwar, 2008).

IMPLICATIONS FOR PRACTICE

There is consensus about the direct link between the type of questions used and children's suggestibility. For this reason, it is recommended that interviewers only use open-ended questions at the start of the investigative interview and, if possible, throughout it. Since these questions involve recall memory, research has consistently shown that the information provided is more likely to be accurate although, from a forensic standpoint, it is often incomplete. Their wording does not give the child any information about the nature of the response that is expected. When possible, directive questions should be preferred over option-posing questions. However, when the child has not revealed information – for example, the words spoken by the alleged perpetrator – it is less suggestive to ask the child, "Did he tell you something?" This question allows the child to answer "No." Saying to the child "What did he say to you?" or "Tell me more about what he said" puts pressure on the child to report words that may never have been said or that they don't remember. It is also recommended when using specific questions to pair them with open-ended questions, such as "Did he say something to you?" – "Yes" – "Tell me all about that." With a return to open questioning, the pressure on the children to provide a precise or detailed answer is reduced, and they are allowed to choose more freely what details to retrieve from memory. However, this combination of questions should be limited during the investigative interview since some studies have observed, in young children, that specific yes-or-no questions or misleading questions followed by a request to describe more may elicit false information, especially when the children have heard this information outside of the interview or the question asked about peripherical details (e.g., description of clothes) (Brown et al., 2013).

3.2 Repeated questions and multiple investigations

Questions can be repeated within an interview or in different interviews, and repeated questions can be non-leading or highly suggestive. Research to date (Andrews & Lamb, 2014; Howie, Kurukulasuriya, Nash, & Marsh, 2009; Howie, Nash, Kurukulasuriya, & Bowman, 2012) indicates that children tend to modify their response when a question is repeated, particularly when it is option-posing rather than open-ended. Although the majority of children under the age of 7 have difficulty explaining why a question is repeated, many 7-year-olds suggest that if the question is repeated, their first answer has to be wrong. This interpretation is consistent with the fact that, in everyday conversations with their children, parents tend to repeat the same question when they have doubts about the child's answer (e.g., "Do you have any homework to do tonight?" – "No." – "You don't have homework to do?"). However, even for open-ended questions, it is best not to repeat a question (e.g., "Tell me more about his hand rubbing your stomach") since, if the child does not provide the expected information, it is possible that the information is not accessible in memory using that prompt. Andrews and Lamb (2014) observe that, in interviews with children aged 3 to 12 years old, questions were repeated three times on average. Usually, the question was repeated to clarify (53.1%) but also to test the child's response by including details that were expected (24%) or for no apparent reason (20%). Most of the time, this led children to simply repeat the content (54%) and more rarely to elaborate (31.5%) but sometimes to contradict themselves (11%). These contradictions occurred most often, in 70% of the cases, when the repeated question was a closed yes-or-no question, a multiple-choice question, or even a suggestive question. Repeated option-posing questions were responsible for 64% of contradictions and suggestive questions for 19%.

In the legal context, it is common for children to be interviewed repeatedly and often over long periods of time. Malloy and her colleagues (Malloy, Lyon, & Quas, 2007) report, in a sample of sexual abuse cases identified in Los Angeles, that children were formally interviewed an average of 4.26 times, with a range of between 1 and 25 times. As for informal interviews with the non-abusive parent, with siblings, with therapists, or with other professionals (teachers, social workers, doctors), they can range from 0 to 7 times for an average of 1.65 (Bottoms, Najdowski, & Goodman, 2009). Therefore, in the majority of cases, children will have to recount their experiences more than 5 times.

The results of research conducted to date continue to fuel controversy over the beneficial or harmful effects of these multiple interviews (La Rooy, Katz, Malloy, & Lamb, 2010). In general, repetition of interviews has a negative effect on children's memory when these interviews are suggestive to the point where, after several repetitions, it becomes difficult to distinguish whether the events described are true or not (Ceci & Bruck, 1995; Ceci, Kulkofsky, Klemfuss, Sweeney, & Bruck, 2007). In addition, with the repetition of interviews, whether they are done in a formal (investigation, evaluation) or non-formal context (questions from parents, teachers, doctors, etc.), children can confuse the information they have taken from their memory with new information that they may have learned during these interviews, particularly as a result of leading questions or speculation made by the interviewer. Thus, they may end up incorporating information that comes from answers to previous questions.

In addition, between interviews, children may be exposed to information from other sources that can be remembered (errors recording the source of information or social pressure). When children give inconsistent accounts from one interview to another, reflecting errors of omission or commission, their credibility may be judged negatively (Lamb et al., 2018).

The desire to cooperate and the confusion of authentic memory may explain why children put up with tendentious repeated questions and become less and less accurate during multiple hearings. When interviews are repeated, children may also assume that their previous answers were not correct, and they will tend to change their answers and, therefore, increase their inaccuracy over time. Several studies conducted by Ceci and his colleagues (Bruck et al., 2002; Ceci, Loftus, Leichtman, & Bruck, 1994) have shown that, with very young children, repeated interviews increase the amount of inaccurate information. Finally, both children and adults tend to use few qualifiers of uncertainty in their later responses to repeated questions such as "I'm not sure, but . . ."; this makes their answers appear more confident than the original answer might have been.

On the other hand, when it comes to non-suggestive interviews, it may be beneficial to repeat interviews for at least five reasons (La Rooy et al., 2010; Malloy & Quas, 2009). First, children report different details in different interviews. Thus, the use of open-ended questions can provide access to new information. For all children, being able to retell what they have been through may allow for reminiscence (adding new details) or hypermnesia (increasing the amount of detail).

Second, repeating the account of the event in successive interviews decreases the loss of information that naturally occurs over time and, therefore, appears particularly beneficial if the child has to testify after a long delay. Each investigative interview reactivates the memory of the original event and helps to maintain that memory, decreases forgetting, decreases suggestibility, and increases recollection. The strength of a consolidating interview is sometimes greater when the first investigative interview comes soon after disclosure rather than several weeks after and also when the initial investigative interview produces a detailed narrative. In the study by Quas and colleagues (2007), children aged 3 to 5 were interviewed either after three weeks or weekly for three weeks in a biased and unbiased way. The worst performance was for children who had a single biased interview. The memory and suggestibility of this group were less accurate than that of children in the other groups. These results suggest the importance of conducting the first investigative interview quickly, which has the effect of protecting the child against the effects of forgetting and bias and suggestion.

Third, repeating the interviews can teach the child how to recount their memories, and therefore, they will need fewer specific questions to fully relate the events.

Fourth, when there are multiple events to report and the child is tired, continuing with a second investigative interview may elicit the details not yet disclosed.

Finally, when the child is reluctant and there is good reason to believe that something has happened, a second investigative interview helps to deepen the bond of trust with the child and perhaps to obtain a disclosure. However, the time between these interviews should be short (less than six months) since some studies have observed that newly provided information is more likely to be inaccurate after long delays.

IMPLICATIONS FOR PRACTICE

It is important to avoid repeating the same question during an interview, especially if it is a very closed question since research tells us that children will tend to modify their answer, thinking that the earlier answer was not good or that it did not satisfy the interviewer. In addition, the number of formal interviews to which the child will be subjected should be limited as much as possible; these should all be recorded audio-visually. Indeed, in practice, it often happens that the children participate in only one filmed interview, but beyond this interview, they are questioned again about the events by a social worker, a psychologist, a prosecutor, or a doctor, not to mention the many informal questions that the children may be asked. Unless you can ensure that the questions asked of the child are all open-ended and not suggestive, there is a risk that their memories will be skewed when probed in subsequent interviews.

3.3   Interviewer biases

Interviewer biases are important in assessing the impact of questions on children's suggestibility. Interviewer bias exists when the interviewer has a priori beliefs about what happened and directs the investigative interview to maximize revelations that are consistent with his/her beliefs (Ceci & Bruck, 1995; Cyr & Bruneau, 2009). Thus, the use of certain questions may introduce bias without the questions appearing inherently suggestive. In addition to looking only for information that confirms their hypotheses, these interviewers prevent revelations that could produce contradictory information. In a synthesis of studies that have focused on interviewer bias, Ceci and Bruck (1995) demonstrate that when interviewers are allowed to interview a child in the way they wish, but having created mistaken beliefs about what the child has been through, the majority of children end up saying what the interviewer wants to hear.

IMPLICATIONS FOR PRACTICE

It is important for interviewers to be aware of their expectations and prejudices before starting an investigative interview with the child. Approaching a case or an investigative interview with a preconceived opinion brings a narrow view of things, whereas any professional should work to obtain information from multiple sources and to analyze all of that information from a perspective of multiple hypotheses. It can also be helpful to indicate to children, before the start of an interview, that they can correct the interviewer if the latter is wrong or reports inaccuracies. Indeed, it is imperative that children feel comfortable enough to reject the interviewer's suggestions. In addition, children should know that the interviewer has no knowledge of the event in question. Children understand the difference between uninformed adults and informed adults and they can modify or adjust their responses accordingly (Malloy & Quas, 2009).

3.4   Selective reinforcement

Selective reinforcement is another strategy that, alone or in combination with interviewer bias or misleading questions, increases the degree of suggestibility in children. This reinforcement can be positive, such as approving or agreeing with what the child has just said, praising them, using other rewards, or even indicating that they are showing desirable qualities like being smart and kind. Selective reinforcement is negative if it consists of criticizing or disapproving of a statement made by the children or telling them that their response is incomplete, inadequate, or disappointing.

Two studies carried out by Garven and her colleagues are particularly enlightening. A week after the visit to the school of a man who read a story to them and gave them candy, the authors (Garven, Wood, Malpass, & Shaw, 1998) questioned young children under two experimental conditions: one including social strategies including reinforcement and the other neutral. Where social pressure was exerted, 58% of preschoolers made false claims about the visit, while in the control situation, only 17% of the children did so. In another study with somewhat older children, 5 to 7 years old (Garven, Wood, & Malpass, 2000), the authors attempted to distinguish between the effects of using selective reinforcement (giving positive support to desired responses) and of suggesting that information has been revealed by another witness. The results indicated that selective reinforcement dramatically increased the rate of false allegations while the use of disclosures from another witness was not influential. When asked about "fantastic" and highly improbable events (e.g., leaving school in a helicopter), children who received reinforcement made 10 times more false allegations than children in the group control. Moreover, two weeks later, the majority of the children upheld the false claims they had made. This suggests that, over a short period of time, children remain consistent in their claims even if they are false.

It is important to emphasize that, in these studies, the reinforcements were contingent on specific types of responses. This is to be distinguished from being warm and supportive during an investigative interview in a noncontingent fashion, which seems to decrease suggestibility rather than increase it (Saywitz, Wells, Larson, & Hobbs, 2019), as we see in the next section.

IMPLICATIONS FOR PRACTICE

Interviewers should be as aware as possible of their bodily and nonverbal signals, which can also serve as subtle selective reinforcement when, for example, "um, um" and "ah, yes!" are used only after certain types of responses from the child. Likewise, criticism or praise should not be made in response to specific information provided by the child: information the interviewer wanted to hear.

3.5   The interviewer's unsupportive attitude

Another important factor that can increase children's suggestibility is the emotional climate that prevails during the interview. Thus, through their verbal and nonverbal attitude, the interviewers can create an atmosphere in which the children feel comfortable or, conversely, intimidated at the idea of communicating their memories. This attitude can be cold, distant, or confrontational and, thus, foster the interviewer's dominance. The results of a meta-analysis indicate that the interviewer's non-supportive attitude increases children's suggestibility compared to a neutral or supportive investigative interview (Saywitz et al., 2019). This result was consistent in fourteen of the fifteen studies identified. This could be explained by the fact that being warm and friendly with the children, often smiling at them and giving random reinforcements, such as "You are doing a good job" or "You have a good memory," would reduce the stress experienced by the children. Therefore, children are less suggestible to deceptive or direct questions when the interviewer is more supportive. The value of providing support to counter stress or anxiety during an investigative interview has been experimentally validated by directly measuring the stress level or by asking children after investigative interviews (Saywitz et al., 2019). Children who do not have to manage their anxiety have more emotional and cognitive resources to regulate their behavior and concentrate their efforts on the cognitive task at hand, namely searching for details. This is also true for adolescents. A study using the Gudjonsson suggestibility grid observed that adolescents, when pressured, became more sensitive to interviewer suggestions than adults (Gudjonsson & Singh, 1984).

However, Underwager and Wakefield (1990) caution workers against overly supportive investigative interviews that could influence children to respond in a biased manner just to please the interviewer. Overvaluing children (e.g., "How good you are" or "You are so smart") can increase their suggestibility. This is also true for adolescents who, in their stage of development, are more aware of social rejection (Ansado et al., 2014). The Revised NICHD Protocol prescribes supportive interventions that are not suggestive (see Chapter 6).

IMPLICATIONS FOR PRACTICE

The results obtained concerning positive and negative reinforcements indicate to us that interviewers must be attentive to their behavior and that they must be careful not to reinforce children to provide specific answers so as not to make them suggestible. On the other hand, this does not mean that we must adopt a neutral, distant, or even cold attitude. Children perform best when they feel comfortable with the interviewer, and for this reason, a smiling, relaxed, calm, and warm attitude on the part of the interviewer should be fostered. Positive encouragement or reinforcement is also necessary to support children's efforts and motivate them to continue. However, these should be about the task (e.g., "You have told me a lot of things, and it really helps me understand what happened") and not the person of the child ("You are very good"; "Ah! How intelligent you are"). In addition, encouragement and reinforcement should be used during the investigative interview at times of transition, such as after training the child to relate a neutral event, before bringing up the topic of the investigative interview (see Chapter 6), or during the account of the event investigated during natural breaks in the interview.

4   Other suggestive strategies used by the interviewer

Other strategies used by the interviewer during the investigative interview that are likely to increase the suggestibility of children include social pressure, inviting the child to speculate about what may have happened, or the introduction of stereotypes about the alleged perpetrator. Social pressure may consist of telling the child that the interviewer has already received information from another person regarding the event. This strategy is often used by interviewers when interviewing a sibling. They think it will help a shyer or more fearful child to speak up if they tell them that their brother or sister has already told them something bad has happened. This strategy is also used in situations where several children could have been victims or witnesses of an event, such as in the cases that would have occurred in a nursery/kindergarten, a school, or a sports club. Using this strategy, the interviewer puts pressure on the children to change their accounts in order to be consistent with those of others. Research (see Ceci & Bruck, 1995; Garven et al., 1998) indicates that children and even adults tend to respond in ways that conform to the group norm.

From the highly suggestive interviews carried out in the McMartin daycare case in the United States in the early 1990s, Garven and her colleagues (Garven et al.,1998) observe several situations in which the children were invited to speculate or give their opinion on past events. They involved asking children to use their imagination during the investigative interview ("Suppose . . ."), to solve a mystery ("If we tried to understand, to solve . . ."), or to pretend ("Suppose and let's see what could have happened . . ."; "What do you think could have happened?"). Although there has been no research to verify the effect of these techniques, appealing to the imagination or assumptions can make children suggestible since, as we noted earlier, children who are more creative and imaginative are also more suggestible.

Ceci and Bruck (1995) point out that the introduction of stereotypes increases the suggestibility of children. Interviewers introduce a stereotype when they convey negative characteristics about an event or about a person to the child that may be true or false. For example, telling the child that the alleged perpetrator "did things that were wrong" or "tried to scare the child" can influence the child's story to accommodate the perceptions of the interviewer. These stereotypes can also be induced before the hearing, which we will discuss a little further on.

IMPLICATIONS FOR PRACTICE

Although the motivation of an interviewer is often to help or encourage children who are not saying much to reveal their experiences, these suggestive strategies should not be used in forensic interviews since they cause children to conform to the interviewer's perceptions or to the supposed perception of other people. They also promote the use of the child's imagination instead of keeping it in the real world. Even in a context where a child from the same family or the same class at school has revealed something, the interviewer cannot assume that this other child has been a witness or a victim; the interviewer has to work with multiple hypotheses.

5   Pre- and post-event information

Children do not need suggestive questions to absorb misinformation or to meet social expectations. Thus, any information that children receive in informal settings prior to being interviewed may influence the accuracy of their responses to suggestive and non-suggestive questions in formal settings. In a study by Bruck and colleagues (Bruck, Ceci, Francoeur, & Barr, 1995), children were exposed to misinformation in the weeks following a medical examination before being interviewed. In response to the question "Tell me everything that happened," 48% of false allegations were made spontaneously by children who had been influenced beforehand. In contrast, for children who were not influenced, all information given was correct except for one child who erred in answering the direct question "who."

Children may also be exposed to stereotypes and expectations before the investigative interview, which are likely to influence their responses to all types of questions. For example, Leichtman and Ceci (1995) show that when stereotypes were learned before the suggestive interview, 46% of young children (3–4 years) and 30% of older children (5–6 years) made false accusations in their free account. This rate increased to 72% among young children who accused Sam, the person involved in the event, of one or more wrongdoings in response to more specific questions. These findings are especially important to consider in child custody disputes when children hear negative comments about either parent from the other. Negative stereotypes also affect children in complicated cases involving multiple victims where children can overhear conversations before being interviewed. Likewise, the Mr. Science study (Poole & Lindsay, 1995) clearly revealed that parents' accounts influence children's memories and subsequent accounts of events. In this study, the children confused what was said by parents when reading the story of Mr. Science's visit with what they had experienced during this visit by Mr. Science. In addition to answering yes to suggestive questions, the children gave descriptions of events that had not happened.

IMPLICATIONS FOR PRACTICE

It can be very difficult to determine after the fact how and by whom the children may have been influenced before the interview. The investigator should attempt to retrace the course of events to find out how the children may have been influenced either by questions from those around them or by comments or opinions from those around them. Poole and Lamb (1998) draw an analogy between a knife found at a crime scene and the facts reported during the investigative interview of a child. In the first case, the prosecutor will have to describe how the knife was placed in a bag, transported for storage, and then kept secure. In other words, the prosecution will have to demonstrate that there were no loopholes that could introduce errors into the knife's chain of custody. Similarly, in the case of children's statements, the chain of custody must be documented to see if and how the child's memory could have been altered.

6   Child's implicit expectations about the interview

Children also have interview expectations that arise from implicit social rules that they have learned during their conversations with adults. For example, social conventions dictate that children should try to answer questions and be cooperative when a parent addresses them or a teacher asks them a question. This social rule frequently leads them to say yes to multiple-choice or yes-or-no questions. Believing that they are supposed to answer adult questions can exacerbate memory impairments (e.g., providing requested information that is not available), making specific questions problematic, especially when interviewers use yes-or-no questions or those that offer options. Also, with respect to interviews, children may not know what is essential to report. In other words, they do not understand what the interviewer wants or needs to know. Thus, because children usually refer to the authority of the adult, they are likely to follow the adult's suggestions even if they know that a particular suggestion is incorrect (Poole & Lamb, 1998).

IMPLICATIONS FOR PRACTICE

Lamb and colleagues (Lamb et al., 2018) suggest teaching children about the communication rules they can use during investigative interviews (see Chapter 6). So children should know that they don't have to answer a question if they don't know the answer. In addition, Poole and Lamb (1998) suggest doing an exercise with the children using a recent event unrelated to the subject of an investigative interview to make them understand the amount and nature of details that the one wishes to get during the interview. Children learn to participate in interviews, and this step is particularly important for improving the quality of the child's participation in the interview. Moreover, this recommendation, which has been empirically verified (Sternberg et al., 1997), has been included in several practice guides (e.g., Step-Wise Interview, Memorandum of Good Practice, APSAC guidelines, the NICHD Protocol; see Chapter 5). Children should also be informed that the interviewer knows nothing about the facts of the event in question. Thus, not taking for granted that the interviewer knows what happened encourages children to give more information to the interviewer. Finally, children should know that they can correct an interviewer who makes a mistake or says something that is not true; in other words, they should know that they don't have to accept a suggestion that is wrong.

Distinguishing true from false: the effects of suggestive interviews

Previous sections have documented that people who ask children questions can be suggestive in many ways and thus lead children to give accounts that are not accurate or do not reflect the truth. According to Ceci and Bruck (2007), it is never possible for an expert to be able to determine with certainty whether the child's words are true or false unless there is a witness to the facts. Ceci and colleagues (1994) have shown that professionals are unable to distinguish between true narratives and false descriptions. It is difficult to tell them apart, among other things, because many false reports contain certain characteristics that professionals believe are associated with true testimony, such as personal details and spontaneous corrections. In a study (Bruck, Hembrooke, & Ceci, 1997) of preschool children, different types of true and false stories about positive and negative events were compared. The researchers also varied the techniques: (a) a basic interview; (b) suggestive interviews involving visualization techniques, repeated misinformation, and selective reinforcement; (c) an interview in which the child used a puppet to describe the events; and finally (d) an interview with a research assistant unfamiliar with the child. With repeated interviews, subtle differences between true and false reports disappeared, and the accounts became more elaborate and consistent. For example, there was no longer a significant difference between the amount of detail reported, and the fake stories contained more emotional and descriptive terms than the real stories; on the other hand, in the first interview, conducted using non-suggestive techniques, there was a clear differentiation between true and false stories. This was mainly due to the child denying the false story, and therefore, this one contained less detail. However, with repeated interviews, false stories quickly became similar to a true story in terms of the number of details given, the spontaneity of the report, the number of new details, the contradictions in the stories, the elaboration of the details, and the cohesion of the story. Only consistency across the narrative differentiated those who were true from false events. So when false stories are repeated in suggestive interviews, they acquire additional qualities that make them more and more believable, sometimes even more so than real stories. This also indicates that if the children's first words were taken during a very suggestive interview, there is a high risk that this will taint their story and that these inaccuracies will persist over time.

Although some parts of the scientific literature maintain that accounts produced as a result of suggestive interviewing contain more elaboration and are less consistent over time than real accounts, this criterion cannot be used to differentiate what is true or false in a child's story. Jurors often regard the consistency of narratives as indicative of truth and their inconsistency as a reflection of poor accuracy. In addition, in the judicial context, during cross-examination, elements of testimony that appear inconsistent are considered to undermine the credibility of the witness (see also chapter 8, research on testimony). Despite these claims, inconsistencies and false narratives are statistically unrelated (Malloy & Quas, 2009). In fact, inconsistencies are quite common in children's accounts of real experiences. By inconsistency we meant changes in the child's story or the inclusion of new information. These inconsistencies are not necessarily synonymous with contradictions. Contradictions are frequently observed when children change their answers to direct questions, such as yes-or-no questions, and to the same questions asked in one or more interviews. Thus, the contradictions are more likely to be the result of the interviewer's questions than of the child's memory (Orbach & Lamb, 2001).

Inconsistencies can emerge for several reasons. First, children can imagine that when asked the same question a second time in an investigative interview or different interviews, they often introduce different and new information; this brings about changes in the narrative. Second, children can remember new and different information when asked at different times about a past event. When questioned with open-ended questions, children, especially very young children, tend to report a high percentage of new information that is accurate – up to 75% of the information reported in a second investigative interview (Hamond & Fivush, 1991). Comparing two interviews about physical and sexual abuse, Ghetti and colleagues (Ghetti, Goodman, Eisen, Qin, & Davis, 2002) observe that children aged 6 to 16 were more consistent than the youngest ones (3 to 5 years old). Girls were also more consistent than boys, and children were more consistent when reporting sexual abuse rather than physical abuse. This could be explained by the fact that physical abuse was more often done by multiple perpetrators and tended to be more frequent than sexual abuse. However, the veracity of the information could not be verified in this study. In conclusion, inconsistencies must be distinguished from contradictions. Inconsistencies can reveal a different narrative, but it can be accurate, which can happen when the child is asked repeated yes-or-no questions.

7   Conclusion

Despite the considerable number of studies carried out on the subject of suggestibility in children, we cannot draw many definitive conclusions. Indeed, the research clearly indicates that the style of questions used by the interviewer has a potent impact on children's suggestibility. For this reason, open-ended questions should always be preferred, and directive questions should, where possible, be used instead of option-posing questions. In addition, beyond the questions, the interviewers' attitude is very important since they can subtly convey their hypotheses or a priori beliefs and thus influence the child's account. As for the child's personal characteristics, as Bruck and Melnyk (2004) underline in their review, we cannot, on the basis of the research carried out, identify the profile of the child most at risk of being very suggestible. In addition, a major limitation of the research conducted to date on children's personal characteristics is that the majority of research has focused on preschool children. Studies clearly demonstrate the complexity of suggestibility; this is often not linked to a single cognitive or psychosocial variable but probably to a combination of these variables. As Poole and Lamb (1998) point out, the quality of a child's testimony is determined by the intersection of social and cognitive maturity, experiences outside of formal hearings, and the context of the child interview.

References

Andrews S. J., Lamb M. E. (2014). "The effects of age and delay on responses to repeated questions in forensic interviews with children alleging sexual abuse", *Law and Human Behavior*, 38(2), 171–180.

Ansado J. Chiasson V., Beauchamp M. H. (2014). "Croissance cérébrale et neurodéveloppement à l'adolescence [Adolescent brain growth and neurodevelopment]", in Claes M., Lannegrand-Willems L. (Éds.), *La psychologie de l'adolescence*, Montréal, Les Presses de l'Université de Montréal, 45–71.

Bottoms B. L., Najdowski C. J., Goodman G. S. (Eds.). (2009). *Children as victims, witnesses, and offenders: Psychological science and the law*, New York, Guilford.

Brown D. A., Lamb M. E., Lewis C., Pipe M. E., Orbach Y., Wolfman M. (2013). "The NICHD investigative interview protocol: An analogue study", *Journal of Experimental Psychology: Applied*, 19(4), 367–382.

Bruck M., Ceci S. J., Francoeur E., Barr R. J. (1995). "'I hardly cried when I got my shot!': Influencing children reports about a visit to the pediatrician", *Child Development*, 66, 193–208.

Bruck M., Ceci S. J., Hembrooke H. (2002). "The nature of children's true and false narratives", *Developmental Review*, 22(3), 520–554.

Bruck M., Hembrooke H., Ceci S. J. (1997). "Children's reports of pleasant and unpleasant events", in Read J. D., Lindsay D. S. (Eds.), *Recollections of trauma: Scientific evidence and clinical practice*, New York, Plenum Press, 199–213.

Bruck M., Melnyk L. (2004). "Individual differences in children's suggestibility: A review and synthesis", *Applied Cognitive Psychology*, 18(8), 947–996.

Carrick N., Quas J. A. (2006). "Effects of discrete emotions on young children's ability to discern fantasy and reality", *Developmental Psychology*, 42(6), 1278–1288.

Ceci S. J., Bruck M. (1995). *Jeopardy in the courtroom: A scientific analysis of children's testimony*, Washington, DC, American Psychological Association.

Ceci S. J., Bruck M. (2007). "Loftus's lineage in developmental forensic research: Six scientific misconceptions about children's suggestibility", in Garry M., Hayne H. (Eds.), *Do justice and let the sky fall: Elizabeth Loftus and her contributions to science, law, and academic freedom*, Mahwah, Lawrence Erlbaum Associates Publishers, 65–77.

Ceci S. J., Kulkofsky S., Klemfuss J., Sweeney C. D., Bruck M. (2007). "Unwarranted assumptions about children's testimonial accuracy", *Annual Review of Clinical Psychology*, 3, 311–328.

Ceci S. J., Loftus E. F., Leichtman M. D., Bruck M. (1994). "The possible role of source misattributions in the creation of false beliefs among preschoolers", *International Journal of Clinical and Experimental Hypnosis*, 42, 304–320.

Chein J., Albert D., O'Brien L., Uckert K., Steinberg L. (2011). "Peers increase adolescent risk taking by enhancing activity in the brain's reward circuitry", *Developmental Science*, 14(2), 1–10.

Cyr M., Bruneau G. (2009). "Assessing false allegations of child sexual abuse", in Yves St-M., Tanguay M. (Eds.), *Psychology of criminal investigations: The search for the truth*, Toronto, ON, Thomson – Carswell, 199–228.

Daignault I. V., Hébert M. (2009). "Profiles of school adaptation: Social, behavioral and academic functioning in sexually abused girls", *Child Abuse & Neglect*, 33(2), 102–115.

Davis S. L., Bottoms B. L. (2002). "The effects of social support on the accuracy of children's reports: Implications for the forensic interview", in Eisen M. L., Quas J. A., Goodman G. S. (Eds.), *Memory and suggestibility in the forensic interview*, Mahwah, Lawrence Erlbaum Associates Publishers, 437–457.

Dion J., Bouchard J., Gaudreault L., Mercier C. (2012). "L'agression sexuelle envers les enfants ayant une déficience intellectuelle: Investigation, traitement et prévention [Sexual abuse on children with intellectual disabilities: Investigation, treatment and prevention]", in Hébert M., Cyr M., Tourigny M. (Éds.), *L'agression sexuelle envers les enfants*, vol. 2, Québec, Les Presses de l'Université du Québec, 9–44.

Dion J., Cyr M. (2008). "The use of the NICHD protocol to enhance the quantity of details obtained from children with low verbal abilities in investigative interviews: A pilot study", *Journal of Child Sexual Abuse*, 17(2), 144–162.

Earhart B., La Rooy D. J., Brubacher S. P., Lamb M. E. (2014). "An examination of 'don't know' responses in forensic interviews with children", *Behavioral Sciences & the Law*, 32(6), 746–761.

Eigsti I.-M., Cicchetti D. (2004). "The impact of child maltreatment on expressive syntax at 60 months", *Developmental Science*, 7(1), 88–102.

Eisen M. L., Goodman G. S., Qin J., Davis S., Crayton J. (2007). "Maltreated children's memory: Accuracy, suggestibility, and psychopathology", *Developmental Psychology*, 3(36), 1275–1294.

Feltis B. B., Powell M. B., Snow P. C., Hughes-Scholes C. H. (2010). "An examination of the association between interviewer question type and story-grammar detail in child witness interviews about abuse", *Child Abuse & Neglect*, 34(6), 407–413.

Finlay W. M. L., Lyons E. (2002). "Acquiescence in interviews with people who have mental retardation", *Mental Retardation*, 40(1), 14–29.

Garven S., Wood J. M., Malpass R. S. (2000). "Allegations of wrongdoing: The effects of reinforcement on children's mundane and fantastic claims", *Journal of Applied Psychology*, 85(1), 38–49.

Garven S., Wood J. M., Malpass R. S., Shaw J. S. (1998). "More than suggestion: The effect of interviewing techniques from the McMartin preschool case", *Journal of Applied Psychology*, 83(3), 347–359.

Ghetti S., Goodman G. S., Eisen M. L., Qin J., Davis S. L. (2002). "Consistency in children's reports of sexual and physical abuse", *Child Abuse & Neglect*, 26(9), 977–995.

Goodman G. S., Bottoms B. L., Rudy L., Davis S. L., Schwartz-Kenney B. M. (2001). "Effects of past abuse experiences on children's eyewitness memory", *Law and Human Behavior*, 25(3), 269–298.

Goodman G. S., Quas J. A., Batterman-Faunce J. M., Riddlesberger M., Kuhn J. (1997). "Children's reactions to and memory for a stressful event: Influences of age, anatomical dolls, knowledge, and parental attachment", *Applied Developmental Science*, 1(2), 54–75.

Gudjonsson G. H., Singh K. K. (1984). "Interrogative suggestibility and delinquent boys: An empirical validation study", *Personality and Individual Differences*, 5, 425–430.

Hamond N. R., Fivush R. (1991). "Memories of Mickey Mouse: Young children recount their trip to Disneyworld", *Cognitive Development*, 6(4), 433–448.

Harris L. S., Goodman G. S., Augusti E.-M., Chae Y., Alley D. (2009). "Children's resistance to suggestion", in Kuehnle K., Connell M. (Eds.), *The evaluation of child sexual abuse allegations: A comprehensive guide to assessment and testimony*, Hoboken, NJ, John Wiley & Sons, 181–202.

Henry L. A., Bettenay C., Carney D. (2011). "Children with intellectual disabilities and developmental disorders", in Lamb M. E., LeRooy D. G., Malloy L. C., Katz C. (Eds.), *Children's testimony: A handbook of psychological research and forensic practice*, 2nd ed., New York, Wiley, 251–283.

Henry L. A., Gudjonsson G. H. (1999). "Eyewitness memory and suggestibility in children with mental retardation", *American Journal on Mental Retardation*, 104(6), 491–508.

Henry L. A., Gudjonsson G. H. (2003). "Eyewitness memory, suggestibility, and repeated recall sessions in children with mild and moderate intellectual disabilities", *Law and Human Behavior*, 27(5), 481–505.

Howie P., Kurukulasuriya N., Nash L., Marsh A. (2009). "Inconsistencies in children's recall of witnessed events: The role of age, question format and perceived reason for question repetition", *Legal and Criminological Psychology*, 14(2), 311–329.

Howie P., Nash L., Kurukulasuriya N., Bowman A. (2012). "Children's event reports: Factors affecting responses to repeated questions in vignette scenarios and event recall interviews", *British Journal of Developmental Psychology*, 30(4), 550–568.

Jens K. G., Gordon B. N., Shaddock A. J. (1990). "Remembering activities performed versus imagined: A comparison of children with mental retardation and children with normal intelligence", *International Journal of Disability, Development and Education*, 37, 201–213.

Lamb M. E., Brown D. A., Hershkowitz I., Orbach Y., Esplin P. W. (2018). *Tell me what happened: Questioning children about abuse*, 2nd ed., Hoboken, NJ, John Wiley & Sons Inc.

Lamb M. E., Fauchier A. (2001). "The effects of question type on self-contradictions by children in the course of forensic interviews", *Applied Cognitive Psychology*, 15, 483–491.

La Rooy D., Katz C., Malloy L. C., Lamb M. E. (2010). "Do we need to rethink guidance on repeated interviews?" *Psychology, Public Policy, and Law*, 16(4), 373–392.

Leichtman M. D., Ceci S. J. (1995). "The effects of stereotypes and suggestions on preschoolers' reports", *Developmental Psychology*, 31(4), 568–578.

Lyon T. D., Malloy L. C., Quas J. A., Talwar V. A. (2008). "Coaching, truth induction, and young maltreated children's false allegations and false denials", *Child Development*, 79(4), 914–929.

Malloy L. C., Lyon T. D., Quas J. (2007). "Filial dependency and recantation of child sexual abuse allegations", *Journal of the American Academy of Child & Adolescent Psychiatry*, 46(2), 162–170.

Malloy L. C., Quas J. A. (2009). "Children's suggestibility: Areas of consensus and controversy", in Kuehnle K., Connell M. (Eds.), *The evaluation of child sexual abuse allegations: A comprehensive guide to assessment and testimony*, Hoboken, NJ, John Wiley & Sons Inc., 267–297.

Mazzoni G. (1998). "Memory suggestibility and metacognition in child eyewitness testimony: The roles of source monitoring and self-efficacy", *European Journal of Psychology of Education*, 13(1), 43–60.

Melinder A., Alexander K., Cho Y. I., Goodman G. S., Thoresen C., Lonnum K., Magnussen S. (2010). "Children's eyewitness memory: A comparison of two interviewing strategies as realized by forensic professionals", *Journal of Experimental Child Psychology*, 105(3), 156–177.

Michel M. K., Gordon B. N., Ornstein P. A., Simpson M. A. (2000). "The abilities of children with mental retardation to remember personal experiences: Implications for testimony", *Journal of Clinical Child Psychology*, 29(3), 453–463.

Orbach Y., Lamb M. E. (2001). "The relationship between within-interview contradictions and eliciting interviewer utterances", *Child Abuse & Neglect*, 25(3), 323–333.

Orbach Y., Lamb M. E., Abbott C., Hershkowitz I., Pipe M.-E. (2016). "Do allegedly abused children's responses to suggestion differ depending on the type of eliciting suggestions?" Unpublished manuscript.

Poole D. A., Lamb M. E. (1998). *Investigative interviews of children: A guide for helping professionals*, Washington, DC, American Psychological Association.

Poole D. A., Lindsay D. (1995). "Interviewing preschoolers: Effects of nonsuggestive techniques, parental coaching, and leading questions on reports of nonexperienced events", *Journal of Experimental Child Psychology*, 60(1), 129–154.

Quas J. A., Goodman G. S., Bidrose S., Pipe M.-E., Craw S., Ablin D. S. (1999). "Emotion and memory: Children's long term remembering, forgetting, and suggestibility", *Journal of Experimental Child Psychology*, 72, 235–270.

Quas J. A., Malloy L. C., Melinder A., Goodman G. S., D'Mello M., Schaaf J. (2007). "Developmental differences in the effects of repeated interviews and interviewer bias on young children's event memory and false reports", *Developmental Psychology*, 43(4), 823–837.

Saltzstein H., Dias M. da G., Millery M. (2004). "Moral suggestibility: The complex interaction of developmental, cultural and contextual factors", *Applied Cognitive Psychology*, 18(8), 1079–1096.

Saywitz K. J., Wells C. R., Larson R. P., Hobbs S. D. (2019). "Effects of interviewer support on children's memory and suggestibility: Systematic review and meta-analyses of experimental research", *Trauma, Violence, & Abuse*, 20(1), 22–39.

Sternberg K. J., Lamb M. E., Hershkowitz I., Yudilevitch L., Orbach Y., Esplin P. W., Hovav M. (1997). "Effects of introductory style on children's abilities to describe experiences of sexual abuse", *Child Abuse & Neglect*, 21(11), 1133–1146.

Underwager R., Wakefield H. (1990). *The real world of child interrogations*, Springfield, Charles C. Thomas Pub Ltd.

Vrij A., Bush N. (2000). "Differences in suggestibility between 5–6 and 10–11 year olds: The relationship with self confidence", *Psychology, Crime & Law*, 6, 127–138.

Walker A. G. (2013). *Handbook on questioning children: A linguistic perspective*, Washington, DC, ABA Center on Children and the Law.

Chapter 4

Children's development

- Which factors in children's development are most important in predicting children's performance in auditions?
- Do children who go to school and learn to read and count use language like adults?
- Can children who are able to count report the number of times they have been abused if there were few?
- Can children with intellectual disabilities or other developmental problems be reliable witnesses?

One of the big challenges for anyone interviewing a child is assessing and adjusting to their level of development. It is easy to imagine that the constraints of an interview with a 4-year-old child will be different from those of an interview with a 10-year-old child, and the capacities of children to participate in such interviews increase with age. However, for the same age group, there may also be great variability in children's capacities and in their level of development; thus, interviewing two 4-year-olds will require adjustments reflecting the differences between them. Differences in age can be explained, on the one hand, by the acquisition of cognitive and language skills and, on the other hand, by socioemotional development. Cognitive and language skills allow children to use better mnemonic strategies, in addition to increasing their understanding of the questions asked and their ability to answer them (Korkman, Santtila, Drzewiecki, & Sandnabba, 2008; Walker, 2013). In addition, the socioemotional development of children allows them to adapt to the particular situation of the interview (Alexander et al., 2002; Chae & Ceci, 2005). Unfortunately, research indicates that investigative interviews often involve language that exceeds the cognitive and linguistic level of the children being interviewed (Korkman et al., 2008; Brennan & Brennan, 1988; Cederborg, La Rooy, & Lamb, 2008; Korkman, Santilla, & Sandnabba, 2006). In addition, interviewers do not always take into account the anxiety or temperament of the child.

From the point of view of an adult, the child's story during an interview is more likely to be considered comprehensible and complete if it includes the following six components:

1 a context that introduces the places and the actors
2 how the incident began
3 central action

DOI: 10.4324/9781003265351-4

4   people's motivation and goals
5   the initial responses (attitudes and emotions of the people involved)
6   the consequences or conclusion

In addition, it is useful to add details that put life to the story, including a description of sounds, feelings, behaviors, and signs, reporting what people have said. This scheme is organized chronologically and has two functions. It provides a structure for encoding information or remembering the event and retrieving it later. This scheme, therefore, includes the who, what, where, when, why, and how of events, which are the elements often sought in the context of an investigation. Children begin to use this form of narrative reporting around the age of 2 (Fivush, Gray, & Fromhoff, 1987), and it matures as the child develops cognitive, language, conversational skills, and theory of mind. This allows the child to understand the behavior, namely that s/he and others have mental states and, therefore, desires, emotions, intentions, and beliefs and that both actions and interactions can be explained or be interpreted in the light of these mental states (Milligan, Astington, & Dack, 2007). An essential skill in producing narratives is to gain control over the concept of time, which helps to structure the order in which the elements of the story appear (before and after) and the time of the reported event. Among the other skills required is the metacognitive ability to note your own mistakes while speaking and then to self-correct, to check the understanding of the person listening and to adjust your account accordingly, to use references to appropriate pronouns, and to use linguistic skills to point out new or old information. Until all of these skills are learned, around age 10, children's narratives tend to be incomplete and disorganized by adult standards. In addition, it is only around the age of 12 that typically developing children incorporate interpretive elements reflecting their unique perspective into their accounts – information that refers to their desires, emotions, and thoughts or to those of others; younger children focus on the facts (Pasupathi & Wainryb, 2010). It is important to stress that even adolescents and adults frequently forget to report information about where the event happened, why it happened this way, and their own subjective perspective (e.g., emotion, thought, evaluation) (Bauer, 2015).

Incomplete narratives are more difficult to judge in terms of accuracy or truthfulness, with truth being the crucial test of narratives in a judicial context. To help children provide the types of detail they are developmentally able to provide, interviewers must therefore adjust their expectations and requests in order to capitalize on the child's strengths and avoid accentuating their weaknesses. Talking about child development is a large and complex subject that goes beyond the focus of this chapter. Therefore, in the next sections, cognitive, language, and socioemotional development will be reviewed, but only to the extent that they are relevant to the context of the investigative interview. A section of this chapter will be devoted to the difficulty of documenting the frequency of events and when they occurred. Finally, the challenges posed by children with intellectual disabilities or other forms of developmental delay will be discussed before concluding this chapter.

I   Cognitive development

The work carried out by Piaget (1926) sheds light on our understanding of the major stages in child development and enables us to realize that children do not think like little adults. Piaget identifies four major stages of development with concrete implications for children's abilities to understand the world and things, including language, numbers, and notions of time. The first stage, which extends from birth to about 2 years of age, is the sensorimotor stage; the second, the preoperational stage, covers the period between 2 and 7 years; the concrete operational period extends from 7 to 11 years; and the formal operational period begins at 11 years and continues until 16.

1.1   The sensorimotor stage

The sensorimotor stage is when the child discovers the world through the movements made and the sensations felt. Taking objects, throwing them, handling them, putting them in the mouth are different means that allow the child to develop cognitive structures to understand the world around him/her. Toward the end of the first year, the notion of the permanence of the object is acquired – that is to say, that the child comes to understand that the object continues to exist even if the object is not visible.

1.2   The preoperational stage

The preoperational stage is when the child begins to use language, which allows him/her to participate in the interviews. At the age of 2, most children are able to use two-word sentences. At the age of 3, they usually know their name, gender, and age, and their vocabulary is much larger. They then make complete sentences and use plurals and pronouns. At the age of 4, the child's speech is understandable, and the child knows his/her address. At the age of 5, the child knows the date of his/her birthday, and defines concrete names by their function (e.g., "Mum is someone who takes care of me") (Walker, 2013). Children at this age recognize letters and sounds, write their names and simple words, and begin to read independently and ask for the meanings of abstract terms. They begin to distinguish the past from the future, but they remain very concrete and very anchored in the present.

With the acquisition of language, the child learns to use words to symbolize objects, actions, and notions, like categories. However, the categories used are few, and they are often used rigidly. As Walker (2013) points out, pajamas or swimsuits might not fall into the clothing category. This means that a child might answer no to the question "Did he take your clothes off?" whereas later in the interview, she might say that the perpetrator took off her pajamas. Similarly, an apartment might not be included in the house category. For the same reasons, questions like "Did something like this happen to you?" may not be understood by the child who will not put "something else" in the category of sexual acts committed against him/her. In addition, children may use words or terms such as "old," "short," and "tall" in sentences when they have not mastered or understood these concepts. For example, the questions "How old is he?" "Is he older than me?" and "Is he taller than I am?" are liable to introduce errors for various reasons. For very young children, age is directly related to height. For such children, "big" and "old" are directly related. Comparing an old but short lady with a younger but tall lady, children under the age of 8 will choose the taller as the oldest. When the investigation involves a stranger or if it is important to have an idea of the age of the alleged perpetrator, Walker (2013) suggests that it is useful after a question such as "How old do you think he is?" to ask the child, "What makes you think he's old?" However, this type of question remains very difficult for all children under the age of 12 and should only be used when clearly necessary.

At these ages, children are also egocentric, which means they have difficulty anticipating or seeing reality from other people's perspectives. This ensures that they do not have expectations or an understanding of the needs of the interviewer and that, for them, giving as much detail as possible during the interview remains an abstract directive with which they may have difficulty complying. This egocentricity also implies that they have difficulty understanding that their interlocutor does not know about the event they are describing (Lamb & Brown, 2006). When it comes to dimensions, for 2- to 6-year-olds, some things may appear bigger or wider than they currently are. They have difficulty comparing objects. For them, a house is big, and it remains big even when compared to a building containing several apartments. Between the ages of 5 and 7, the child's attention span increases dramatically, and this development facilitates the amount of information that the child can store in memory and communicate to an interviewer.

1.3 The concrete operational stage

It is during this period, which extends from 7 to 11 years, that children develop logical thinking, although their thought remains concrete. They can explain or reason about everyday experiences, but they have difficulty thinking in an abstract way (e.g., "What would have happened if you hadn't gone to the park at night?"). It is during this period that children's abstraction skills enable them to grasp mathematics and to perform such operations on observable phenomena.

At this stage, children develop a greater awareness of the motivations and intentions of others in social situations and consequently better understand the perspective of their interlocutor during interviews (Ginsburg & Opper, 1969). Their narratives are better organized with a beginning, a middle, and an end. They also begin to integrate their emotions, their intentions, and those of others into their story. At these ages, children might begin to answer "why" questions, such as "Why didn't you say that before?" or "Why did he tell you not to talk about it?" but the question "why" is not an appropriate question for children under the age of 10. Indeed, as in the previous examples, this question asks the child to think about a mental state, and this calls for a sophisticated skill that does not emerge until 8 to 10 years, in relation to their own mental states, and not before 10 to 13 years, in relation to the motives of others (Walker, 2013). In addition, answering these questions often implies that the child must justify himself/herself, which can put him/her on the defensive. When that happens, it becomes difficult to get an adequate response. It is also the question most often used by parents when they are dissatisfied with an action or inaction on the part of their child (e.g., "Why haven't you finished tidying up your room?"). These questions are, therefore, perceived as critical or accusatory by children.

At this stage of development, children improve their mastery of categories, and they become more competent at placing objects, events, or people into more specific and appropriate categories; they also have an easier time making comparisons between objects and events. It is between 8 and 10 years that the understanding of temporal categories also emerges (Orbach & Lamb, 2007); we will come back to this important notion later in this chapter. Regarding the ranking of family figures, Walker (2013) highlights several difficulties that can be encountered with children under the age of 10. For a 9-year-old child, a term like "parent" can be considered the equivalent of "adult" regardless of whether or not the person in question has children. "Uncle George" could, for young children, correspond to the full name of this person and not be regarded as a category of kinship combined with a first name. For some children, only children can have siblings, and parents automatically become grandparents when they are older. As their attention span improves, children aged 6 to 10 are better able to recognize the components of a face (e.g., eyes, ears, beard, skin color) than younger children because they can focus on the face longer and focus their attention on several of its components at the same time. However, describing a perpetrator physically remains a very difficult task for children, as well as for many adults.

1.4   *The formal operational stage*

From the age of 11 or 12 and up to 16, children enter the last stage of development described by Piaget, a stage characterized by the acquisition of abstract thinking. Here, children begin to perform hypothetico-deductive reasoning and establish abstract relationships. They become able to answer questions starting with: "what if . . ." At the end of this period, they, like adults, can reflect on and discuss moral or abstract concepts such as justice. However, they still have difficulty connecting their current actions with a future consequence and this sometimes puts them in difficult situations (e.g., sending a boyfriend or girlfriend nude or suggestive selfies without thinking about what might happen to these photographs if a breakup occurs).

Believing that the linguistic and cognitive development of preadolescents and adolescents is almost complete, adults often treat them as if they were adults, and this can be detrimental to them during interviews (Walker, 2013). Adults have high expectations regarding the capacities of adolescents to understand legal language. They also have difficulty interpreting improbable answers like "Four hundred" to questions such as "How many times has this happened?" adults often see such answers as lies rather than mere metaphors (Walker, 2013). Likewise, much more than young children who have less understanding of interview issues, adolescents are likely to be anxious and feel pressured to give the "right answer." As a result, they are more at risk of being misjudged. It should also be noted that, since Piaget, research has shown that the brains of adolescents are not mature and that they continue to develop until around the age of 21 (see Given-Wilson, Hodes, & Herlihy, 2018, for a review; Jensen & Nutt, 2015). The fact that the brain's prefrontal cortex continues to develop into the twenties has many implications for the testimony of adolescents. In fact, this part of the brain is particularly involved in attentional processes that play a crucial role in building up memories. Studies have shown that this brain area is less activated in adolescents than in adults, which explains why they have more difficulty perceiving and encoding information about an event (Bastin, Van der Linden, Michel, & Friedman, 2004; Konrad et al., 2005). This area is also involved in the recording, organization, and storage of information in memory, as well as in its retrieval, and that could explain why adolescents of the same age do not provide the same amount of information.

It is important to stress that all of the developmental stages described above are greatly influenced by the environment in which the child develops. Thus, the stimulation offered by the family and social environment, the quality of care (e.g., food, material, and emotional security) are all factors that influence the development of the child. Abused children are three to four times more likely than non-abused children to have health problems, learning difficulties, language, vision or hearing disorders, intellectual disabilities, conduct disorders, or affective disorders (Cicchetti & Toth, 2015; Sullivan & Knutson, 2000). Several studies (Daignault & Hébert, 2009; Dion, Cyr, Richard, & McDuff, 2006; Eigsti & Cicchetti, 2004) have reported delays in cognitive development and language in sexually abused children. For example, children who were sexually assaulted had a verbal intelligence quotient (a measure of developmental level) indicating an average delay of 1.5 years (Dion et al., 2006). This means that the level of understanding and functioning of an 8-year-old interviewee may not exceed that of a 6.5-year-old child.

IMPLICATIONS FOR PRACTICE

Cognitive development and understanding of the world develop progressively in children, and the interviewer should have realistic expectations of the capacities of the person they are interviewing. Interviewers must also consider that the background from which the child comes may have caused a significant delay in his/her development. Thus, it is always preferable to underestimate the age and ability of the child, even if it means readjusting if one observes that the child understands better and participates better than was expected. By respecting the capacities of the child, one avoids making him/her feel incompetent to understand and answer questions. The more competent and comfortable the child feels, the more his/her collaboration is encouraged and the longer the interview is likely to last.

Since children have difficulty with categorization, it is best not to use synonyms when talking about places, clothes, or objects; it is better to use exactly the same words as the child, even if you may think that the term is not ideal. In such cases, there will always be time to get the child to clarify what the word means to him/her once all the important details about the event have been gathered. Children are also very concrete in their descriptions and, therefore, make few assumptions or provide little explanation about their motivation or that of others. Difficult questions, and therefore those that are likely to exceed their capacity, should be relegated to the end of the interview and be limited in number. In addition, each time you want to tackle a question that is likely to exceed the child's capacities, it is important to take the time to remind the child that if s/he does not understand the question or has no answer, it is entirely appropriate to simply say so and that s/he doesn't have to answer to please the interviewer.

1.5   Additional considerations about teenagers

Some studies have focused specifically on adolescents and, in particular, on the development of their autobiographical memory skills and their capacity to provide narratives. Because of their greater autonomy and their numerous activities outside the family, adolescents are exposed to more violence and aggression than children are. Statistics Canada data indicates that 737,000 adolescents aged 15 to 24 report having been victims of violent crimes, including 321,000 sexual assaults, 334,000 aggravated assaults, and 82,000 robberies (Statistics Canada, 2015). Thus, adolescents are frequently invited for forensic interviews. However, not much is known concerning their ability to participate in these interviews.

Adolescence is the period between childhood and adulthood, roughly between 12–13 and 18–21 years of age. It has been described by some as a period of transition characterized by many conflicts and difficulties and by others as a period of discovery and development (Lerner & Steinberg, 2004). Indeed, adolescence is a period when important changes take place on many different levels: physical, hormonal, cognitive, emotional, social, and psychological. We have already noted that the brain of teenagers continues to develop until around the early twenties. This neurobiological process could explain why adolescents report more details about experiences than children do, although fewer than adults do, with autobiographical accounts becoming more complex and more coherent with age (Jack, Leov, & Zajac, 2014). The ability to produce coherent narratives improves between ages 12 and 16 but does not fully mature until age 20 (see Given-Wilson et al., 2018, for a review). The same is true of the ability to make causal inferences that permits individuals to describe causes and motivations (Habermas & Reese, 2015). Temporal consistency also increases during adolescence, resulting in younger adolescents having more action-based narratives providing less information about location or time than older adolescents whose narratives better incorporate these elements. Adolescence is a period where autobiographical memories weave reports of single events into a cohesive life narrative that contributes to the development of an understanding of personal identity or personhood (Fivush, Habermas, Waters, & Zaman, 2011). Adolescents who were exposed to maltreatment during their childhoods produce shorter and more general memories than those who were not maltreated (Given-Wilson et al., 2018; Greenhoot, Johnson, Legerski, & Mccloskey, 2009; Valentino, Toth, & Cicchetti, 2009). Adolescents who suffer from depression or post-traumatic stress disorder also produce more general autobiographical accounts containing less emotional or sensory content and more often narrate from an observer's perspective (Given-Wilson et al., 2018).

On the psychological and relational levels, studies have shown that adolescents are more hesitant to report the violence they have suffered because of shame, the fear of stigma or not being believed, facing parental sanctions, or that their friends/acquaintances might find out because of the investigation (McElvaney, Greene, & Hogan, 2012; Staller & Nelson-Gardell, 2005). Police officers also perceive that adolescents are often more easily embarrassed than children or adults (Marcil, 2021). In forensic interview settings, adolescents who understand the possible repercussions better than young children are likely to be anxious and to feel pressure to give the "right answer" (Walker, 2013). As for their suggestibility, which is said to be lower than that of children, research indicates that they become very easily influenced when a question, by its wording or the tone used by the interviewer, suggests that certain information is expected (Gudjonsson, 2013). These findings put into context the fact that adolescents have lower capacities than adults often attribute to them and that these deficiencies can have adverse consequences in the context of the interviews.

In addition, the investigators' beliefs and attitudes also have a role to play in the conduct of these interviews. Although adolescent victims may use significantly fewer strategies than children do to protect themselves during sexually abusive events (e.g., saying "no" to the perpetrator) (Leclerc, Wortley, & Smallbone, 2010), beliefs in their higher capacities to avoid sexual abuse (e.g., by making the decision to run away) undermine their credibility (Tabak & Klettke, 2014). In France, Dodier (2017) observes that police officers consider deliberate lying to be a salient problem (38.2%)

during interviews with adolescents, although there is no empirical data showing this. Rather, in Canada, police officers indicate that compared to children or adults, adolescents do not lie more often but rather fail to inform the police of important elements, which can modify the officers' understanding of the situation (having used substances such as alcohol or drugs, carrying a knife, etc.) for fear of parental or police sanctions (Marcil, 2021). According to police investigators, the more frequent manifestations of resistance by adolescents compared to adults (Marcil, 2021) could be explained by deficiencies in their reflection and decision-making. Absence of answers, silence, or a failure to answer is another difficulty reported by 55.3% of investigators (Dodier, 2017). Data from a national survey in France regarding investigative techniques indicate that investigators justified the use of suggestive interventions to assess the consistency of adolescents' accounts, to help them overcome their shyness, to help them develop their accounts, to remember and obtain additional information, or to detect a lie (Dodier, 2017). These investigative strategies are very likely to create either a stereotypical or simplistic view of events. A recent study that compared 44 interviews with children aged 7–10 and adolescents aged 13–16 confirmed these strategies and differences (Larose-Grégoire, Cyr, & Dion, submitted). Unlike interviews with children, interviewers asked more suggestive questions of adolescents, and adolescents provided more elaborate responses to these types of prompts than children did. However, even after an elaborated response, suggestive questions tend to be used as subsequent statements on the part of the investigators instead of an invitation that will be more appropriate.

Practical implications

Adolescents present many challenges for investigators. Indeed, they are often intimidated, more often feel guilty, and are ashamed of the situations in which they find themselves, thus making their disclosure more difficult. Because their abilities are not yet those of adults, their sometimes partial or inconsistent narratives arouse suspicion and are sometimes interpreted as a sign that they are making false allegations. Since interviewers tend to use more suggestive strategies on adolescents than on children, the contradictions they cause in adolescent narratives also fuel suspicion. The dynamics of the interviews described above, where even elaborate answers are followed by suggestive questions, can both reflect high expectations on the part of the investigators regarding the number of details expected or even doubts about the information provided.

Thus, it appears desirable that interviewers be better informed about the issues specific to adolescents and the need to take the time to develop rapport. The discomfort and greater reluctance observed among adolescents also indicate that the level of support offered by interviewers should be more frequent and adjusted as needed. In this sense, the Revised NICHD Protocol offers several relevant tools that will be discussed in Chapter 6.

2 Language

The language skills of children are a crucial element that influences the whole interview process. Recent studies have observed that expressive language skills, which represent the children's ability to use words to describe their experience, are associated with the accuracy of what they say, while receptive language skills, which reflect the child's ability to understand what is said, are correlated with their resistance to leading questions (Klemfuss, 2015). Language development is a complex learning process that involves phonetics and the acquisition and use of vocabulary and syntax. The elements most relevant to interviews with children will be reviewed in the next paragraphs, starting with language learning.

2.1 Language learning

The child is dependent on language not only to encode experiences in memory but also to relate them; this does not exclude the fact that images and sensations can also be recorded in autobiographical memory (Fivush, 2011). Language is learned from what children see, hear, and experience (real-world context), as well as by listening to how words are placed in sentences (linguistic context). For example, depending on the interactions they have with the people around them, children will learn that questions do not all have the same function. For example, while the question "Do you want another cookie?" is a request for information, "Do you want to have another spanking?" is not (Walker, 2013). Research findings confirm the importance of interactions between children and their parents not only for language learning but also for the development of children's skills to use language to report the events they have experienced. Autobiographical memory and the capacity to report one's emotions and thoughts and those of others depend on the quality of parent-child conversations (Fivush, Reese, & Haden, 2006; Salmon & Reese, 2015). When interactions between parent and child have been few and of poor quality, the child is likely to have a limited capacity to recall experiences in an organized and consistent manner, both because of its limits in terms of vocabulary and its narrative competence.

Bernstein (1972) identifies two main categories of discourse that can be found in families: families of "talkers" versus families of "pointers." In talkers' families, parents name objects, articulate their thoughts, and try to provide clear meaning to requests made to the child. These families tend to be precise in the choice of words used and make few assumptions about the knowledge of the listener. These parents have been identified by other authors (Reese & Fivush, 1993; Fivush, Marin, McWilliams, & Bohanek, 2009) as having a high development style. Thus, they assist the child by confirming his/her memory when s/he tries to remember and when s/he recounts common experiences. They also use questions to help the child build a more comprehensive narrative. Families of pointers give less explanation to their children about the nature of objects and people, use more impersonal pronouns (e.g., "that," "there," "we"), are less precise, and tend to take for granted that the listener knows what it is about. Parents with a low elaboration style ask their child a few questions when telling a story, and they tend to repeat the same question to try and get a full story instead of diversifying the questions. When you meet a child who gives a vague and unfinished story, it is possible that this is due to the family context in which s/he is growing up and not to the fact that s/he is reluctant to reveal things or even to the fact that s/he has made a false allegation.

Therefore, the family environment that promotes early language development is also the one that allows the creation of a secure attachment through the presence of a caring, consistent, and available adult who knows how to adjust to the child's needs.

This relationship allows the learning of cultural conventions associated with language (reciprocity, eye contact, speaking, common reference) and also supports the development of social cognition and empathy (Cohen, 2001). Several studies have shown important links between early secure attachment, the presence of receptive parents, and the child's receptive and expressive language skills (Salmon & Reese, 2015). Parents who discuss positive and negative lived events with their child in a sensitive and supportive way allow them to develop their memory and their emotional regulation. This style of elaboration of reminiscences becomes internalized toward the end of the preschool period and allows the child to remember a wide range of events and relate them in narratives that are more comprehensive. Unfortunately, as Snow, Powell, and Sanger (2012) point out, these stimulating and supportive family conditions are often absent for children and adolescents who are in contact with protection or justice services. Several studies have shown that the cognitive and academic skills of young people are affected as much by abuse (e.g., physical, sexual, verbal) as by neglect (e.g., physical, emotional, educational) (see Cicchetti & Toth, 2015; Hildyard & Wolfe, 2002, for a review).

2.2   Phonetics

The pronunciation of words can also present difficulties for the interviewer in the presence of young children. Before the age of 4, many sounds are not yet mastered, and up to 10% of 8-year-olds still cannot pronounce all sounds (Reich, 1986). The most common pronunciation errors include inversion, suppression, addition, assimilation, and substitution of sounds (Reich, 1986; de Villiers & de Villiers, 1978). It is common to observe that when a word is not understood, interviewers tend to either suggest a similar word to the child or even ignore the word (Warren, Woodall, Hunt, & Perry, 1996). Since children often tend to say yes and not correct interviewers when they are wrong, it is best to have the child repeat the word and ask questions that may clarify its meaning (Walker, 2013).

2.3   Vocabulary

Vocabulary is another essential acquisition for the child to be able to communicate. If 2-year-old children have mastered around two hundred words, this number grows exponentially, reaching between eight thousand and fourteen thousand words by the age of 6 (Stoel-Gammon & Vogel Sosa, 2007). However, the individual differences are very strong and can mainly be explained by the family context. A word can be difficult to understand because it is not used in the child's environment, because it appeals to a concept that has not yet been cognitively mastered or because it is part of a sentence whose structure is too complex or unusual for the child. In addition, young children often use words that they do not understand as adults do.

Walker (2013) has listed several elements related to vocabulary that can complicate either the interviewer's questions or the child's answers. Since children are very concrete (see above, regarding their cognitive development), their answers are often literal. Berliner and Barbieri (1984) report that during a trial, a 5-year-old girl answered "no" to the question "Have you ever put your mouth on daddy's penis?" because it did not reflect the literal truth. It was not the child who made the gesture (who put his mouth), but it was dad who put his penis in the mouth (who is the agent of the action). This concrete thinking and literal approach to language are very important in very young children and even some older children.

Preschoolers have difficulty with references to pronouns. They don't always remember whom the "they," "us," or "them" refers to. If the child has named them, it becomes easier to use nouns and places instead of pronouns. For example, it is easier for the child to answer "What did Albert say?" rather than "What did he say?" or again "Were there a lot of people in the living room?" rather than "Were there a lot of people there?" (Walker, 2013). Under 8 or 9 years, children do not always understand that using a pronoun means that we are talking about the same person last referenced. In addition, an interviewer who uses his/her first name in reference to himself/herself (e.g., "Tell Mireille everything that happened") may confuse children who do not remember the interviewer's first name after a few minutes (Walker, 2013). It is, therefore, preferable to use "I" or "me" (e.g., "Tell me everything that happened"). Young children and those being interviewed in a second language can also make mistakes in the use of "he/she," "my/your," and so on (e.g., "My cousin Peter she hurt me").

Prepositions are simple words that are necessary, among other things, to interpret gestures accurately, but they can cause several difficulties. Walker (2013) has reviewed and illustrated many of these. Children begin to use prepositions between 1.5 and 2 years old, but not all of them are learned before the age of 5.5. During the learning period, children make many mistakes. For example, a 3-year-old could use "inside" or "in" to mean "between" or use "on" to mean "beside," thus altering the meaning of "Daddy put his penis in my butt." A 4-year-old can confuse "above" with "below" or "in front." The prepositions "before" and "after" (e.g., before lunch, after dinner) can pose special problems for preschool children, and often these concepts are not mastered until the age of 6.5 or older. Adverbs like "always" and "never" are often confused by children who tend to interpret this pair of words as positive or negative. The questions "Do you always tell the truth?" or "Have you never told a lie?" ask the child to undertake detailed research into the past to answer it correctly. Since adults have difficulty with this type of cognitive operation, it is, therefore, reasonable to assume that children have similar difficulties. Likewise, answering a question that includes the word "none" or "no," such as "no thing," "no person," and "no place," also requires a global search of all the possibilities in order to be able to answer accurately. These questions regularly generate inconsistent answers. Usually, children will answer "no" to the questions "Did something else happen?" and "Did he say something else?" yet later in the interview, they will apparently contradict themselves. It is not uncommon for young children to answer a question like "Was there anyone else?" by saying "No, only Peter."

Walker (2013) indicates that the word "more" is an easy word for children, but initially, it means simple repetition (e.g., "I want more milk"). The comparative use of this term is not understood until the age of 6, especially when used in relation to the word "less" (e.g., "Was it more or less than such and such a thing?"). Before the age of 10, this type of comparison is not recommended.

Words that can take on multiple meanings are also a problem for young children (Korkman et al., 2008; Walker, 2013). For example, the word "touch" can include at least a dozen different touches or gestures (e.g., "hitting," "throwing," "squeezing") between objects, body parts, or instruments. For young children, touching may be limited to describing a single type of gesture that is done with the hand. So a 6-year-old could deny having been touched but later say that something was put in his mouth. "Move" is another example of a word that can have multiple meanings. It can be difficult for children under the age of 7 to understand that a penis is moving. It is for this reason that they usually use simpler terms like "push" and "pull." Obviously, legal terms (e.g., "lawyer," "court") and terms used in investigations (e.g., "incident," "event," "scene") are abstract and complex for children, often up to the age of 12, and should therefore be avoided (Walker, 2013; Saywitz, Jaenicke, & Camparo, 1990). Using the child's words is a better solution (e.g., "We are going to talk about the second time" rather than "We are going to talk about the second event").

An interesting fact about vocabulary has been observed by Simcock and Hayne (2002, 2003) in their studies; it seems that when the child recounts what happened to him/her, s/he may use the level of language s/he had at the time of encoding, therefore at the time of the event, and not the current level of language that is the one at the time of the recall. This means that if an 8-year-old child reports an assault experienced at the age of 5, it is possible that the vocabulary used to describe it may appear immature. Interviewers' expectations must therefore be adjusted accordingly.

We have examined in detail the content and words used by children to describe their perpetrator (Landry, 2018), the actions (Côté, Cyr, & Dion, 2017), and the location (Marcil, Cyr, & Dion, 2019) of experienced events by comparing reports by three equal-sized groups of children aged 3 to 5, 6 to 8, and 9 to 12 years old interviewed by police officers in the course of their work. The scope of this work is limited by the fact that it was not possible to classify the children in groups according to their language functioning as assessed objectively using a standardized test. As expected, for all categories, children's capacities increase with age. From the age of 6 to 9 years, children's descriptions become more complex through the use of qualifying adjectives, adverbs, and prepositions that help to clarify information.

When talking about their perpetrator, all children older than 3 mentioned the name. So when the perpetrator is a familiar person, children are able to indicate who they are. Physical descriptions by younger children are very general, as are descriptions of clothes for which they use simple common names (e.g., "old," "clothing"). Older children, especially those aged 9 to 12, are able to use information about nationality, culture, occupation, or family ties to describe their perpetrators who are known to them. They are also better able to bring out particular distinguishing elements in appearance (e.g., false teeth).

Regarding the perpetrators' actions, children mostly reported physical contact and, to a lesser extent, noncontact gestures, such as showing parts of the body or pornographic films and taking pictures, and in some situations, use of physical force or violence. Young children are able to name the parts of their body that are involved in actions. They use simple verbs like "touch," "put on," and "play," while children aged 6–9 and older use verbs that describe more specific gestures like "caress," "stroke," "lick," or "kiss," reflecting a better understanding of sexual gestures. As for their own behavior, the children reported few elements. These concern a few gestures with contact on the private parts of the perpetrator or relate to the fact of having seen these things. They can also relate to active resistance strategies such as hitting, pushing, and passively resisting, such as by not looking. Very few children and none of the very young made any reference to sensations or even calls for help.

The description of the location where the assault took place is a very important element in corroborating the child's comments and, in certain situations, in recovering evidence. Children speak very generally about the place, the room, the furniture it contained, or other objects. Here, too, the descriptions offered by very young children are very general and broad (e.g., in the house). However, from the age of 6, descriptions refer to specific places (e.g., in the boys' locker room). These children are also able to describe in a clear and precise way any objects that were used (e.g., hairy brown towel, small laptop computer, gray camera), unlike children under 6, whose descriptions are limited and vague (e.g., one thing, thing).

This content analysis makes it possible to mark out what can be expected from children according to their age. Even though their abilities are less developed, young children are able to name who their perpetrator is, but they have little ability to describe the perpetrator, to indicate the parts of their body that were involved in the acts committed, and to describe in general terms the perpetrator's actions. They are also able to identify where the abuse took place without being able to provide a very detailed description. It is important to respect children's descriptive skills and to use open-ended questions to access content. The use of more specific questions or option-posing questions increases the probability that children will provide inaccurate answers.

2.4 Syntax

Syntax refers to the rules for combining words to make sentences. A simple sentence consists of a subject, a verb, and a complement. It is this type of sentence that is best understood by children and should be preferred during the interview. In addition, sentences should be as short as possible since children's attention spans are limited. For this reason, it is important not to use summaries of all the facts since very often the children will not have the capacity to follow this sequence of sentences and correct the interviewer if necessary. Likewise, it is preferable to avoid having to make short summaries that serve as an introduction to the question or to put a context (e.g., "Earlier, you told me that you arrived at her house and you went to the living room and then sat on the sofa. Tell me what happened in the living room"). These sentences are long and require a good attention span to be understood. It is better to use a shorter sentence like "Tell me what happened after you sat on the couch." Thus, the first factor that makes a sentence complex for a child is its length.

A second factor that makes a sentence complex is whether it contains two ideas or two questions. Walker (2013) indicates that questions like "When and where was the last time?" and "Did it happen because it happened or because your mother told you to tell us that?" are difficult for children aged 4 to 6 to understand. In addition, the question "Do you remember being in the kitchen?" is complex for children since, unlike adults, they do not fully understand that they must answer the second part of the question. For example, a "yes" response from a young child could mean "yes, I remember" or "yes, I went to the kitchen." It is, therefore, preferable to split this type of question into two parts and remind the child that if s/he does not know the answer to a question, s/he can say I don't know or don't remember. The question asked could, for example, take the following form: "If you don't know the answer, tell me you don't know. Did you go to the kitchen?" In a study that focused specifically on questions that included more than one request for information, Katz and Hershkowitz

(2012) observe that these questions had negative effects on the length of children's responses. None of the 65 children aged 4 to 9 reported that they did not understand the question, that they had difficulty answering, or that they needed clarification. Yet in 24% of cases, the responses were unintelligible. In cases where the children produced relevant answers, they mainly answered the last part of the multiple questions; they rarely provided a response to the two requests for information included in the question.

Walker (2013) points out that sentences that include embeddings – that is, one sentence within another sentence – are also difficult to understand and should be worded differently. For example, "Did you cry when he touched you?" is easier to understand than "Did you, when he touched you, cry?" or "What did you do after school?" is a simpler sentence than "What, after school, did you do?"

Questions that include negatives (e.g., "Didn't he kiss you?") are often used in interviews and even more so in cross-examinations (see Chapter 8, questions during testimony). These phrases are not reliable tools for obtaining information from either adults or children. A study by Perry and colleagues reported by Walker (2013) indicates that, on average, children from kindergarten to college correctly answered only 50% of the questions containing a simple negation (e.g., "Didn't you see the woman in the video?") or double negation (e.g., "Isn't it true that Sam didn't jump over the blocks?"). When these questions are not asked negatively, 70% to 100% of the time children answer correctly.

Walker (2013) also indicates that asking questions starting with "I suggest to you," "I submit to you," "I believe you told us," or "Isn't it" are all inappropriate for children being cross-examined (see also Powell, Westera, Goodman-Delahunty, & Pichler, 2016). Even adults have difficulty understanding the meaning of these questions, given their asymmetric nature. As we pointed out in the chapter on suggestibility, children tend to believe that adults know everything and are right about things (Walker & Warren, 1995). Thus, if an adult in a position of authority "suggests" that something has happened, it is extremely difficult if not impossible for children under the age of 12 to disagree with what is being said, assuming that the question thus asked has been understood, which is not always the case.

Another difficulty for children is the use of passive voice in sentences (e.g., "Were you touched by Peter?"). Three-year-olds tend to ignore passive forms. Thus, they will interpret the question "Were you chased by him?" as "Did you chase him?" Some studies indicate that children do not understand the passive forms before the age of 10 to 13.

IMPLICATIONS FOR PRACTICE

Several implications for the conduct of an interview stem from the observations made with regard to language.

1   It is important to speak to the child using correct pronunciation and not to use childish language (Poole & Lamb, 1998). Since children are likely to pronounce certain words differently from adults, one should also avoid guessing what the child said if the words used were pronounced poorly or if they were not understood. It is better to ask the child to repeat than to make a suggestion of what may have be said (e.g., "I didn't hear correctly. Can you repeat?").

2   As children sometimes use words idiosyncratically (e.g., an 8-year-old girl said she was raped, but the reality was that she had only had her arm squeezed tightly), in a more restrictive way (e.g., pajamas are not considered as clothing) or even a more inclusive way (e.g., "in" and "between" are confused), it is, therefore, important to clarify what the child wants to say by asking other questions, if possible open-ended (e.g., "I am not sure I understood correctly, tell me more about . . .").

3   It is difficult to choose the correct words when interviewing children, and it is best choice to use the child's words and not attempt to replace them either with words that appear more accurate (e.g., "penis" instead of "pee") or by synonyms (e.g., "injury" for "boo-boo"). It is useful to ask parents before an interview what words the child uses to refer to the private parts since these can vary considerably from one family to another (see appendix 6). In any case, it is better to have the children provide the word s/he uses to designate parts of the body rather than suggest them.

4   Similarly, Poole and Lamb (1998) suggest, when a child talks about a person, asking other questions to ensure that there is no ambiguity about the identity of the person (e.g., "my uncle Peter" can be a friend of the family or one of two or three Peters in the extended family). As suggested by Walker (2013), replace the abstract words ("here," "there," "that," "we") with the correct words when they have been previously named by the child (e.g., "Was your sister Sophie with you in the living room?" instead of "Was she there with you?").

5   With regard to syntax, the sentences must be as short and as simple as possible – that is, the sentence must include only a subject, a verb, and a complement. Avoid starting sentences with "I would like you to tell me," "Can you," or "Will you," which unnecessarily lengthens them. Summaries and short recaps at the beginning of sentences should also be avoided if possible since these additions make the question more complex (e.g., "Earlier you told me he had put cream on your peepee and then he hurt you with his fingers. Where did he get this cream?").

Sentences that contain more than one idea, more than one question, or negative terms are all too complex for children and should be avoided. If this is not possible, it is better to remind the child before asking the question that if s/he does not understand it or does not know the answer, s/he should simply say so.

"Why" questions should be avoided since they lead children to justify themselves; they can be replaced by "what is" (Walker, 2013). Here's an example: "Why didn't you tell your mom right after?" could be replaced by "What is the reason for which you did not tell your mom?"

It is common for the interviewers to correct themselves by rephrasing their questions while formulating them. This process unnecessarily complicates questions and can even confuse children. It is, therefore, important for the interviewer to take the time to design questions that are simple and as short as possible before asking them.

In addition, the child must be allowed the necessary time to understand the question and answer it. These cognitive operations take more time for children than for adults, and it is not uncommon for interviewers to repeat their question or add another because the child has not answered within seconds.

In order to better hear a child who does not speak loudly, it may be helpful to keep speaking loudly rather than adjusting to the child's sound level. Be tolerant of language difficulties and avoid correcting the child unnecessarily so that s/he does not feel inadequate.

3   Socioemotional development

Many abused children manifest delayed socioemotional development, which can affect their participation in the interview. These children have poorer relationships with their parents, and this can have many repercussions. In their review of the literature, Pipe and Salmon (2009) indicate that abused children had deficiencies in their ability to recognize, express, understand, and control their emotions (Cicchetti & Toth, 2015). They also tend to reverse caregiver roles and exhibit controlling behaviors more than other children (Toth, Cicchetti, Macfie, & Emde, 1997). These children also have a more negative image of themselves, and girls specifically report more feelings of shame and fewer feelings of pride (Cicchetti & Toth, 2015; Kim & Cicchetti, 2006).

In terms of attachment, abused children are more often identified as presenting an insecure pattern of attachment (Toth, Maughan, Manly, Spagnola, & Cicchetti, 2002). Among the possible consequences that result from this, Beaudoin and Hébert (2012) indicate that these children often have less confidence in their capacities to control their environment and to reach objectives; they, therefore, have less self-confidence, and they demonstrate lower self-esteem; they adapt less easily to different social interactions and to related demands. Preschool and school-age children with insecure attachments adopt less adequate conflict resolution strategies, becoming more frustrated and less empathetic. It is, therefore, not surprising that abused children experience more internalized (e.g., anxiety, depression, posttraumatic stress disorder, attention deficit) or externalized (e.g., conduct disorder, aggression) types of symptoms and are also less capable of resisting various environmental stressors. Abused preschoolers often experience anxiety when asked to separate from a parent figure to accompany a stranger into an unfamiliar room. However, children with an assured pattern of attachment (secure pattern) are able to better manage their distress, and they report more information than children who are insecurely attached. In addition, the results of studies conducted to date empirically support the existence of a significant relationship between attachment pattern and children's memory (Alexander, Quas, & Goodman, 2002; Chae et al., 2014; Quas et al., 1999) or the memory of adults who experienced childhood sexual assault (Edelstein et al., 2005). Securely attached children report more details about the events they have experienced than insecurely attached children. This pattern is also observed in adults.

The temperament of children is another factor influencing their participation in forensic interviews. For example, some children are more open and collaborative, while others are more withdrawn and shy. Temperament refers to the behavioral tendencies of persons, and there are important individual differences. These trends have a certain biological basis, and they appear very early on. In addition, they are relatively stable over time and in various situations (Chess & Thomas, 1996). Among the components that define temperament, we note

- approach/withdrawal, which indicates the ease or difficulty in accommodating new social situations;

- the emotional intensity or vigor with which negative effects are expressed;
- adaptability, or the ease of adjustment to new situations;
- persistence, or the tendency to continue an activity despite any difficulty;
- the level of distraction, or the tendency to redirect one's attention;
- activity level, or the level of motoric vigor;
- rhythmicity, or the regularity of biological functions, such as sleep and diet;
- the tolerance threshold, or the sensitivity to and tolerance for environmental stimuli; and
- the quality of mood, or the positive or negative mood of the child in general.

All of these components are often grouped under two dimensions: inhibition (which represents the tendency to withdraw or to be upset in the face of social situations involving a stranger) and impulsivity (which represents difficulties self-regulating emotional reactions, motor activity, and attention). Some studies based on a medical examination (Gordon et al.,1993; Merritt, Ornstein, & Spicker, 1994) or a staged event (Chae & Ceci, 2005; Geddie, Fradin, & Beer, 2000) indicate that the more inhibited a child's temperament, the less information s/he will report. Shy children and those who are very adaptable are also more suggestible when asked specific questions (Greenhoot, Ornstein, Gordon, & Baker-Ward, 1999; Roebers & Schneider, 2001). Children with more anxious temperaments and those who are anxious during the interview are also more suggestible (Almerigogna, Ost, Bull, & Akehurst, 2007).

IMPLICATIONS FOR PRACTICE

It is important to remember that the associations between the variables discussed in this section and children's testimony only account for part of the observed variability in children's performance. Other factors are likely to influence the child's ability and willingness to share the events experienced. However, it should be noted that a child's pattern of attachment, particularly if insecure, and temperament, whether inhibited, shy, or withdrawn, will pose particular challenges to interviewers. The challenges will be particularly great during interviews in which the interviewer meets for the first and only time the child with whom s/he must create a trusting relationship sufficient for the child to feel comfortable talking about what s/he has experienced or observed. This is why it is necessary, as prescribed in the pre-substantive phase of the NICHD Protocol, to take the time to create a bond of trust with the child and to support and encourage him/her with non-suggestive reinforcements such as those discussed in Chapter 6 and Appendix 6.

4   Temporal attributes

As Pipe and Salmon (2009) point out, the temporal attributes of an event, such as the number of times it happened, the sequence of events, and the date, are essential elements to be documented in forensic contexts. From the age of 4 or 5, children are able to name the days of the week, the months of the year, the numbers, and the time. Often these lists are learned by heart. However, it is important to remember that just because a child knows the days of the week does not mean that s/he can tell the day on which an event took place. The child's ability to recite such lists tells us only that s/he has acquired the vocabulary and not the child knows the meaning of the words learned.

To be able to indicate the frequency of an event, it is necessary to know how to count. Some suggest that number skills develop rapidly and remain constant between ages 5 and 20, while others suggest that they gradually increase and improve with age (Walker, 2013). Walker points out that children can easily look unreliable when they give high numbers (10,000) in response to questions about the number of times something happened. Usually, children use this type of metaphor to mean that something has happened to them multiple times like in this sample of an interview with a 12-year-old boy:

INTERVIEWER: Approximately how many times?
VICTIM: Eight times.
INTERVIEWER: OK. Why do you remember those two times? Once in the living room and once in the kitchen?
VICTIM: I remember them.
INTERVIEWER: OK. But other times, do you remember them too?
VICTIM: Not a lot.
INTERVIEWER: Not a lot. But why do you think he touched you about eight times?
VICTIM: Because I remember it's a lot of times, it took like a week.

This excerpt illustrates the difficulty, even for a child of 12 years, of quantifying the number of times sexual abuse has occurred. In addition, it illustrates several communication problems. As we have already pointed out, asking "why" makes a question difficult since it focuses on internal processes or motivations, and the child's capacity to deal with these notions is not acquired until after age 10 to 13. In addition, as noted earlier, the question "why" is often perceived as critical or accusatory by children; this causes them to become defensive, making it difficult to obtain an adequate response. To the first "why," the child's answer "I remember them" indicates his inability to answer the question. Also, his answer "not a lot" to the question "But other times, do you remember them too?" indicates that the child is not sure of his answer, either because his memory is unreliable or because the question is beyond his capacity to give an exact answer. In such a context, it is important to respect the child's limits. In that sense, the metaphor he uses – "it took like a week" – is the best answer he can offer. Friedman (2007) observes that before the age of 12, children are not able to use their metacognition to explain how they could estimate when an event has occurred.

Counting the occurrences of an event that has happened two or three times is a task that some children can accomplish, but as soon as the circumstances in which the events have occurred multiply, it is very difficult for them to determine the frequency. Research seems to indicate that children tend to underestimate the number of times and especially to change the number of times if they are asked for this information again (Sharman, Powell, & Roberts, 2011). Sometimes they manage to indicate the number of times things have happened (e.g., "It happens every time I go to Daddy" or "It happens every time I have a babysitter and my brothers are not at home"). As an adult, it is easy to appreciate the level of difficulty this can represent if you ask yourself, for example, how many times we have done a fairly frequent activity in the past year, such as skiing, going to the cinema, or eating out. Establishing the exact frequency of the specified events requires cognitive and memory capacities first to mentally identify each of the events and then to add them up, assuming that these events have all been stored in memory. Usually, to answer such questions, adults who have much more developed cognitive skills than children estimate the number of times (e.g., "I go skiing every two weeks, throughout a season that lasts about five months, so ten times").

Studies conducted in a laboratory setting with children, the majority of whom were between the ages of 4 and 10, report that, from the age of 4, children are able to indicate whether an event has occurred one or more times with a high accuracy rate (Brubacher, Powell, & Roberts, 2014, for a review). However, this sensitivity to frequency does not allow children to say how many times this has happened or to associate specific details with a specific episode (Connolly & Gordon, 2014; Sharman et al., 2011). For example, in the case of a single situation, 85% to 96% of children aged 4 to 8 accurately indicated that the event had happened once; this rate was 72% to 100% for children who had experienced the event several times, but of those, fewer than 25% accurately quantified the number of events (Roberts et al., 2015; Sharman et al., 2011). Thus, children are able to report that different things happened from one situation to another without being able to associate them with specific episodes. Compared to the sequence, analogous studies tell us that school-age children can generally locate the temporal order of two events, but when there are more than two, answering the question is difficult (Roberts et al., 2015).

Orbach and Lamb (2007) observe, in interviews conducted with presumed victims of sexual abuse between the ages of 4 and 10 years, that children speak little spontaneously about the frequency and duration of events; they also note that the more details they give, the more they relate to time. However, references to the number of times the event has occurred are very infrequent, and it is only from the age of 10 that children begin to report this type of information.

Another very complex task for children is to indicate when the event occurred. To achieve this, three types of skills are needed:

- the ability to remember information about the weather when the event occurred (e.g., "it was dark," "cold," "trees had leaves," "back from school");
- general knowledge of temporal referents (e.g., day, month, year); and
- executive functions that control the integration of the two preceding forms of information – that is to say, to seek the relevant information associated with the event, to evaluate it, and to interpret it according to the child's general knowledge about time.

We can refer to time by talking about the sequence of events in relation to one another, by invoking the distance between the event and the moment when the child narrates it or by locating it at a precise moment using a date, a day of the week, or an hour.

In interviews conducted with sexually abused children between the ages of 4 and 10, Orbach and Lamb (2007) observe that the temporal sequences (e.g., "then") are the most frequently discussed. This could be specific to this study and to the use of the NICHD Protocol (see chapters 5 and 6), which seeks to elicit a free narrative that is sequenced from start to finish. They also note that, contrary to their assumptions, children of all ages more often use concrete time references (e.g., "it was

Monday") than more vague notions (e.g., "a long time ago"). This can be explained by the fact that sexual abuse usually occurs in familiar everyday activities and that the temporal structuring task allows young children to make the connection between the time of the event and familiar everyday activities (e.g., "every day when I come home from school"). One of the limitations of Orbach and Lamb's study is that it was not possible to verify whether the information given by the children was correct.

Because professionals, especially those in the legal field, often assume that referring to milestone events (e.g., Christmas, Halloween, birthday) will help the child to properly judge the time of year for the target event, Friedman and Lyon (2005) tried to verify this hypothesis and failed to do so, even when the interviews occurred three months after a significant event. In their study, they created an event in the classes of a school a few days before or a few days after a milestone event, such as Halloween, which is a very important holiday for North American children. They interviewed them three months later and observed that the children spontaneously gave little temporal information in response to open questions or in a free narrative. When asked about the timing of the event (e.g., "What month?" "What day?" "What time of day?"), children were able to respond using the correct time scale. However, the responses of children under the age of 8 or 9 were not very accurate regarding the time of day. As for the month, up to 40% of children 13 years old and under made mistakes. Regarding the season, 20% of the information reported by children 11 years and over was erroneous. Another study (Jack, Friedman, Reese, & Zajac, 2016) observes that children from the age of 9 and adolescents are as able as adults to identify the time of day and the season in which an event took place eight months later. However, children and adolescents are less accurate than adults for indicating the day and month. This confirms that several temporal notions are not mastered before the end of childhood.

The results of a study examining data obtained from abused children aged 6 to 10 and their placement history and their visit to the court indicate even less developed capacities (Wandrey, Lyon, Quas, & Friedman, 2012). Only half of the children were able to identify their age at the time of the last or first placement or during their last court visit. This data was incorrect, and the error varied from nine to twelve months for placements and six months for the court visit. Only 10% of the children were able to provide an exact date for any of these events. Just over 50% of older children were able to establish the month of their most recent court visit, indicating their limited ability to date events. Using the season to determine the timing of the event was only accurate a third of the time. Children were also unable to give an exact number of times they had come to court, and 35% of children were wrong when asked if it had happened more than once, more than five times, or more than ten times. This ability to quantify the frequency of incidents does not improve with age but seems to be influenced by the number of incidents experienced. This indicates that children have some understanding of frequency even if they have difficulty putting exact numbers on it. It is important to note that children seem to be unaware of their weakness in dating or quantifying events since they rarely say that they do not know or that they do not remember an event, regardless of the age of the child. This low awareness of their ignorance about their ability to date events is also reported by Friedman (2007) for children under 12 years old.

IMPLICATIONS FOR PRACTICE

Research tells us quite clearly that concepts related to time, number, or frequency are difficult for children under the age of 10 to use accurately, and these difficulties may continue even until the end of adolescence. Children gradually develop their ability to designate time scales; thus, from the age of 4, they are able to talk about specific times of the day (e.g., in the morning); at six, they can talk about the time of the year; and from 6 to 7 years, they usually know several relevant cues for interpreting time (e.g., day, week, month). However, it should not be concluded that these skills give them the real capacity to indicate when something has happened to them. Research tells us that if we ask a child to say when something happened, s/he will be able to respond using the correct temporal referent (e.g., "What day did that happen?" Response: "Thursday"). Unfortunately, that doesn't mean the answer is correct. From the age of 10, the ability of children improves greatly, and consequently, so does the accuracy of their answers.

For all these reasons, it is preferable to delay questions relating to the frequency or even the time when the event occurred as far as possible so as not to embarrass children with questions that they have difficulty answering. It is also advisable to indicate to the child before asking the question that if s/he does not know the answer or does not remember, s/he should say so instead of attempting an answer. If the child gives an answer, then continue with open-ended questions (see Chapter 6) instead of asking other specific questions that may cause the child to modify his/her answer. Here is an example of what is recommended:

INTERVIEWER: If you don't know the answer or you don't remember it, tell me. When did it happen?
CHILD: Last Saturday.
INTERVIEWER: Tell me all about that (instead of "When, last Saturday?").

Finally, investigators should not use the hesitations, the difficulties, or the inconsistencies in the responses by children to cast doubt on the veracity of their testimony because this does not take into account their capacities and their limits. Studies clearly show that children are able to report accurate information about events they have experienced even if they cannot report the number of times or the timing of these events.

5   Children with developmental delays

Children with intellectual or developmental delays present particular challenges for investigative and assessment interviews. These children are very vulnerable since they are between four and eight times more likely to be victims of sexual abuse than children who have a so-called typical development (see Jones et al., 2012, for a meta-analysis; see Wissink, van Vugt, Moonen, Stams, & Hendriks, 2015, for a review of the literature). Hershkowitz and colleagues (Hershkowitz, Lamb, & Horowitz, 2007) studied the intellectual characteristics of 40,430 children suspected of being victims of sexual or physical abuse. They observed that children of all ages with intellectual disabilities tend to be overrepresented among suspected victims of sexual abuse.

In addition, children with intellectual disabilities experience more severe forms of sexual abuse, more intrusive violence, more incidents, and a higher number of other incidents involving threats and the use of force. They are more often victimized by their parents. The greater the degree of impairment, the more the children are at risk of being abused. In addition, these children disclose the sexual abuse less often, and when they do, the length of the delays increases with the degree of severity of their intellectual disability.

The vulnerability of these children is compounded by several factors such as lack of communicational and social skills, their heavy reliance on caregivers, frequent exposure to different workers, and a lack of sex education (Wissink et al., 2015). Due to their cognitive impairments, these children are often underserved by justice systems insensitive to their limits (Cederborg & Lamb, 2006). They are considered unreliable witnesses because of their poorer memories, their reduced capacity to describe events, and their greater sensitivity to suggestions (Gudjonsson, 2003; Milne & Bull, 2001).

Because the investigative interview aims to obtain an autobiographical narrative – that is, a narrative that is generally based on the willingness and ability to express information rather than the mere ability to remember it (Lamb, Hershkowitz, Orbach, & Esplin, 2008) – it is not surprising that children with intellectual disabilities have more difficulty cooperating. When children have limited language skills, which is often the case with those with intellectual disabilities, investigators are more likely to have difficulty understanding their allegations, and children do not fully grasp the requests and the objectives of investigators (Walker, 2013).

Developmental delays include intellectual disability, Down syndrome, autism, and Williams syndrome. Each of these conditions has specific characteristics that affect the nature of the difficulty. Intellectual disability is defined as a deficit from the normal cognitive level (i.e., an intelligence quotient below 70 as assessed using standardized tests). This delay can be mild (50–69), moderate (35–49), or severe (less than 35). In addition to intellectual difficulties, children with intellectual disabilities also have adaptive difficulties, such as problems with communication, social development, interpersonal skills, autonomy, and personal care. Almost 80% of diagnoses of intellectual disability are mild. Several studies have focused on the abilities of children with intellectual disabilities and shed light on their capacities in forensic contexts.

Dion and her colleagues (Dion, Bouchard, Gaudreault, & Mercier, 2012) indicate that many of the skills required to produce an autobiographical account can be acquired in children with intellectual disabilities, but to a lesser degree. Thus, the episodic memory of these children is acquired more slowly, and the percentage of information stored in memory is lower than in typically developing children, so their accounts are less detailed. They often have communication and language difficulties because their skills develop at a slower pace or with deficits. Expressive language problems include difficulties in articulation, limited fluency and incorrect grammar, restricted and immature vocabulary, inadequate conversational skills, a tendency to repeat the speech heard (echolalia), inconsistencies, and lack of nuance and precision.

The results of laboratory studies (Agnew & Powell, 2004; Brown & Pipe, 2003a, 2003b; Henry & Gudjonsson, 2003; Henry & Gudjonsson, 1999, 2004; Jens, Gordon, & Shaddock, 1990), studies concerning a medical examination (Eisen, Qin, Goodman, & Davis, 2002; Michel, Gordon, Ornstein, & Simpson, 2000), and a study carried out with children presumed to be victims of sexual abuse (Dion et al.,

2006) report that children with intellectual disabilities perform less well than typically developing children when asked to remember an event. However, some studies have suggested that children with mild to moderate intellectual disabilities can provide useful and medico-legal information that is accurate and that they are not more suggestible than children with typical development, as long as they are compared to children of the same mental age (Brown, Lewis, Lamb, & Stephens, 2012; Brown, Lewis, & Lamb, 2015; Dion & Cyr, 2008; Henry & Gudjonsson, 1999, 2003; Jens et al., 1990; Michel et al., 2000).

Here, the type of questions used may partly explain these differences obtained since the accuracy of the information reported by children with intellectual disabilities in response to open-ended questions is generally as high as that of typically developing peers of the same chronological age (Henry, Bettenay, & Carney, 2011; Brown et al., 2012; Brown et al., 2015). Research also indicated that the questioning strategies often differed with more focused and fewer open-ended questions asked to children with intellectual disabilities both in forensic interviews (Agnew, Powell, & Snow, 2006; Cederborg & Lamb, 2008; Cederborg, La Rooy, & Lamb, 2008; Cederborg, Danielsson, La Rooy, & Lamb, 2009; Cederborg et al., 2012) and in interviews about a staged event (Brown, Lewis, Stephens, & Lamb, 2017).

With the exception of Roebers and Schneider (2001), researchers who assessed intellectual and cognitive abilities with the scales of the Wechsler intelligence test concluded that verbal intelligence has the most important impact on the quality of the child's testimony (Chae & Ceci, 2005; Dion et al., 2006; Brown & Pipe, 2003a). For example, children with poor verbal intelligence skills were less likely to provide details about an event (Geddie et al., 2000; Elischberger & Roebers, 2001). However, one of our studies with suspected victims (Dion & Cyr, 2008) showed that children with poor verbal intelligence can nonetheless provide relevant information on the dimensions used to describe aggression. A number of recent studies have demonstrated that the use of the NICHD Protocol helped children with intellectual disabilities to provide relevant and accurate details; these will be presented in Chapter 7.

Down syndrome, also called trisomy 21, is a genetic abnormality in chromosome 21. Children with it are distinguished by a body shape that includes a flattened face, poor muscle tone, and usually moderate intellectual disability, although some adults with Down syndrome have learned to read or write. Regarding investigative interviews, these children have a marked deficit in expressive language, which implies deficiencies in vocabulary, sentence length, sentence construction or syntax, and intelligibility (Henry et al., 2011). Short-term memory deficits also influence their understanding of long utterances. On the other hand, the receptive language of these children is better than their expressive language, indicating that they understand better than what they are able to express. Thus, these children might find it easier to communicate information nonverbally (by gestures or tracing).

Children with developmentally delayed autism spectrum disorder may exhibit a variety of symptoms, the three main ones being difficulties in reciprocal social interaction, communication difficulties, and restricted or repetitive behaviors and interests. These symptoms vary in severity, ranging from children with a high level of functioning, such as those with Asperger syndrome, where language and intelligence are preserved, to children with severe symptoms. All of these children have difficulty picturing other people's thoughts and feelings as their own. Thus, they do not understand jokes, metaphors, and lies. They also have more difficulty with pronouns (me, you) and words describing space and time (here, there, coming, going). Anxiety is often present, especially with strangers or when routines are broken. Between 50 and 80% of autistic children also have an intellectual disability. In terms of memory, they have difficulty remembering the essential elements (gist) of the event, although they can remember certain facts precisely in more detail than most people if it matches one of their interests. Talking about an event from their perspective is not easy given their difficulty with social relationships and their self-understanding. In addition, the recognition of faces or voices, recent or familiar, is deficient. Two studies (see Henry et al., 2011) have found that older children with Asperger syndrome did not differ from children of the same mental age in the accuracy and suggestibility of their response. However, they gave less information, particularly on the social details of the event or the personal relevance of the event. A recent study (Almeida, Lamb, & Weisblatt, 2019) done with an adaptation of the Revised NICHD Protocol shows that autistic children are able to answer open-ended questions accurately, and their performance after a delay is similar to that of typical children (see Chapter 7 for more detail).

IMPLICATIONS FOR PRACTICE

Children with developmental delays can provide accurate information about events they have experienced if questioned appropriately. Under the right conditions, the performance of these children could be similar to that of a typical child of the same mental age. In other words, if a 15-year-old has an intellectual disability equivalent to a mental age level of 6, this child should understand and answer questions like a 6-year-old.

All the recommendations previously made on cognitive abilities, language, and temporal concepts also apply to children with developmental delay, depending on their mental age level.

In addition, some additional precautions should be taken. The presence of a third party, either a trusted person or a person who knows the child well, may be beneficial, specifically when the child has communication difficulties or wishes to be accompanied. This trusted person could also introduce the interviewer to children and provide support. This presence will be short – that is, the time for a brief neutral conversation (e.g., during the pre-substantive phase of the NICHD Protocol; see Chapter 6), and then leaving the interviewer and the interviewee alone to broach the subject of the interview. Since children with developmental delays can be rather fearful or confused in the presence of a stranger, it may be useful to meet them twice; a first meeting to create a relationship of trust and to discuss pleasant events and a second meeting to address the subject of the interview. This approach reduces the length of each interview and is particularly beneficial with children who have lower attention spans and lower fatigue resistance than typical children.

It may also be easier to conduct the interview in a location familiar to the child but free from distraction (Henry et al., 2011). Given the language and short-term memory delays, questions should be short, to the point, and open-ended. Questions offering a choice and repeated questions increase the suggestibility of these children and should be avoided. These children require more supportive statements from the interviewer, more time to think through their response, and more frequent pauses. Finally, it is recommended to use a structured interview protocol like that of NICHD, which, as the most recent research has shown, helps children with developmental delays to provide more accurate and detailed reports; these studies are detailed in Chapter 7.

6   Conclusion

Children of all ages with minimal language proficiency, and even those with cognitive deficits, can be good informants about the events they have experienced if the interviewer knows how to adjust his/her requests to their level of development. For a child, producing an account of what s/he has experienced is a task that requires mastering several skills, be they cognitive, linguistic, mnemonic, or social. The individual differences in performance can be explained by the variations in the acquisitions made in each of these skills. For example, a child who has been abused, compared to children of the same age who have not experienced abuse, might perform at a lower level on one or more of these dimensions. The quality of the familial, social, and educational environment can also account for these differences. It may, therefore, be useful to try to identify these contexts before meeting the child (see appendix 6).

The quality of the relationship that the interviewer will be able to implement in the short time allotted to him/her is another important factor that will influence the child's motivation to speak up and, in some cases, to overcome the feelings of shame, responsibility, and blame the child can experience. Asking questions that are simple and clear, helping the child to develop the account using open-ended questions, and making him/her feel confident about answering the questions because these are adjusted to the child's capacity will enhance the quality of this exchange. To help set up superior conditions for carrying out the interview, interviewers should adjust to the child's temperament (whether s/he is calm, introverted, responsive, curious, or anxious) and take into account the child's needs to feel close to the interviewer or to keep a physical distance, depending on his/her attachment style.

To assess the child's developmental level, the interviewer should have a certain period of time to observe the child. Ideally, this observation period should include tasks or activities that mimic those that will be asked of the child when it comes to the subject being investigated or evaluated. The NICHD Protocol offers such a structure during the pre-substantive phase of the interview, and this will be described in detail in Chapter 6. There is no doubt that the interviewer must be adaptable and flexible when conducting interviews with children because the variability and degree of difficulty posed by children are surely greater than those by adults.

References

Agnew S. E., Powell M. B. (2004). "The effect of intellectual disability on children's recall of an event across different question types", *Law and Human Behavior*, 28(3), 273–294.

Agnew S. E., Powell M. B., Snow P. C. (2006). "An examination of the questioning styles of police officers and caregivers when interviewing children with intellectual disabilities", *Legal and Criminological Psychology*, 11(1), 35–53.

Alexander K. W., Goodman G. S., Schaaf J. M., Edelstein R. S., Quas J. A., Shaver P. R. (2002). "The role of attachment and cognitive inhibition in children's memory and suggestibility for a stressful event", *Journal of Experimental Child Psychology*, 83(4), 262–290.

Alexander K. W., Quas J. A., Goodman G. S. (2002). "Theoretical advances in understanding children's memory for distressing events: The role of attachment", *Developmental Review*, 22, 490–519.

Almeida T. S., Lamb M. E., Weisblatt E. J. (2019). "Effects of delay, question type, and socio-emotional support on episodic memory retrieval by children with autism spectrum disorder", *Journal of Autism and Developmental Disorders*, 49(3), 1111–1130.

Almerigogna J., Ost J., Bull R., Akehurst L. (2007). "State of high anxiety: How non-supportive interviewers can increase the suggestibility of child witnesses", *Applied Cognitive Psychology*, 21(7), 963–974.

Bastin C., Van der Linden M., Michel A.-P., Friedman W. J. (2004). "The effects of aging on location-based and distance-based processes in memory for time", *Acta Psychologica*, 116(2), 145–171.

Bauer P. J. (2015). "A complementary processes account of the development of childhood amnesia and a personal past", *Psychological Review*, 122(2), 204–231.

Beaudoin G., Hébert M. (2012). "La sécurité d'attachement: Un concept prometteur pour l'analyse des profils des victimes d'agression sexuelle? [Attachment security: A promising concept for analyzing sexual assault victim profiles]", in Hébert M., Cyr M., Tourigny M. (Éds.). *L'agression sexuelle envers les enfants* [Sexual abuse on children], vol. 2, Montréal, Presses de l'Université du Québec, 261–314.

Berliner L., Barbieri M. (1984). "The testimony of the child victim of sexual abuse", *Journal of Social Issues*, 40, 125–137.

Bernstein B. (1972). "Social class, language and socialization", in Giglioli P. (Ed.), *Language and social context*, New York, Penguin Books, 157–178.

Brennan M., Brennan R. E. (1988). *Strange language: Child victims under cross examination*, 3rd ed., Wagga Wagga, Riverina Literacy Center.

Brown D. A., Lewis C. N., Lamb M. E. (2015). "Preserving the past: An early interview improves delayed event memory in children with intellectual disabilities", *Child Development*, 86(4), 1031–1047.

Brown D. A., Lewis C. N., Lamb M. E., Stephens E. (2012). "The influences of delay and severity of intellectual disability on event memory in children", *Journal of Consulting and Clinical Psychology*, 80(5), 829–841.

Brown D. A., Lewis C., Stephens E., Lamb M. (2017). "Interviewers' approaches to questioning vulnerable child witnesses: The influences of developmental level versus intellectual disability status", *Legal and Criminological Psychology*, 22(2), 332–349.

Brown D. A., Pipe M.-E. (2003a). "Individual differences in children's event memory reports and the narrative elaboration technique", *Journal of Applied Psychology*, 88(2), 195–206.

Brown D. A., Pipe M.-E. (2003b). "Variations on a technique: Enhancing children's recall using narrative elaboration training", *Applied Cognitive Psychology*, 17(4), 377–399.

Brubacher S. P., Powell M. B., Roberts K. P. (2014). "Recommendations for interviewing children about repeated experiences", *Psychology, Public Policy, and Law*, 20(3), 325–335.

Cederborg A. C., Danielsson H., La Rooy D., Lamb M. E. (2009). "Repetition of contaminating question types when children and youths with intellectual disabilities are interviewed", *Journal of Intellectual Disability Research*, 53(5), 440–449.

Cederborg A.-C., Hultman E., La Rooy D. (2012). "The quality of details when children and youths with intellectual disabilities are interviewed about their abuse experiences", *Scandinavian Journal of Disability Research*, 14(2), 113–125.

Cederborg A.-C., Lamb M. E. (2006). "How does the legal system respond when children with learning difficulties are victimized?" *Child Abuse & Neglect*, 30(5), 537–547.

Cederborg A.-C., Lamb M. E. (2008). "Interviewing alleged victims with intellectual disabilities", *Journal of Intellectual Disability Research*, 52(1), 49–58.

Cederborg A. C., La Rooy D., Lamb M. E. (2008). "Repeated interviews with children who have intellectual disabilities", *Journal of Applied Research in Intellectual Disabilities*, 21, 103–113.

Chae Y., Ceci S. J. (2005). "Individual differences in children's recall and suggestibility: The effect of intelligence, temperament, and self-perceptions", *Applied Cognitive Psychology*, 19(4), 383–407.

Chae Y., Goodman G. S., Larson R. P., Augusti E.-M., Alley D., VanMeenen K. M., . . . Coulter K. P. (2014). "Children's memory and suggestibility about a distressing event: The role of children's and parents' attachment", *Journal of Experimental Child Psychology*, 123, 90–111.

Chess S., Thomas A. (1996). *Temperament: Theory and practice*, Philadelphia, Brunner/Mazel.

Cicchetti D., Toth S. L. (2015). "Child maltreatment", in Lamb M. E., Lerner R. M. (Eds.), *Handbook of child psychology and developmental science*, vol. 3, New York, John Wiley & Sons, 513–563.

Cohen N. J. (2001). *Language impairment and psychopathology in infants, children and adolescents*, Thousand Oaks, CA, Sage.

Connolly D. A., Gordon H. M. (2014). "Can order of general and specific memory prompts help children to recall an instance of a repeated event that was different from the others?" *Psychology, Crime & Law*, 20(9), 852–864.

Côté É., Cyr M., Dion J. (2017). "Description des gestes d'agression rapportés par les enfants victimes d'agression sexuelle lors de l'entrevue d'enquête policière [Description of abuse actions reported by child victims of sexual abuse during police investigative interview]", Poster presented at *the 14th Annual meeting of CRIPCAS*, Québec.

Daignault I. V., Hébert M. (2009). "Profiles of school adaptation: Social, behavioral and academic functioning in sexually abused girls", *Child Abuse & Neglect*, 33(2), 102–115.

Dion J., Bouchard J., Gaudreault L., Mercier C. (2012). "Agression sexuelle envers les enfants ayant une déficience intellectuelle [Sexual abuse of children with intellectual disabilities]", in Hébert M., Cyr M., Tourigny M. (Éds.). *L'agression sexuelle envers les enfants* [Sexual abuse on children], vol. 2, Montréal, Les Presses de l'Université du Québec, 9–54.

Dion J., Cyr M. (2008). "The use of the NICHD protocol to enhance the quantity of details obtained from children with low verbal abilities in investigative interviews: A pilot study", *Journal of Child Sexual Abuse*, 17(2), 144–162.

Dion J., Cyr M., Richard N., McDuff P. (2006). "L'influence des habiletés cognitives, de l'âge et des caractéristiques de l'agression sexuelle sur la déclaration des présumées victimes [The influence of cognitive skills, age and characteristics of sexual assault on the reporting of alleged victims]", *Child Abuse & Neglect*, 30(8), 945–960.

Dodier O. (2017). *Les adolescents en situation de témoignage occulaire [Adolescents as occular witness]*. Thèse de doctorat déposée au département de psychologie, sciences sociales et sciences de l'éducation [Doctoral thesis in the Department of Psychology, Social Sciences and Education]. Université Clermont Auverge, France.

Edelstein R. S., Ghetti S., Quas J. A., Goodman G. S., Alexander K. W., Redlich A. D., Gordon I. M. (2005). "Individual differences in emotional memory: Adult attachment and long-term memory for child sexual abuse", *Personality and Social Psychology Bulletin*, 31(11), 1537–1548.

Eigsti I.-M., Cicchetti D. (2004). "The impact of child maltreatment on expressive syntax at 60 months", *Developmental Science*, 7(1), 88–102.

Eisen M. L., Qin J., Goodman G. S., Davis S. (2002). "Memory and suggestibility in maltreated children: Age, stress arousal, dissociation, and psychopathology", *Journal of Experimental Child Psychology*, 83, 167–212.

Elischberger H. B., Roebers C. M. (2001). "Improving young children's free narratives about an observed event: The effects of nonspecific verbal prompts", *International Journal of Behavioral Development*, 25(2), 160–166.

Fivush R. (2011). "The development of autobiographical memory", *Annual Review of Psychology*, 62, 559–582.

Fivush R., Gray J. T., Fromhoff F. A. (1987). "Two-year-olds talk about the past", *Cognitive Development*, 2(4), 393–409.

Fivush R., Habermas T., Waters T. E., Zaman W. (2011). "The making of autobiographical memory: Intersections of culture, narratives and identity", *International Journal of Psychology*, 46(5), 321–345.

Fivush R., Marin K., McWilliams K., Bohanek J. G. (2009). "Family reminiscing style: Parent gender and emotional focus in relation to child well-being", *Journal of Cognition and Development*, 10(3), 210–235.

Fivush R., Reese E., Haden C. A. (2006). "Elaborating on elaborations: Role of maternal reminiscing style in cognitive and socioemotional development", *Child Development*, 77(6), 1568–1588.

Friedman W. J. (2007). "The development of temporal metamemory", *Child Development*, 78(5), 1472–1491.

Friedman W. J., Lyon T. D. (2005). "Development of temporal-reconstructive abilities", *Child Development*, 76(6), 1202–1216.

Geddie L., Fradin S., Beer J. (2000). "Child characteristics which impact accuracy of recall and suggestibility in preschoolers: Is a get he best predictor?" *Child Abuse & Neglect*, 24(2), 223–235.

Ginsburg H., Opper S. (1969). *Piaget's theory of intellectual development: An introduction*, Englewood Cliffs, Prentice Hall.

Given-Wilson Z., Hodes M., Herlihy J. (2018). "A review of adolescent autobiographical memory and the implications for assessment of unaccompanied minors' refugee determinations", *Clinical Child Psychology and Psychiatry*, 23(2), 209–222.

Gordon B. N., Ornstein P. A., Nida R. E., Follmer A., Crenshaw C. M., Albert G. (1993). "Does the use of dolls facilitate children's memory of visits to the doctor?" *Applied Cognitive Psychology*, 7(6), 459–474.

Greenhoot A. F., Johnson R. J., Legerski J., McCloskey L. A. (2009). "Stress and autobiographical memory functioning", in Quas J. A., Fivush R. (Eds.), *Emotion and memory in development: Biological, cognitive, and social considerations*, New York, NY, Oxford University Press.

Greenhoot A. F., Ornstein P. A., Gordon B. N., Baker-Ward L. (1999). "Acting out the details of a pediatric check-up: The impact of interview condition and behavioral style on children's memory reports", *Child Development*, 70(2), 363–380.

Gudjonsson G. H. (2003). *The psychology of interrogations and confessions: A handbook*, New York, Wiley.

Gudjonsson G. H. (2013). "Interrogative suggestibility and compliance", in Ridley A. M., Gabbert F., La Rooy D. J. (Eds.), *Suggestibility in legal contexts: Psychological research and forensic implications*, Chichester: Wiley Blackwell, 45–61.

Habermas T., Reese E. (2015). "Getting a life takes time: The development of the life story in adolescence, its precursors and consequences", *Human Development*, 58(3), 172–201.

Henry L. A., Bettenay C., Carney D. (2011). "Children with intellectual disabilities and developmental disorders", in Lamb M. E., La Rooy D. G., Malloy L. C., Katz C. (Eds.), *Children's testimony: A handbook of psychological research and forensic practice* (2nd ed.), New York, Wiley, 251–283.

Henry L. A., Gudjonsson G. H. (1999). "Eyewitness memory and suggestibility in children with mental retardation", *American Journal on Mental Retardation*, 104(6), 491–508.

Henry L. A., Gudjonsson G. H. (2003). "Eyewitness memory, suggestibility, and repeated recall sessions in children with mild and moderate intellectual disabilities", *Law and Human Behavior*, 27(5), 481–505.

Henry L. A., Gudjonsson G. H. (2004). "The effects of memory trace strength on eyewitness recall in children with and without intellectual disabilities", *Journal of Experimental Child Psychology*, 89(1), 53–71.

Hershkowitz I., Lamb M. E., Horowitz D. (2007). "Victimization of children with disabilities", *American Journal of Orthopsychiatry*, 77(4), 629–635.

Hildyard K. L., Wolfe D. A. (2002). "Child neglect: Developmental issues and outcomes", *Child Abuse & Neglect*, 26, 679–695.

Jack F., Friedman W., Reese E., Zajac R. (2016). "Age-related differences in memory for time, temporal reconstruction, and the availability and use of temporal landmarks", *Cognitive Development*, 37, 53–66.

Jack F., Leov J., et Zajac R. (2014). "Age-related differences in the free-recall accounts of child, adolescent, and adult witnesses", *Applied Cognitive Psychology*, 28(1), 30–38.

Jens K. G., Gordon B. N., Shaddock A. J. (1990). "Remembering activities performed versus imagined: A comparison of children with mental retardation and children with normal intelligence", *International Journal of Disability, Development and Education*, 37, 201–213.

Jensen F. E., Nutt A. E. (2015). *The teenage brain*, New York, NY, Harper.

Jones L., Bellis M. A., Wood S., Hughes K., McCoy E., Eckley L., et al. (2012). "Prevalence and risk of violence against children with disabilities: A systematic review and meta-analysis of observational studies", *The Lancet*, 380, 899–907.

Katz C., Hershkowitz I. (2012). "The effect of multipart prompts on children's testimonies in sexual abuse investigations", *Child Abuse & Neglect*, 36, 753–759.

Kim J., Cicchetti D. (2006). "Longitudinal trajectories of self-system processes and depressive symptoms among maltreated and nonmaltreated children", *Child Development*, 77(3), 624–639.

Klemfuss J. Z. (2015). "Differential contributions of language skills to children's episodic recall", *Journal of Cognition and Development*, 16(4), 608–620.

Konrad K., Neufang S., Thiel C. M., Specht K., Hanisch C., Fan J., Fink G. R. (2005). "Development of attentional networks: An fMRI study with children and adults", *Neuroimage*, 28, 429–439.

Korkman J., Santtila P., Drzewiecki T., Sandnabba K. N. (2008). "Failing to keep it simple: Language use in child sexual abuse interviews with 3–8-year-old children", *Psychology, Crime & Law*, 14(1), 41–60.

Korkman J., Santilla P., Sandnabba K. N. (2006). "Dynamics of verbal interaction between interviewer and child in interviews with alleged victims of child sexual abuse", *Scandinavian Journal of Psychology*, 47(2), 109–119.

Lamb M. E., Brown D. A. (2006). "Conversational apprentices: Helping children become competent informants about their own experiences", *British Journal of Developmental Psychology*, mars, 24(1), 215–234.

Lamb M. E., Hershkowitz I., Orbach Y., Esplin P. W. (2008). *Tell me what happened: Structured investigative interviews of child victims and witnesses*, Hoboken, John Wiley & Sons Inc.

Landry S. (2018). "Analyse de la description des personnes par les enfants lors des entrevues d'enquête policière [Analysis of people description by children during police investigative interviews]", Master thesis, Canada, Université de Montréal.

Larose-Grégoire É., Cyr M., Dion J. (submitted). "Dynamique des entrevues auprès des mineurs victimes d'agression [Dynamics of Interviews with Minor Victims of Assault]", Manuscript submitted for publication in *Revue Criminologie*.

Leclerc B., Wortley R., Smallbone S. (2010). "An exploratory study of victim resistance in child sexual abuse: Offender modus operandi and victim characteristics", *Sexual Abuse*, 22(1), 25–41.

Lerner R. M., Steinberg L. (2004). "The scientific study of adolescent development: Past, present, and future", in Lerner R. M., Steinberg L. (Eds.), *Handbook of adolescent psychology*, Hoboken, NJ: John Wiley & Sons, 1–12.

Marcil M.-P. (2021). "Les entrevues d'enquête réalisées auprès des adolescents victimes d'agression sexuelle: L'expérience des policiers [Investigative interviews with sexually abused adolescents: The police investigators perspective]", Thèse de doctorat [Doctoral thesis], Canada, Université de Sherbrooke.

Marcil M-P., Cyr M., Dion J. (2019). "La description des lieux lors de l'entrevue d'enquête chez les jeunes victimes d'agression sexuelle [Description of the locations during the investigative interview among young victims of sexual abuse]", Criminologie, 52, 218–238.

McElvaney R., Greene S., Hogan D. (2012). "Containing the secret of child sexual abuse", Journal of Interpersonal Violence, 27(6), 1155–1175.

Merritt K. A., Ornstein P. A., Spicker B. (1994). "Children's memory for a salient medical procedure: Implications for testimony", Pediatrics, 94(1), 17–23.

Michel M. K., Gordon B. N., Ornstein P. A., Simpson M. A. (2000). "The abilities of children with mental retardation to remember personal experiences: Implications for testimony", Journal of Clinical Child Psychology, 29(3), 453–463.

Milligan K., Astington J. W., Dack A. (2007). "Language and theory of mind: Meta-analysis of the relation between language ability and false-belief understanding", Child Development, 78, 622–646.

Milne R., Bull R. (2001). "Interviewing witnesses with learning disabilities for legal purposes", British Journal of Learning Disabilities, 29(3), 93–97.

Orbach Y., Lamb M. E. (2007). "Young children's references to temporal attributes of allegedly experienced events in the course of forensic interviews", Child Development, 78(4), 1100–1120.

Pasupathi M., Wainryb C. (2010). "On telling the whole story: Facts and interpretations in autobiographical memory narratives from childhood through mid-adolescence", Developmental Psychology, 46(3), 735–746.

Piaget J. (1926). The language and thought of the child, London, Routledge & Kegan Paul.

Pipe M.-E., Salmon K. (2009). "Memory development and forensic context", in Courage M. L., Cowan N. (Eds.), The development of memory in infancy and childhood (2nd ed.), New York, Psychology Press, 241–282.

Poole D. A., Lamb M. E. (1998). Investigative interviews of children: A guide for helping professionals, Washington, DC, American Psychological Association.

Powell M. B., Westera N., Goodman-Delahunty J., Pichler A. S. (2016). An evaluation of how evidence is elicited from complainants of child sexual abuse. www.childabuseroyalcommission.gov.au/research

Quas J. A., Goodman G. S., Bidrose S., Pipe M. E., Craw S., Ablin D. S. (1999). "Emotion and memory: Children's long-term remembering, forgetting, and suggestibility", Journal of Experimental Child Psychology, 72(4), 235–270.

Reese E., Fivush R. (1993). "Parental styles of talk about the past", Developmental Psychology, 29, 596–606.

Reich P. A. (1986). Language development, Eglewood Cliffs, Prentice-Hall.

Roberts K. P., Brubacher S. P., Drohan-Jennings D., Glisic U., Powell M. B., Friedman W J. (2015). "Developmental differences in the ability to provide temporal information about repeated events", Applied Cognitive Psychology, 29(3), 407–417.

Roebers C. M., Schneider W. (2001). "Individual differences in children's eyewitness recall: The influence of intelligence and shyness", Applied Developmental Science, 5, 9–20.

Salmon K., Reese E. (2015). "Talking (or not talking) about the past: The influence of parent – child conversation about negative experiences on children's memories", Applied Cognitive Psychology, 32, 791–801.

Saywitz K., Jaenicke C., Camparo L. (1990). "Children's knowledge of legal terminology", Law and Human Behavior, 14(6), 523–535.

Sharman S. J., Powell M. B., Roberts K. P. (2011). "Children's ability to estimate the frequency of single and repeated events", International Journal of Police Science and Management, 13, 234–242.

Simcock G., Hayne H. (2002). "Breaking the barrier? children fail to translate their preverbal memories into language", *Psychological Science*, 13, 225–231.

Simcock G., Hayne H. (2003). "Age-related changes in verbal and nonverbal memory during early childhood", *Developmental Psychology*, 39, 805–814.

Snow P. C., Powell M. B., Sanger D. D. (2012). "Oral language competence, young speakers, and the law", *Language, Speech, and Hearing Services in Schools*, 43(4), 496–506.

Staller K. M., Nelson-Gardell D. (2005). "'A burden in your heart': Lessons of disclosure from female preadolescent and adolescent survivors of sexual abuse", *Child Abuse & Neglect*, 29(12), 1415–1432.

Statistics Canada. (2015). "Criminal victimization in Canada", *Juristat*, 35(1).

Stoel-Gammon C., Vogel Sosa A. (2007). "Phonological development", in Hoff E., Shatz M. (Eds.), *The Blackwell handbook of language development*, Malden, MA, Blackwell Publishing, 238–256.

Sullivan P. M., Knutson J. F. (2000). "Maltreatment and disabilities: A population-based epidemiological study", *Child Abuse & Neglect*, 24(10), 1257–1273.

Tabak S. J., Klettke B. (2014). "Mock jury attitudes towards credibility, age, and guilt in a fictional child sexual assault scenario", *Australian Journal of Psychology*, 66(1), 47–55.

Toth S. L., Cicchetti D., Macfie J., Emde R. N. (1997). "Representations of self and other in the narratives of neglected, physically abused, and sexually abused preschoolers", *Development and Psychopathology*, 9(4), 781–796.

Toth S. L., Maughan A., Manly J. T., Spagnola M., Cicchetti D. (2002). "The relative efficacy of two interventions in altering maltreated preschoolchildren's representational models: Implications for attachment theory", *Development and Psychopathology*, 14(4), 877–908.

Valentino K., Toth S. L., Cicchetti D. (2009). "Autobiographical memory functioning among abused, neglected, and nonmaltreated children: The overgeneral memory effect", *Journal of Child Psychology and Psychiatry*, 50(8), 1029–1038.

Villiers J. G. de, Villiers de P. A. (1978). *Language acquisition*, Cambridge, MA, Harvard University Press.

Walker A. G. (2013). *Handbook on questioning children: A linguistic perspectives*, Washington, DC, ABA Center on Children and the Law.

Walker A. G., Warren A. R. (1995). "The language of the child abuse interview: Asking the questions, understanding the answers", in Ney T. (Ed.), *True and false allegations of child sexual abuse: Assessment and case management*, Philadelphia, Brunner/Mazel, 153–162.

Wandrey L., Lyon T. D., Quas J. A., Friedman W. J. (2012). "Maltreated children's ability to estimate temporal location and numerosity of placement changes and court visits", *Psychology, Public Policy, and Law*, 18(1), 79–104.

Warren A. R., Woodall C. E., Hunt J. S., Perry N. W. (1996). "'It sounds good in theory, but . . .': Do investigative interviewers follow guidelines based on memory research?" *Child Maltreatment*, 1(3), 231–245.

Wissink I. B., van Vugt E., Moonen X., Stams G. J. J. M., Hendriks J. (2015). "Sexual abuse involving children with an intellectual disability (ID): A narrative review", *Research in Developmental Disabilities*, 36, 20–35.

Chapter 5

Investigative protocols and tools

- What are the steps in a good investigative interview?
- What are the best protocols for interviewing children?
- Do dolls or body diagrams help children to produce accurate accounts?

The studies reviewed in the previous chapters on memory, suggestibility, and child development have led to the development of a consensus about the guidelines to be followed when conducting investigative interviews. These recommendations have been disseminated in various interviews protocols and in the majority of training programs on non-suggestive interviewing with children. In this chapter, we first give a brief presentation of the main recommendations that have achieved scientific consensus. Subsequently, we briefly present investigative interview protocols that have been widely disseminated, namely the Cognitive Interview, the Step-Wise Interview, the NICHD Protocol, and the CornerHouse Forensic Interview Protocol. Then we discuss strategies such as mental or physical reinstatement of the context, the use of drawing, dolls or body diagrams, and dog-assisted interviewing. By the end of this chapter, the reader should have a better understanding of the recommended aids and their usefulness in the field.

1   Guidelines for conducting a non-suggestive investigative interview

The abundance of research on children's development and capacities to accurately report experienced events has made it possible to establish a consensus among both clinicians and researchers on guidelines to conduct investigative interviews (Saywitz & Camparo, 2009; Lamb, Brown, Hershkowitz, Orbach, & Esplin, 2018).

The first recommendation that should influence all aspects of investigative interviews is that interviewers should adapt their approach to the child's developmental level. This involves, among other things, formulating questions that are adapted to the child's level of language acquisition and cognitive development, as well as only asking questions when the child has acquired the necessary knowledge to answer accurately.

Second, it is important to take the time to establish trust and rapport with the child in a non-suggestive way and to foster a supportive, caring, and unthreatening atmosphere throughout the investigative interview.

Third, it is also important to establish ground rules and to provide precise explanations of our expectations to the child. This implies that the child should be asked to

DOI: 10.4324/9781003265351-5

speak only of what really happened to him/her, to tell the truth and not to pretend or invent anything. The child should also recount everything s/he can remember from beginning to the end, including even the smallest details. Regarding the questions asked by the interviewer, the child should be informed that asking for clarification of a question not understood and correcting the interviewer if the latter says something that is wrong are allowed during the interview. It is also important to indicate to the child that s/he can say "I don't know" if s/he does not know the answer to the question or "I don't remember" if s/he does not remember the details requested. It is also useful to let the child know that the interviewer was not present during the alleged event and, therefore, cannot know what happened unless the child tells him/her.

Fourth, the child should be given the opportunity to practice recounting events in detail, in response to open-ended questions, before introducing the subject about which the child is being interviewed. This allows the child to become familiar with the type of the questions and the nature of the task s/he will have to perform. It also allows the interviewer to observe the child and assess his/her ability to understand and respond adequately to questions.

Fifth, the initial questions relating to the event under investigation should be as non-suggestive as possible. Interviewers should favor the use of open-ended questions, which require multi-word answers and follow-up invitations to help the child to elaborate further in his/her own words (e.g., "What happens next?" "Tell me more about that?"). If important details are still missing, the interviewer can then proceed to ask more specific questions in a specific sequence. Thus, directive questions (e.g., where, who, when, what, how) can be used to seek details about the features of an incident already disclosed by the child. If necessary, option-posing questions (multiple-choice or yes-or-no) can be used but only when really important legal information is still missing.

Sixth, the interviewer should remain as objective and as neutral as possible about the veracity of the allegations. The interviewer should try to explore hypotheses and alternative explanations and check for possible biases. In addition, s/he should avoid suggestive techniques that mislead, introduce bias, reinforce interviewer expectations, apply peer pressure (e.g., telling the child that a sister/brother/friend revealed things to the interviewer), or deploy a stereotype about the perpetrator (e.g., a bad person or someone who does bad things); the interviewer should also avoid inviting the child to pretend or speculate or asking questions that are coercive.

It is also recommended that the investigative interview take place in a private environment, appropriate for the child's age, and with minimal distractions. In addition, the investigative interview should be recorded for accountability purposes, information sharing with other professionals involved in the investigation (e.g., prosecutor, child welfare worker), supervision, and feedback.

IMPLICATIONS FOR PRACTICE

Any investigative interview should respect these recommendations, which are based on solid empirical foundations. As they have been described in a very concrete way, they will not be repeated here. The challenge for professionals dealing with a child is to take all of these recommendations into account and apply them appropriately. It is for this reason that investigative interview protocols have been developed and are presented in the next sections.

2   Investigative protocols

Investigative protocols have been developed in order, on the one hand, to eliminate the use of inadequate techniques and, on the other hand, to promote the adoption of best practices. Among the large body of articles and books that suggest a variety of practices, a few have received more attention and are reviewed in this section.

2.1   The Cognitive Interview

The Cognitive Interview, developed in the early 1980s by Fisher and Geiselman for adult witnesses (1992; Edward Geiselman & Fisher, 1988), has been modified for children (Geiselman & Padilla, 1988; Saywitz, Geiselman, & Bornstein, 1992). This interview guidance takes into account the specificity of memory, general cognitive processes (e.g., re-creation of the context of the event, multiple encoding, guided imagery, change of narrative order, change of perspective), and principles of communication and social interaction (e.g., developing rapport, handing over control of the investigative interview to the victim/witness, using questions tailored to the victim/witness). These strategies are based on two theoretical principles relating to memory: (1) memories are composed of multiple aspects, and their recovery is based on an overlap between the elements of the memory and the cues used in the questions (encoding specificity principle; Tulving & Thomson, 1973), and (2) any particular memory can be retrieved via a variety of paths, so if one path does not work, another might work (Bower, 1967).

The four main investigative interview techniques most often used in the Cognitive Interview are

- to allow the victim to reinstate the context (environmental and personal) that existed at the time of the event;
- then, to allow the interviewee to start reporting everything that happened that comes to mind, whether it is trivial, is out of chronological order, or even contradicts a statement made earlier;
- to report the sequence of the event in a variety of ways (e.g., beginning to end, end to beginning); and
- to report events from various perspectives (e.g., that of the perpetrator or a witness).

The Cognitive Interview takes place in five stages: the introduction, the open narration, the exploration stage (during which the interviewer guides the witness to exhaustively recount the content of his/her memory), the revision stage (during which the interviewer verifies the accuracy of his/her interview notes and provides the witness/victim with additional opportunities to remember the event), and ultimately the closure (Fisher & Geiselman, 1992).

Field and laboratory studies indicate that Cognitive Interview elicits 35% more accurate details from adults without increasing the error rate (see also meta-analysis by Memon, Meissner, & Fraser, 2010). Because the protocol proved to be less effective for children, it was revised to be more developmentally appropriate (Geiselman & Padilla, 1988; Saywitz et al., 1992; Verkampt & Ginet, 2010), and that increased its effectiveness. Indeed, for young children, the protocol can present certain difficulties; for example, requests for repeated retrieval, for retrieval in varied temporal orders, and for retrieval from a variety of perspectives may exceed the cognitive capacities of young children. Additionally, imagining the event from another person's perspective can cause children or adolescents to distance themselves from reality and not report real events (Olafson, 2012). Changes made to the basic protocol (e.g., context reinstatement, ground rules presentation) have enhanced the effectiveness of this revised protocol for children (see Memon et al., 2010, for a meta-analysis).

It is important to stress that the Cognitive Interview was designed to collect testimonies from people about events that are known to have occurred. Poole and Lamb (1998) point out that, in the case of investigative interviews with suspected victims of child abuse, it is not certain that the child was the victim, and this may pose additional challenges when using certain techniques included in this interview.

IMPLICATIONS FOR PRACTICE

The Cognitive Interview is undoubtedly a first choice for use with adult witnesses and victims, as well as adolescents. Indeed, the latter have sufficient cognitive and language skills to be able to produce a detailed account of high quality, with the help of a few clear instructions. Its application with suspected child victims must be done with care so that the child feels free to say that s/he has not experienced maltreatment or abuse if this is the case.

2.2 The Step-Wise Interview

The Step-Wise Interview (Yuille, Hunter, Joffe, & Zaparnuik, 1993) is a protocol that has been adopted by the police and workers in child welfare centers in several locations in Canada, the United States, and Europe. It was developed specifically to collect testimonies from children. The Step-Wise Interview comprises nine successive stages: building rapport, the recollection of two specific but neutral events, a discussion concerning the need to tell the truth, the introduction of the topic of the investigative interview, a free narrative, open-ended questioning, specific questions (if necessary), the use of special techniques to support the interview, and the conclusion of the investigative interview.

During rapport building, the interviewer should spend enough time discussing neutral topics until the child is relaxed. This may involve discussing school interests (with a teenager) or playing with coloring books (with a preschooler).

Next, the interviewer asks the child to recount two unrelated events. Three objectives are pursued here:

- To allow a rough estimate of the quantity and quality of details that the child can report about specific experiences, which will serve as a basis for evaluating the quantity and quality of details provided about the target events.
- To continue to develop the relationship and allow the interviewer to show interest in the experiences of the child.
- To illustrate the form that the investigative interview will take in the substantive part, especially concerning the questioning using open-ended and non-direct questions.

The concept of truth is then discussed by the interviewer and the child, either by a focus on truth and lies in a general or a more specific context. The interviewer can also use a story in which one of the characters tells a lie and ask the child about the meaning and consequences of that lie.

The subject of the investigative interview is then introduced in successive stages. Very open general questions are first tried before more specific questions are introduced. Under no circumstances should the name of the suspect be mentioned or suggestions be made about what happened during the alleged acts. As soon as the child reveals that something has happened to them, they are asked to describe the event from beginning to end.

The next step is to use general open-ended questions to allow the child to recall as many details as possible about the events and things that were described in the free narrative. These questions should be based only on the information given by the child and should use the child's words (e.g., "You said _____. Do you know anything more about it?"). It is important that the interviewer reminds the child that s/he can answer no to such questions.

When important information remains to be obtained, specific questions can be asked. Some components of the Cognitive Interview can also be used: for example, the interviewer may tell the child to mentally reconstruct the context of the event ("Do you remember what you did before _____?").

Before concluding the investigative interview, the interviewer can ask their partner if they have any additional questions for the child. Then the interviewer thanks the child for their participation, regardless of the conclusion of the investigative interview. The interviewer can also explain what should happen next in the investigation process.

The effectiveness of the Step-Wise Interview in collecting details with open-ended questions has been the subject of little systematic research. Yuille and his colleagues (Yuille et al., 1993) indicate that the quality of the interviews made with the protocol as only 5% of these interviews included too many leading questions that contaminated the content reported compared with 35% for the interviews of the control group.

IMPLICATIONS FOR PRACTICE

The Step-Wise Interview is an investigative interview protocol that incorporates several of the recommendations from the research listed at the beginning of this chapter. Thus, it appears to be quite suitable. Its main weakness is that it does not offer enough examples about how open-ended questions should be worded; therefore, interviewers who use it tend to ask a lot of directive and option-posing questions.

2.3 The NICHD Protocol and its revision

The NICHD Protocol was developed in the late 1990s and revised in 2014 by Michael Lamb and his colleagues (Lamb, Hershkowitz, Orbach, & Esplin, 2008; see Lamb et al., 2018, for a review) by drawing inspiration from, among others, the procedures of Cognitive Interview and Step-Wise Interview. The NICHD Protocol uses four strategies that have received significant empirical support in laboratory and field studies (see Chapter 7).

- First, the interviewer creates a supportive interview environment free from distractions.
- Second, in order to help the child to cooperate with the investigative interview, the interviewer gives a series of instructions regarding the importance of telling the truth and saying "I don't know" or "I don't understand the question" and of correcting the interviewer when the interviewer misstates something.
- Third, the interviewer establishes rapport with the child to ensure that s/he feels comfortable with the interviewer and trusts the interviewer enough to discuss personal or embarrassing events.
- Fourth, before discussing the topic of the investigative interview, the interviewer gives the child the opportunity to practice providing a detailed and comprehensive account of a recent event unrelated to the investigative interview in response to open-ended questions and reinforces the efforts made by the child.
- Fifth, during the substantive part of the investigative interview, especially if the child reports multiple incidents, the interviewer asks him/her to report specific events, especially the last and the first event in the series, to reduce the likelihood that the child only reports generic or script memory-based information.
- Sixth, the interviewer tries to elicit as much information as possible using a variety of open-ended questions before asking directive questions and then, as a last resort and only after a break to allow them to be carefully composed, option-posing questions.

This investigative interview protocol has been the subject of a considerable number of empirical studies (Lamb, Orbach, Hershkowitz, Esplin, & Horowitz, 2007; see La Rooy et al., 2015, for a review; Orbach, Hershkowitz, Lamb, Sternberg, and Horowitz, 2000; Sternberg, Lamb, Orbach, Esplin, & Mitchell, 2001), carried out in several countries and drawing upon more than forty thousand field investigative interviews which have shown that use of the NICHD Protocol increases the quality of investigative interviews. A subsequent revised version added enhanced focus on the motivational and relational aspects of the interview and is presented in detail in the next chapter.

IMPLICATIONS FOR PRACTICE

The NICHD Protocol is currently the most widely recommended protocol for investigative interviews with children. It was developed specifically for investigative interviews with children, and it incorporates the main recommendations mentioned at the beginning of this chapter. It provides the interviewer with concrete guidance and a selection of open-ended questions to use when eliciting the child's account. It respects the developmental capacities of the child, and the revised version focuses more attention on motivational and relational interventions to build a trusting and collaborative bond with the child. A full chapter is devoted to a presentation of the Revised NICHD Protocol.

2.4 The Narrative Elaboration Technique

The Narrative Elaboration Technique (NET) developed by Saywitz and her colleagues (Camparo, Wagner, & Saywitz, 2001; Saywitz & Snyder, 1996) is an intervention for training memory that helps to structure the child's recall by providing him/her with external visual aids or recall cards and drawings representing specific categories of information (e.g., participants, setting, actions, conversational and affective states relevant to the target event). Described as a procedure for preparing and training children for questioning and as a format for investigative interviews, this original procedure had four main components:

- Interview preparation that includes the rationale and an introduction to the strategy for organizing and reporting the narrative in relation to the four categories represented by the cards, the introduction of these cards, practice using the strategy with feedback and modeling, and a review immediately after practicing each of these steps.
- Free recall of the target event.
- Cued reminders that involve presenting the child with each of the cards one by one and saying "Does this card remind you of anything more?" or "Tell me about the people" or using verbal cues for each category ("Who was there?" "What was their name?" "What did these people say?").
- Specific follow-up questions.

This procedure has been adapted for preschool children (Dorato & Saywitz, 2001) and for children with learning difficulties (Nathanson, Crank, Saywitz, & Ruegg, 2007). It also helps reduce the effects of a low IQ on children's ability to report details (Brown & Pipe, 2003a, 2003b).

It should be noted that the gains obtained with the Narrative Elaboration Technique can also be obtained using only a verbal cue from the same categories as those used in the cards, without training in how to talk about a past event (Bowen & Howie, 2002; Brown & Pipe, 2003a) so simply asking children to talk about what they have seen and heard or to talk about different categories of information can increase the number of details elicited (Larsson & Lamb, 2009). In addition, all the studies that have used the narrative elaboration procedure were carried out in the laboratory rather than in forensic contexts, so children were asked to talk about neutral topics or enjoyable experiences and therefore were unlikely to be reluctant to talk. As the Narrative Elaboration Technique has not been used in legal contexts, it should be noted that the time at which visual or verbal cues are introduced may be important in determining the suggestibility of these interventions. For this reason, the Narrative Elaboration Technique could perhaps be used more safely during pre-interview training sessions rather than in investigative interviews.

IMPLICATIONS FOR PRACTICE

The Narrative Elaboration Technique might be particularly useful with children who have limited attentional skills and for whom using pictorial aids in addition to verbal instructions might help to capture their attention longer. Children and adults with intellectual disabilities could also benefit from such a procedure. However, care must be taken when using these kinds of techniques to avoid using overly specific questions that could be suggestive. Questions should be kept open, with limited numbers of directive questions and no option-posing or suggestive questions.

2.5   The CornerHouse Forensic Interview Protocol

The CornerHouse Forensic Interview Protocol, formerly known as the Rapport, Anatomy Identification, Touch Inquiry, Abuse Scenario, and Closure (RATAC) guide, is an investigative interview protocol that was developed by the CornerHouse and is an integral part of a course entitled "ChildFirst" developed by the American Prosecutors Research Institute (Anderson et al., 2010; Walters, Holmes, Bauer, & Vieth, 2003). This protocol, which is semi-structured and responsive to the child's development, can be used with child victims and witnesses who have experienced all forms of abuse, neglect, or other violent crimes. This protocol, similar to the Step-Wise Interview, includes different stages: the creation of alliances, body part labeling, questions about touching, the abusive event, and the closure (Walters et al., 2003). Recently, a narrative practice was incorporated into the interview format (Anderson, Anderson, & Gilgun, 2014) and was shown to increase the number of details reported about the abuse.

This CornerHouse Forensic Interview Protocol is widely used in the United States, although it has only been the subject of a few studies designed to demonstrate the effectiveness of the interview format or the effectiveness of training in modifying interviewers' practices (Lyon, Lamb, & Myers, 2009). In addition, this interview protocol uses anatomically detailed dolls and body diagrams for anatomy identification and to describe the actions experienced, although the use of these aids is controversial. We address this issue in the next sections.

IMPLICATIONS FOR PRACTICE

It seems premature to recommend the use of the CornerHouse Forensic Interview Protocol since we do not have enough empirical evaluation on its effectiveness. In addition, the inclusion of aids whose use remains controversial leads us to be cautious.

3   Props and strategies to support children's disclosure

3.1   The use of anatomically detailed dolls and body diagrams

The use of anatomically detailed dolls and body diagrams of a child's or adult body seen from the back and front, naked or clothed, was initiated to make it easier for young children to reveal their sexual abuse. This practice has been used in clinical settings with children in the belief that interaction with dolls would allow children to disclose difficult emotional issues and problems (Poole, Bruck, & Pipe, 2011). The objective pursued by the use of these nonverbal aids is to help children to be less embarrassed, to illustrate what they cannot describe due to lack of vocabulary, or to help them focus their memory on certain elements of the abuse. These tools are also used to ascertain how the child labels the parts of his/her body, to obtain the disclosure of sexual abuse, or to verify that the body labels verbalized by the child correspond to the labels understood by the interviewer.

It is important to point out that this practice was imported into forensic practice before researchers were able to verify whether the dolls or the body diagrams actually helped children to provide more information about their abuse and, especially, whether information so elicited was accurate. Several reviews of the extensive research that has been carried out both in laboratory settings with staged events, after medical exams, and in forensic interview settings conclude that the answer to these two questions is no (Poole et al., 2011; Pipe & Salmon, 2009). Indeed, children provide more details when using these aids, but some of those details are wrong. In addition to reducing the accuracy of the details shared by children, the use of these aids leads some of them to report touching that had never taken place. This is particularly true for very young children (2–4 years) with whom these aids are most likely to be used. In addition, investigators tend to use more specific questions (e.g., "Did he touch you here?" [pointing to a part of the body]), which are not recommended in the context of investigative interviews because they tend to elicit inaccurate information from young victims or witnesses or do not increase the amount of accurate information about touches (Brown, Pipe, Lewis, Lamb, & Orbach, 2007, 2012; Dickinson & Poole, 2017; Salmon, Pipe, Malloy, & Mackay, 2012).

IMPLICATIONS FOR PRACTICE

For all these reasons, the use of these nonverbal props is not recommended in the context of investigative interviews with children, given the increased risk that the child will produce false testimony. In young children, researchers (Poole et al., 2011) assume that two key difficulties (semantic and attentional) limit children's disclosure of abusive incidents they have experienced. Dolls and body diagrams do not help children understand what touch means or that touching can include actions such as tapping or hugging (semantic difficulty). In addition, the use of these nonverbal aids does not resolve the difficulties encountered by the child when encoding the event: the touches are part of a sequence of complex activities (attentional difficulty).

3.2 Drawing

Drawing is a method sometimes used by professionals who work with children. Drawing is a suitable procedure that can also be used to put the child at ease. In studies, children are encouraged to draw freely or to focus on a specific element (e.g., drawing a person or an object). The child can be asked to draw and talk about the event or to draw and then talk about it. This technique has certain advantages over props, such as dolls or body diagrams (Katz & Hershkowitz, 2010; Salmon & Pipe, 2000). First of all, when free drawing is used, the cues retrieved from memory are self-generated by the child. This limits suggestibility and gives the interviewer new details to explore. In addition, the child's drawing provides visual cues that could generate new memory stimuli when visual information was available during the event and during the encoding process. Drawing also helps children organize their retrieval efforts by keeping them focused on the goal of investigative interviewing. And last but not least, since kids love to draw, this procedure might help to maintain their focus for a longer period of time.

Studies examining memories of medical examinations, hospitalizations, emotionally arousing events, or events that take place in laboratories with non-victimized children have shown that this technique helps children to provide more information about the target event (Gross, Hayne, & Drury, 2009; Lev-Wiesel & Liraz, 2007;

Salmon, Roncolato, & Gleitzman, 2003), especially details about objects rather than actions (Butler, Gross, & Hayne, 1995). However, other research has not observed that the use of drawing increases the number of details recalled, and still others have found that drawing increases the number of incorrect details retrieved (Gentle, Powell, & Sharman, 2014; MacLeod, Gross, & Hayne, 2016; Otgaar, van Ansem, Pauw, & Horselenberg, 2016; Salmon et al., 2012). When children are asked open-ended questions about their drawings, the information obtained is accurate. However, when directive or option-posing questions (Wesson & Salmon, 2001; Bruck, Melnyk, & Ceci, 2000) are asked about the drawing, more errors are observed in the reported information. In addition, when children have to draw specific parts of the event (e.g., the nurse or the room), the drawings contain several errors (Salmon & Pipe, 2000). The accuracy of items reported by children also decreases the longer the delay.

In a field study involving alleged sexual abuse victims, Katz and Hershkowitz (2010), after using the NICHD Protocol, had half of these children invited to draw what happened to them. The children in the drawing group disclosed more information about the abuse, but the accuracy of this new information could not be verified. In a study of a staged event involving a pirate, drawing after answering open-ended questions as part of the NICHD Protocol yielded some additional information from children aged 5 to 7, but the accuracy of this information was compromised (Salmon et al., 2012).

With preadolescents, O'Connor (2016) compare the effectiveness of drawing what happened during the event to that of making a sketchplan of the layout of the event in the context of an interview conducted using the NICHD Protocol. Neither the drawing nor the sketchplan yielded a significant number of new details, although the sketchplan elicited more spatial information than drawing did.

IMPLICATIONS FOR PRACTICE

These results suggest that drawing may be a promising tool to help children provide a more comprehensive account of their sexual abuse while using only open-ended questions. However, drawing seems to require some additional considerations. Before recommending routine use in investigative interviews, further studies are needed to assess the risks and benefits. In addition, it is important to note that drawing was used in these studies after the child had made a disclosure to help him/her elaborate rather than to elicit a disclosure from him/her because that could be suggestive. Interviewer questions should also be limited to open-ended questions, which may be difficult given the visual appeal of a drawing and the details it contains.

3.3   Mental context reinstatement

Mental context reinstatement is another technique that can be used to facilitate children's recall. This technique is one of the four important components of the Cognitive Interview discussed previously. It involves mentally reconstructing the environment in which the event occurred (e.g., "Close your eyes and think about that moment, as if you are there again. [Pause.] Think about what is happening around you. [. . .]"). This technique has been tested in the laboratory (see Memon et al., 2010, for a meta-analysis; Dietze, Sharman, Powell, & Thomson, 2013; Gentle et al., 2014; Lamb et al., 2018; Pipe & Salmon, 2009) and with sexually abused children (Hershkowitz, Orbach, Lamb, Sternberg, & Horowitz, 2001; Hershkowitz, Orbach, Lamb, Sternberg, & Horowitz, 2002). Although in the majority of these studies, mental reinstatement of the context was not the only technique used, its presence increases the amount of information retrieved from children. The results of studies are sometimes contradictory regarding the accuracy of the information provided.

It should be noted that drawing and mental reinstatement of the context are two aids based on the idea that the reinstatement of the contexts in which the events occurred will result in a better recall of the details of the event (Tulving's theory of specific encoding memory). As mentioned earlier, this idea stems from the principle of encoding specificity, which predicts that congruence between encoding and recall contexts facilitate the accurate retrieval of memories (Tulving & Thomson, 1973).

IMPLICATIONS FOR PRACTICE

This technique could be used with school-age children or adolescents who have given a poor first narrative to help them focus on the event being discussed. However, it is important in such contexts to inform the child to report only things that s/he is sure to remember and not to add details to satisfy the interviewer.

3.4   Return to the scene of the abuse

Similarly, in accordance with the principle of Tulving's specific encoding memory principle, studies have attempted to assess whether returning to the scene where the event occurred facilitates the child's recall. By either taking children back to the scene or showing them objects from or a model of the place. A review of these studies indicates that children recall more details without adverse effects on accuracy (Pipe & Salmon, 2009). Contextual cues may particularly help young children provide as much detail as older children interviewed without returning to the scene (Salmon, 2001).

Two studies involved sexually abused children who were questioned at the location where their abuse had occurred (Hershkowitz et al., 1998; Orbach et al., 2000). In the first study, after a first NICHD Protocol interview, a second interview at the scene resulted in an average of 23% new details. However, when the location of the abuse was unfamiliar or the time between investigative interview and abuse was long, going back to the scene did not help young children provide further details. It is also possible that the details obtained at the scene of the abuse could be explained by the simple fact of having questioned the child a second time. The second study supports this hypothesis because groups of children reinterviewed in the office or at the scene did not differ with respect to the number of informative details reported.

IMPLICATIONS FOR PRACTICE

Although laboratory studies seem to indicate that this strategy may especially help young children to provide more details, it seems that the two studies conducted with children suspected of being sexually abused are less conclusive. It is possible that, in the case of sexual abuse, the return to the scene of the incident creates a level of stress or anxiety that decreases the children's ability to tell an elaborate narrative. In addition, it may be difficult to move the child to the scene. However, in specific contexts, this strategy could be useful, providing interviewers respect the recommendations made at the beginning of this chapter concerning free narration and open-ended questioning.

3.5 Dog-assisted interventions

Dog-assisted interventions are a new aid that is increasingly being used in investigative interview rooms. The use of dogs (a.k.a. facility dogs) in legal settings began in the United States under the supervision of the Courthouse Dogs Foundation. This practice was first used to provide witnesses with company in court before being used in the investigative interview context on the basis that the presence of a dog has been observed to have positive effects on several biomarkers associated with stress, including blood and salivary cortisol levels (Odendaal, 2000; Viau et al., 2010), blood pressure (Krause-Parello, Thames, Ray, & Kolassa, 2018; Odendaal, 2000), and heart rate (Johnson, 2010; Krause-Parello & Friedmann, 2014; Krause-Parello et al., 2018). In children with autism, researchers have also observed an increase in social interaction (see O'Haire, 2017, for a review). In a therapeutic context, the presence of a dog while narratively recounting sexual abuse has been associated with fewer symptoms than in the absence of the dog (Dietz, Davis, & Pennings, 2012). As for the capacity to describe positively or negatively experienced events, a recent study (Capparelli, Miller, Wright, & London, 2020) observes that when a dog was present, college students reported more details about a negatively experienced event than did students for whom the dog was not present. The dog's presence had no effect on the number of details obtained when reporting positive events.

As for the court process involving young witnesses, the benefits identified to date are more anecdotal in nature (Holder, 2013). For example, since testifying in the presence of the perpetrator can create a lot of stress for the child, the soothing presence of a dog by his/her side could allow the child to communicate more clearly and cooperatively (Holder, 2013). Thus, in such circumstances, one can hypothesize that the child's testimony could be more accurate and complete while limiting the potential risk of further trauma triggered by the presence of the perpetrator or the process. These hypotheses have not been verified empirically, however.

In the context of investigative interview, three studies, which are two carried out with the same 42 children (Krause-Parello & Friedman, 2014; Krause-Parello & Gulick, 2015) and another with a group of 51 children (Krause-Parello et al., 2018), show that the presence of a dog during the investigative interview of alleged victims of sexual abuse led to a reduction in salivary cortisol, heart rate, and blood pressure, all indicators of the stress that an investigative interview can cause. However, it is not known whether there is a link between the reduction in stress and the quality of the testimony collected, so several important questions remain unanswered, including the following: Does the presence of a facility dog facilitate disclosure? Can the dog be a source of distraction? Does its presence increase the children's suggestibility? Does the presence of a dog lead interviewers to employ more suggestive techniques to elicit disclosure or even reduce the number of open-ended questions asked as when dolls are used?

IMPLICATIONS FOR PRACTICE

The use of facility dogs is an attractive idea based on observations in contexts other than investigative interviews. In the absence of rigorous research, the benefits and perhaps the pitfalls associated with the presence of facility dogs, their use during investigative interviews should be conducted with caution. These interviews should follow the prescribed steps for conducting non-suggestive interviews, including the use of numerous open-ended questions as recommended by the NICHD Protocol.

4   Conclusion

Several practical implications emerge from this review. The NICHD Protocol is by now the only forensic interview tool that allows for the integration of the majority of recommendations about which there is scientific consensus. In addition, it is the only structured protocol, along with Cognitive Interview, whose effectiveness has been demonstrated in numerous studies. The Cognitive Interview should be used with adolescents and adults who have greater cognitive abilities than children. Although the NICHD Protocol is ideal for children and for adults with cognitive developmental delays, it is possible that prior training sessions using the Narrative Elaboration Technique can promote better collaboration during an NICHD Protocol interview. Aids such as anatomically detailed dolls or body diagrams should never be used to elicit disclosures during an investigative interview or to obtain more details. Ultimately, their use at the very end of the investigative interview to verify a required judicial detail may be acceptable, provided the interviewer acknowledges that this detail was obtained in a more suggestive way and that there is thus a possibility that it may be wrong. Mental reinstatement of the context or a return to the scene of the alleged event could be of some utility in a limited number of cases. Drawing should be used as a tool only when a child's first free narrative has been obtained, as long as only open-ended questions that use the cues provided by the child are then utilized by the interviewer. Finally, the introduction of facility dogs seems premature, given the lack of knowledge about their effects on the investigative interview context. Studies assessing the effects of different aids have shown that when the investigative interview is conducted using an empirically validated protocol, such as the NICHD Protocol, and even more with the revised version (see chapters 6 and 7), these aids elicit few new details and are not a substitute for high-quality investigative interviews.

References

Anderson G. D., Anderson J. N., Gilgun J. F. (2014). "The influence of narrative practice techniques on child behaviors in forensic interviews", *Journal of Child Sexual Abuse: Research, Treatment, & Program Innovations for Victims, Survivors, & Offenders*, 23(6), 615–634.

Anderson J., Ellefson J., Lashley J., Miller A. L., Olinger S., Russell A., et al. (2010). "The CornerHouse forensic interview protocol: RATAC", *Thomas M. Cooley Journal of Practical and Clinical Law*, 12, 193–331.

Bowen C., Howie P. (2002). "Context and cue cards in young children's testimony: A comparison of brief narrative elaboration and context reinstatement", *Journal of Applied Psychology*, 6, 1077–1085.

Bower G. A. (1967). "Multicomponent view of a memory trace", in Spence K., Spence J. (Eds.), *The psychology of learning and motivation*, vol. 1, New York, Academic Press, 230–325.

Brown D. A., Pipe M.-E. (2003a). "Individual differences in children's event memory reports and the narrative elaboration technique", *Journal of Applied Psychology*, 88(2), 195–206.

Brown D. A., Pipe M.-E. (2003b). "Variations on a technique: Enhancing children's recall using narrative elaboration training", *Applied Cognitive Psychology*, 17(4), 377–399.

Brown D. A., Pipe M.-E., Lewis C., Lamb M. E., Orbach Y. (2007). "Supportive or suggestive: Do human figure drawings help 5- to 7-year-old children to report touch?" *Journal of Consulting and Clinical Psychology*, 75(1), 33–42.

Brown D. A., Pipe M.-E., Lewis C., Lamb M. E., Orbach Y. (2012). "How do body diagrams affect the accuracy and consistency of children's reports of bodily touch across repeated interviews?" *Applied Cognitive Psychology*, 26(2), 174–181.

Bruck M., Melnyk L., Ceci S. J. (2000). "Draw it again Sam: The effect of drawing on children's suggestibility and source monitoring ability", *Journal of Experimental Child Psychology*, 77, 169–196.

Butler S., Gross J., Hayne H. (1995). "The effect of drawing on memory performance in young children", *Developmental Psychology*, 31, 597–608.

Camparo L. B., Wagner J. T., Saywitz K. J. (2001). "Interviewing children about real and fictitious events: Revisiting the narrative elaboration procedure", *Law and Human Behavior*, 25(1), 63–80.

Capparelli A. L., Miller Q. C., Wright D. B., London K. (2020). "Canine-assisted interviews bolster informativeness for negative autobiographical memories", *Psychological Reports*, 123(1), 159–178.

Dickinson J. J., Poole D. A. (2017). "The influence of disclosure history and body diagrams on children's reports of inappropriate touching: Evidence from a new analog paradigm", *Law and Human Behavior*, 41(1), 1–12.

Dietz T. J., Davis D., Pennings J. (2012). "Evaluating animal-assisted therapy in group treatment for child sexual abuse", *Journal of Child Sexual Abuse*, 21, 665–685.

Dietze P. M., Sharman S. J., Powell M. B., Thomson D. M. (2013). "Does free recall moderate the effect of mental context reinstatement instructions on children's cued recall?" *Psychology, Crime & Law*, 19(10), 881–891.

Dorato J. S., Saywitz K. J. (2001). "Interviewing preschoolers from low-and middle-SES communities: A test of the narrative elaboration recall improvement technique", *Journal of Clinical and Child Psychology*, 30, 566–578.

Edward Geiselman R., Fisher R. P. (1988). "The cognitive interview: An innovative technique for questioning witnesses of crime", *Journal of Police and Criminal Psychology*, 4, 2–5.

Fisher R. P., Geiselman R. E. (1992). *Memory-enhancing techniques for investigative interviewing: The cognitive interview*, Springfield, Charles C. Thomas Publisher.

Geiselman R., Padilla J. (1988). "Cognitive interviewing with child witnesses", *Journal of Police Science & Administration*, 16(4), 236–242.

Gentle M., Powell M. B., Sharman S. J. (2014). "Mental context reinstatement or drawing: Which better enhances children's recall of witnessed events and protects against suggestive questions?" *Australian Journal of Psychology*, 66, 158–167.

Gross J., Hayne H., Drury T. (2009). "Drawing facilitates children's reports of factual and narrative information: Implications for educational contexts", *Applied Cognitive Psychology*, 23, 953–971.

Hershkowitz I., Orbach Y., Lamb M. E., Sternberg K. J., Horowitz D. (2001). "The effects of mental context reinstatement on children's accounts of sexual abuse", *Applied Cognitive Psychology*, 15(3), 235–248.

Hershkowitz I., Orbach Y., Lamb M. E., Sternberg K. J., Horowitz D. (2002). "A comparison of mental and physical context reinstatement in forensic interviews with alleged victims of sexual abuse", *Applied Cognitive Psychology*, 16, 429–441.

Hershkowitz I., Orbach Y., Lamb M. E., Sternberg K. J., Horowitz D., Hovav M. (1998). "Visiting the scene of the crime: Effects on children's recall of alleged abuse", *Legal and Criminological Psychology*, 3(Part 2), 195–207.

Holder C. (2013). "All Dogs go to court: The impact of court facility dogs as comfort for child witnesses on a defendant's rights to a fair trial", *Houston Law Review*, 50(4), 1156–1187.

Johnson R. A. (2010). "Psychosocial and therapeutic aspects of human-animal interaction", in Rabinowitz P. M., Conti L. A. (Eds.), *Human-animal medicine: Clinical approaches to zoonoses, toxicants, and other shared health risks*, Maryland Heights, MO, Saunders/Elsevier, 24–36.

Katz C., Hershkowitz I. (2010). "The effects of drawing on children's accounts of sexual abuse", *Child Maltreatment*, 15(2), 171–179.

Krause-Parello C. A., Friedmann E. (2014). "The effects of animal-assisted intervention on salivary alpha-amylase, salivary immunoglobulin A, and heart rate during forensic interviews in child sexual abuse cases", *Anthrozoös*, 27(4), 581–590.

Krause-Parello C. A., Gulick E. E. (2015). "Forensic interviews for child sexual abuse allegations: An investigation into the effects of animal-assisted intervention on stress biomarkers", *Journal of Child Sexual Abuse*, 24(8), 873–886.

Krause-Parello C. A., Thames M., Ray C. M., Kolassa J. (2018). "Examining the effects of a service-trained facility dog on stress in children undergoing forensic interview for allegations of child sexual abuse", *Journal of Child Sexual Abuse*, 27, 305–320.

Lamb M. E., Brown D. A., Hershkowitz I., Orbach Y., Esplin P. W. (2018). *Tell me what happened: Questioning children about abuse* (2nd ed.), Hoboken, John Wiley & Sons Inc.

Lamb M. E., Hershkowitz I., Orbach Y., Esplin P. W. (2008). *Tell me what happened: Structured investigative interviews of child victims and witnesses*, Hoboken, John Wiley & Sons Inc.

Lamb M. E., Orbach Y., Hershkowitz I., Esplin P. W., Horowitz D. (2007). "A structured forensic interview protocol improves the quality and informativeness of investigative interviews with children: A review of research using the NICHD Investigative Interview Protocol", *Child Abuse & Neglect*, 31, 1201–1231.

La Rooy D., Brubacher S. P., Aromäki-Stratos A., Cyr M., Hershkowitz I., Korkman J., et al. (2015). "The NICHD Protocol: A review of an internationally-used evidence-based tool for training child forensic interviewers", *Journal of Criminological Research, Policy and Practice*, 1(2), 76–89.

Larsson A. S., Lamb M. E. (2009). "Making the most of information-gathering interviews with children", *Infant and Child Development*, 18(1), 1–16.

Lev-Wiesel R., Liraz R. (2007). "Drawings vs. Narratives: Drawing as a tool to encourage verbalization in children whose fathers are drug abusers", *Clinical Child Psychology and Psychiatry*, 12, 65–75.

Lyon T. D., Lamb M. E., Myers J. (2009). "Authors' response to Vieth (2008)", *Child Abuse & Neglect*, 33, 71–74.

Macleod E., Gross J., Hayne H. (2016). "Drawing conclusions: The effect of instructions on children's confabulation and fantasy errors", *Memory*, 24(1), 21–31.

Memon A., Meissner C. A., Fraser J. (2010). "The Cognitive Interview: A meta-analytic review and study space analysis of the past 25 years", *Psychology, Public Policy and Law*, 16(4), 340–372.

Nathanson R., Crank J. N., Saywitz K. J., Ruegg E. (2007). "Enhancing the oral narratives of children with learning disabilities", *Reading & Writing Quarterly: Overcoming Learning Difficulties*, 23(4), 315–331.

O'Connor P. (2016). "Mapping memories: Do sketchplans help young adolescents recall more information about an event?" Doctoral thesis, Wellington University, New Zealand, Victoria. http://hdl.handle.net/10063/5062

Odendaal J. S. J. (2000). "Animal-assisted therapy – magic or medicine?" *Journal of Psychosomatic Research*, 49, 275–280.

O'Haire M. E. (2017). "Research on animal-assisted intervention and autism spectrum disorder, 2012–2015", *Applied Developmental Science*, 21(3), 200–216.

Olafson E. (2012). "A call for field-relevant research about child forensic interviewing for child protection", *Journal of Child Sexual Abuse: Research, Treatment, & Program Innovations for Victims, Survivors,& Offenders*, 21(1), 109–129.

Orbach Y., Hershkowitz I., Lamb M. E., Sternberg K. J., Horowitz D. (2000). "Interviewing at the scene of the crime: Effects on children's recall of alleged abuse", *Legal and Criminological Psychology*, 5(Part 1), 135–147.

Otgaar H., van Ansem R., Pauw C., Horselenberg R. (2016). "Improving children's interviewing methods? The effects of drawing and practice on children's memories for an event", *Journal of Police and Criminal Psychology*, 31(4), 279–287.

Pipe M.-E., Salmon K. (2009). "Memory development and forensic context", in Courage M. L., Cowan N. (Eds.), *The development of memory in infancy and childhood* (2nd ed.), New York, Psychology Press, 241–282.

Poole D. A., Bruck M., Pipe M.-E. (2011). "Forensic interviewing aids: Do props help children answer questions about touching?" *Current Directions in Psychological Science*, 20(1), 11–15.

Poole D. A., Lamb M. E. (1998). *Investigative interviews of children: A guide for helping professionals*, Washington, DC, American Psychological Association.

Salmon K. (2001). "Remembering and reporting by children: The influence of cues and props", *Clinical Psychology Review*, 21(2), 267–300.

Salmon K., Pipe M.-E. (2000). "Recalling an event one year later: The impact of props, drawing and a prior interview", *Applied Cognitive Psychology*, 14, 99–120.

Salmon K., Pipe M.-E., Malloy A., Mackay K. (2012). "Do non-verbal aids increase the effectiveness of 'best practice' verbal interview techniques? An experimental study", *Applied Cognitive Psychology*, 26(3), 370–380.

Salmon K., Roncolato W., Gleitzman M. (2003). "Children's reports of emotionally laden events: Adapting the interview to the child", *Applied Cognitive Psychology*, 17, 65–79.

Saywitz K. J., Camparo L. B. (2009). "Contemporary child forensic interviewing: Evolving consensus and innovation over 25 years", in Bottoms B. L., Najdowski C. J., Goodman G. S. (Eds.), *Children as victims, witnesses, and offenders: Psychological science and the law*, New York, Guilford Press, 102–127.

Saywitz K. J., Geiselman R., Bornstein G. K. (1992). "Effects of cognitive interviewing and practice on children's recall performance", *Journal of Applied Psychology*, 77(5), 744–756.

Saywitz K. J., Snyder L. (1996). "Narrative elaboration: Test of a new procedure for interviewing children", *Journal of Consulting and Clinical Psychology*, 64(6), 1347–1357.

Sternberg K. J., Lamb M. E., Orbach Y., Esplin P. W., Mitchell S. (2001). "Use of a structured investigative protocol enhances young children's responses to free-recall prompts in the course of forensic interviews", *Journal of Applied Psychology*, 86(5), 997–1005.

Tulving E., Thomson D. M. (1973). "Encoding specificity and retrieval processes in episodic memory", *Psychological Review*, 77, 1–15.

Verkampt F., Ginet M. (2010). "Variations of the Cognitive Interview: Which one is the most effective in enhancing children's testimonies?" *Applied Cognitive Psychology*, 24(9), 1279–1296.

Viau R., Arsenault-Lapierre G., Fecteau S., Champagne N., Walker C.-D., Lupien S. (2010). "Effect of service dogs on salivary cortisol secretion in autistic children", *Psychoneuroendocrinology*, 35(8), 1187–1193.

Walters S., Holmes L., Bauer G., Vieth V. (2003). *Finding Words: Half a nation by 2010: Interviewing children and preparing for court*, Alexandria, National Center for Prosecution of Child Abuse.

Wesson M., Salmon K. (2001). "Drawing and showing: Helping children to report emotionally laden events", *Applied Cognitive Psychology*, 15, 301–319.

Yuille J. C., Hunter R., Joffe R., Zaparnuik J. (1993). "Interviewing children in sexual abuse cases", in Goodman G., Bottoms B. (Eds.), *Child victims, child witnesses: Understanding and improving testimony*, New York, Guilford, 95–115.

Chapter 6

The Revised NICHD Protocol

- What is the Revised NICHD Protocol?
- How to offer non-suggestive support to children?
- How to organize the interview process to obtain the child's account mostly using open-ended questions?

This chapter is entirely dedicated to the detailed presentation of the Revised NICHD Protocol (see Lamb, Brown, Hershkowitz, Orbach, & Esplin, 2018). Thus, each of its phases is examined along with the associated techniques and procedures. Excerpts from the sections of the protocol are presented in order to illustrate some key features, while the NICHD Protocol in its entirety is available in appendix 1, as well as a transcription of an interview (appendix 2) and the notes taken (appendices 3 and 4). Definitions and examples of the different types of questions and especially supportive techniques used, as well as the organization of note-taking during the interview, are also presented. All of these elements are essential to the effective use of the NICHD Protocol. Finally, the pre-interview preparation, the adaptation of the NICHD Protocol to teenagers and adults, and the recommended training to master the protocol are also discussed.

The NICHD Protocol is divided into three main phases, namely

- the pre-substantive phase, which allows the child to prepare for the substantive part of the interview;
- the transition phase, which allows the child to introduce the possible event under investigation; and
- the substantive phase, which is used to collect information concerning the alleged event the child experienced as a victim or a witness, as well as information related to the disclosure.

It is important to mention that the NICHD Protocol was created and designed so that children as young as 4 years old could understand the questions and collaborate effectively with the interviewer. Nevertheless, in rare circumstances, children of a little over 3 years old can also be interviewed using the NICHD Protocol even if their answers lack many details, given, among other things, their limited vocabulary and attention span. Because the NICHD Protocol is intended for young children, instead of explaining abstract concepts to the child (e.g., "It is important to give a lot of details," "You must correct the interviewer"), concrete activities are proposed in order to allow the

DOI: 10.4324/9781003265351-6

child to understand the ground rules of communication and also to learn the interviewee's task, which is to give as many details as possible about what really happened.

Another important feature of the general structure of the NICHD Protocol is the fact that the first part of open-ended questions (called invitations) is always similar, both making it easier for the child to understand and less demanding of his/her capacity to pay attention. For these reasons, interviewers are advised to follow the NICHD Protocol in its entirety and to try to memorize most of its contents in order to maximize eye contact during the interview. However, the interviewer should have the NICHD Protocol in front of him/her during the interview to ensure that s/he is following the various steps and formulating the questions correctly. Even after years of practice, for personal or professional reasons, interviewers are sometimes less available mentally, which leads them to be disoriented during the interview process. Having the NICHD Protocol close by then becomes a necessity. In addition, after examining many interviews of children, we have observed that when interviewers attempt to rephrase the NICHD Protocol sentences instead of using the carefully crafted ones, sentences are much longer, the vocabulary used is more complex, and the wording of the questions is not always clear.

I   The pre-substantive phase

The main objective of this part of the interview is to prepare the child for the task s/he will have to perform when it becomes time to describe the alleged event. Research has shown that children collaborate best when they understand what is expected of them. To achieve this, different tasks are completed with the child, including

1   introduction,
2   rapport building and narrative training,
3   explaining and practicing ground rules, and
4   training of episodic memory about a recent positive event.

I.I   Introduction

The introduction allows the interviewer to present himself/herself to the child and to indicate that the interview will be recorded. It is recommended that interviewers identify the interview on the recording before the child comes in. Thus, the name of the interviewer, the date, the name of the child, and the location where the interview is taking place should be mentioned.

Once in the interview room, the interviewer begins by welcoming the child and indicating where the camera and microphones are located in the room in order to allow the child to familiarize himself/herself with this new place. This also helps to avoid unnecessary distractions during the interview (e.g., questions about the nature or function of objects in the room, such as the microphone). For the same reasons, the room should be free from any source of distractions, such as toys or decorations on the walls.

The interviewer also briefly explains the purpose of the recording. Depending on the jurisdictions where the NICHD Protocol is being used, it may be legally necessary to give the child other information or other instructions such as that s/he may be accompanied by a trusted person or that there may be another person in the room with the interviewer (e.g., a psychologist, a social worker). Ideally, no one other than the interviewer and the child should be in the room. In addition, the interviewer should avoid wearing any objects (e.g., badges, necklaces, bracelets) that could distract the child. Here is an excerpt from the NICHD Protocol for this part of the interview. The sentence in normal characters are the statements to say, and those in italics offer guidance or comments about different situations.

> Hello, [child's name], I am glad to meet you today. How are you?
> My name is _____ and my job is to talk to children about things that have happened to them. As you can see, we have a video camera here. It will record us talking so I can remember everything you tell me.
> *In the introduction, gestures of goodwill are appropriate:*
> Are you comfortable?
> Can I do anything to make you more comfortable?

1.2 Rapport building and narrative training

The next step is to develop the working relationship and to begin training the child to answer open questions (see section 3 for more details). The objective is to give the child confidence so that s/he can settle into the role s/he will have to play during the interview, talking about things s/he knows and have happened to him/her. To achieve this, the interviewer discusses activities the child likes to do. Additionally, in the Revised NICHD Protocol, the interviewer also discusses something pleasant that happened to the child as well as something unpleasant. This addition was made on the basis of the observation that children expressed little emotion when reporting the events that happened to them (Katz et al., 2012; Castelli & Goodman, 2014; Sayfan, Mitchell, Goodman, Eisen, & Qin, 2008). Research has shown that helping children to talk about their internal states (emotions, sensations, thoughts) allows them to provide more details and more references to these internal states (Karni-Visel, Hershkowitz, & Blasbalg, 2020).

Talking about activities that the child enjoys was included in the NICHD Protocol because it is an easy topic of conversation, and children usually have preferences about their activities. The child is simply asked to talk about the things s/he likes to do. This usually generates a list of activities whose length depends on the age of the child. From the answers given, the interviewer can choose an activity and ask the child to tell him/her about it. When they are not using the NICHD Protocol, interviewers often ask a series of closed questions about family or school (e.g., "Do you have siblings?" "Are you at school?" "Do you live with your mom and dad?") to establish rapport and a trusting environment. Unfortunately, we do not want to favor such closed and specific questions during the interview. In addition, these types of questions make the child dependent on the interviewer's questions. During this stage of the interview, the interviewer should only use open-ended questions to allow the child to talk about the things s/he likes to do, with the objective of familiarizing the child with these new types of questions and reducing the use of closed-ended questions. This also helps to avoid embarrassing the child by asking questions they do not understand or cannot answer.

It is also recommended that interviewers use action verbs to help the child provide details (e.g., "Tell me more about playing soccer" rather than "Tell me about soccer"). Depending on the content of the response, the interviewer may continue with an aspect or detail named by the child (e.g., "Tell me more about you scoring a goal") or, if the content reported was lacking information, choose to address another activity mentioned by the child in response to the initial question (e.g., "Tell me more about cycling with your friends"). Caution is required regarding activities that involve television, video games, electronic games, or other activities involving fantasy and imagination. Indeed, as the child must report real events that have occurred during the interview, it is important to avoid making him/her talk about activities that involve fantasy. This step, considered as a warm-up exercise, should only last a few minutes. The interviewer should be limited to two or three questions for each of the three subsections (something you like to do, something pleasant, something unpleasant). For the two questions dealing more specifically with pleasant and unpleasant activities, the objective is to have the child speak spontaneously about his/her emotions, feelings, or thoughts (e.g., "Tell me about being happy to have won the prize") if the child has given access to this content. It is important to target the places where these pleasant and unpleasant events may have occurred in order to prevent the child from spontaneously and prematurely addressing the reason for the forensic interview. It is thus better to target activities that take place at school or in kindergarten or a place other than the location of the suspected event. If the child is still facing a difficult situation that is causing distress, it is important to take the time to check with him/her if any adult knows about this situation and can offer support.

> B.1 Now, [child's name], I want to get to know you better. Tell me about the things you like to do.
>
> *Wait for the child to respond.*
> *If the child responds, express your appreciation and reinforcement:*
> Thank you for sharing that with me. It helps me get to know you.
> *Or* I'm glad. I am starting to get to know more about you.
> B.3 Now, [child's name], tell me more about [the activity the child already mentioned].
> *Use two to three invitations.*
> B.4 [Child's name], tell me about something fun that has happened to you [at school or kindergarten].
> *Important! Do not mention the location in which the alleged abuse may have taken place.*
> B.5 Tell me about [something the child mentioned]. *Use various invitations to ask about different topics; one of those invitations should focus on internal contents: thoughts, feelings, sensations, or emotions.*
> B.6 You told me about something [happy, pleasant, fun] that has happened to you. Now, tell me about something unpleasant that has happened to you [at school or kindergarten].
> B.7 Tell me about [something the child mentioned]. *Ask various invitations to elicit richer information about a variety of topics; one invitation should focus on the internal contents: thoughts, feelings, sensations, or emotions.*

If the child reveals distressing information, please explore that briefly while making supportive statements. You want to check whether the child has previously reported it.
You told me about [the distressing incident]. Have you told an adult about that?
If the child says no, say: Would you like me to help you tell someone?

B.8 [Child's name], you told me about [pleasant event already described] and [unpleasant event already described], and you shared your [emotions, thoughts] with me [if s/he did]. Thanks for letting me know. It's important that you know you can talk to me about anything, both good things and bad things.

Researchers have observed that children who are reluctant to disclose show signs of reluctance early in the interview process. For this reason, the Revised NICHD Protocol includes supportive comments to use if the child shows embarrassment (verbally or nonverbally) or remains silent:

[Child's name], let me see your eyes.
[Child's name], go ahead and sit close to me.
[Child's name], I can see you're [crying, quiet]. Tell me what is happening so I can help.
[Child's name], thanks for letting me listen to you today. Please tell me about what you're going through.

B.2 I really want to know you better, [child's name]. I would like you to tell me about things you like to do at school, during recess, and after school.

1.3   Explaining and practicing ground rules

The next step is to present communication rules to the child. Some of these allow the child to better understand the task s/he faces, while others aim to help him/her counteract his/her natural suggestibility (see Chapter 3). Four ground rules are presented to the child, namely

1   not understanding the question,
2   not knowing the answer,
3   correcting the interviewer, and
4   telling the truth.

The first ground rule is about understanding the questions. Some studies have shown that, when they have to testify in court, children, like many adults, tend to answer questions even if they do not understand their meaning (Brubacher, Poole, & Dickinson, 2015). Thus, children can give peculiar answers to questions they do not understand. Studies have also noted that warning children that they can say they do not understand the question allows them, especially those of school age, to consider this guideline during the interview.

C.1 [Child's name], I'm interested in you, and I'll be asking you all kinds of questions today. If I ask a question that you don't understand, just say, "[interviewer's name], I don't understand." OK, [child's name]?

Whenever the child later says s/he doesn't understand, the interviewer should praise the child for doing so.

The next rule is to inform the child that s/he should not make up answers to please the interviewer and that s/he can say that s/he does not know the answer or does not remember the information. As pointed out in the chapter on suggestibility, research tells us that children know that adults expect a response when they ask a question (Poole & Lamb, 1998). In addition, when children are asked questions at school by the teacher, they know they have to provide the "right" answer. They, therefore, feel pressure to answer a question even if they do not know the answer. Research also tells us that children are particularly reluctant to respond "I don't know" when asked directive or option-posing questions. However, emphasizing this possibility to them seems to allow some children to tell the interviewer that they do not know the answer (Brubacher et al., 2015). When children respond even when they are unsure of their answer, it can result in errors that are repeated in subsequent interviews, indicating contamination of memory (Brown & Lamb, 2017). To counteract children's natural tendency to answer adult questions, it is important to inform them that in the context of this interview, they should simply say if they do not know the answer. Here, an exercise is done with the child. If the child does not fully understand the instruction and does not complete the exercise successfully, another practice exercise is recommended. In both situations, the exercise ends by emphasizing to the child that when s/he knows the answer, s/he should say so.

> C.2 If I ask a question and you don't know the answer, just tell me, "I don't know." So, [child's name], if I ask you [e.g., "What did I have for breakfast today?"], what would you say?
>
> *Wait for the answer.*
> *If the child says, "I don't know," say:*
> Right, you don't know, [child's name], do you?
> *If the child offers a guess, say:*
> No, [child's name], you don't know me and [e.g., "you weren't with me when I had my breakfast this morning"], so you don't know. When you don't know the answer, please don't guess. Just say you don't know.
> *Pause.*
>
> But if you do know or do remember, it is very important that you tell me. OK, [child's name]?

The third ground rule tells the child to correct the interviewer if s/he makes a mistake. Here, too, the natural tendency of children is to believe that adults are reliable sources of information (Poole & Lamb, 1998). Thus, children tend not to spontaneously correct an adult who erroneously "repeats" some of the information they have given. In the context of an interview, only a third of children do so (Evans, Roberts, Price, & Stefek, 2010; Roberts & Lamb, 1999). For this reason, an exercise is provided to indicate to the child that, if the interviewer makes a mistake (e.g., saying that the child had a blanket on him/her when the child had simply said that there was a blanket during the abuse; it could have been under him/her or beside him), the child should inform the interviewer.

C.3 And if I say things that are wrong, you should tell me. OK, [child's name]?

So if I said that you are a 2-year-old girl [when interviewing a 5-year-old boy, for example], what would you say?

Reinforce the child if s/he gives the right answer: You are right, [child's name], you are not a 2-year-old girl. Now you know you should tell me if I make a mistake or say something that is not right.

If the child only denies and does not correct you, say: You're right! You're not a 2-year-old girl. What would be right?

Correct a wrong answer: No, [child's name], you are not [wrong age]. You are [real age]. So if I say you are standing up, what would you say?

[Child's name], now you understand that if I say something incorrect, you need to correct me and tell me what is right.

Finally, the last ground rule discusses the importance of telling the truth and only talking about things that have actually happened. Research (Lyon & Dorado, 2008; Talwar & Crossman, 2012) has shown that the ability to distinguish between truth and lies is not related to the practice of telling the truth, whereas promising to tell the truth is more often associated with truthful accounts. For this reason, the stated rule is limited to making the child promise to tell the truth.

C.4 Part of my job is to talk to [children, teenagers] about things that have happened to them. I meet with lots of [children, teenagers] so that they can tell the truth about things that have happened to them. [Child's name], it is very important that you tell me the truth today about things that have happened to you. Do you promise to tell me the truth, [child's name]?

It is important to do the short exercises suggested since these allow children to better understand and apply the ground rules (Brubacher et al., 2015; see Chapter 7 for a review of empirical studies). If necessary, during the interview, it is possible to add other rules if they might help the child (Lamb et al., 2018). Thus, interviewers might emphasize to children that all details are important ("Tell me everything that has happened, even the small things") and only to report what they are certain about ("Don't guess. Just tell me what you really know"; "Tell me what happened. You don't have to repeat something you said to someone if that's not what happened") and to be aware that the interviewer does not know the facts ("I don't know what happened"; "I was not there. I did not see what happened").

I.4   *Episodic memory training about a recent positive event*

Episodic memory training is a crucial portion of the NICHD Protocol and of the pre-substantive phase, which cannot be skipped if one wishes to obtain all the benefits of using the NICHD Protocol (see Chapter 7). This exercise allows the child to think back in time and retrieve as much detail as possible about what happened and what s/he experienced. This training in the use of recall memory about a recent actual event that is unrelated to the possible event under investigation serves several purposes for both the child and the interviewer.

For the child, the objectives are

- to make him/her aware of the amount of detail that the interviewer needs to fully understand the event in question;
- to report everything;
- to understand that the interviewer knows nothing about him/her or what s/he has experienced;
- to use memory to inform a narrative about an experienced event;
- to familiarize him/her with open-ended questions that are often used very little or not at all by parents in the child's daily life;
- to make the interview roles concrete (i.e., the interviewer speaks little and asks short questions, while the child talks a lot and gives very elaborate answers);
- to develop a sense of confidence in answering questions;
- to promote and consolidate the relationship of trust and working alliance between the interviewer and the child; and

For the interviewer, this exercise makes it possible to achieve several objectives, particularly

- to have time to observe the reactions of the child (does the child respond by giving the information sought by the question, or does the child have difficulty providing the specific types of details sought?);
- to assess the child's level of development in order to adjust questions and phrasing to accommodate the child's knowledge and abilities;
- to adjust to the child's pace and style (some children need more time to think before responding; others use their bodies a lot to explain what has happened);
- to show interest and consolidate rapport; to promote this bond, it is essential that the interviewer be really interested in the child's story and demonstrate that verbally ("hum-hum," "yes") or with sustained eye contact;
- to train the child to report events in chronological order; and
- to help the child to develop an emotional discourse by naming and exploring the child's emotions to help him/her to disclose and potentially regulate emotions.

This exercise also provides the interviewer with basic information with which to compare the attitudes, behaviors, and responses of the child when s/he is talking about the alleged event. This can facilitate the identification of false allegations if there is a mismatch between the behavior and abilities of children during the memory practice and substantive phases.

Concretely, to carry out this episodic memory training, the interviewer will have previously identified with the parents a recent event that was pleasant for the child, such as a family outing, a birthday party, or a special activity at school. If no parent accompanies the child at the time of the interview, the interviewer can still use an event that usually involves special activities within families (such as Christmas, Passover, Eid, Halloween, or the child's birthday), the first or last day of school, or similar occasions. The interviewer can also ask the child if s/he participated in a special event recently, such as a birthday or a trip. When no special events have occurred, the interviewer may choose to use the activities of the previous day. However, a special event is preferable for various reasons because it is more stimulating for the child to talk about a pleasant special event than an ordinary day like today or yesterday and because a special event will have been better encoded in memory than a more routine event. In addition, this exercise is closer to the task that the child will have to do in the substantive part of the interview, reporting an event that is "special."

To begin this exercise, the interviewer invites the child to tell him/her about everything that has happened during the special event, urging the child to provide the most comprehensive account possible starting from the beginning of the event. To complete the story, the child will likely need the support of the interviewer with prompts, such as "And then what happened?" Once the story has been completed, the interviewer may attempt to clarify some elements using time-segmenting invitations and then cued invitations (the reader can refer to the section on open-ended questions and note-taking at the end of this chapter for more information). This exercise should necessarily include these two types of invitations to determine if the child is able to respond to them because they are the ones that will be favored throughout the substantive part of the interview. This exercise should be long enough to help the child understand the amount of detail the interviewer needs, but at the same time, it should not take too long so as to tire him/her out. Indeed, the results of three studies (Hershkowitz, 2011; Teoh & Lamb, 2010; Davies, Westcott, & Horan, 2000) indicate that, in young children, practice that exceeded seven minutes was associated with fewer substantive details, probably because the children were more tired. Therefore, it remains important to respect the developmental capacities of the child so as not to tire him/her too much. Usually, the time required to complete the pre-substantive part with a child who understands the instructions and is cooperative is approximately fifteen to twenty minutes.

In addition to seeking an account of the event from beginning to the end, interviewers should use at least three time-segmenting invitations (including one very short time segmentations using the information provided by the child) and at least three cued invitations. These should refer to actions, thoughts, feelings, sensations, or emotions mentioned by the child. The other invitations could also relate to descriptions of the location or an object.

Is it also very important to provide support by using the child's name when posing invitations, to thank the child for attempting to provide a full account, and to explore whether the child is having difficulty reporting the event. For example, if the child cannot respond successfully to the time-segmenting invitation or seems not to understand it, the interviewer could explain to the child what is expected (e.g., "You know, [child's name], I wasn't there, and I don't know what happened. I would like you to tell me everything that happened between the moment when you arrived at your friend's house until you started to play"). Emphasis should also be put on the emotions reported by the child by reflecting and exploring them (e.g., "You told me it was exciting. Tell me more about being excited").

If the child understands the questions well and gives detailed answers, the interviewer can move on to the substantive part. However, if the responses are inappropriate or the child is reluctant, it may be best to continue until the child seems more cooperative. In addition, if the special event that had been chosen beforehand appears not to be a good choice, either because the child's memory of it is poor or because s/he does not wish to describe it, the interviewer can identify another event or use the activities of the previous day or the current day to continue the exercise. This exercise concludes with reinforcement for the work done by the child and checking the child's comfort level.

> I'm glad to meet with you today, [child's name], and I would like to get to know you even better.
>
> D.1 A few [days, weeks] ago was [a holiday, birthday party, other event]. Tell me everything that happened on [the event], from beginning to end, as best you can.
>
> D.2 And after that, what happened, [child's name]?
> *Use this question as often as needed throughout this section until you have been given a full account of the event.*
>
> Thank you, [child's name]. You have told me many things [if s/he did]. I want to ask you some more questions about what you just told me.
>
> D.3 [Child's name], I would like you to tell me everything about [the event]. Please tell me everything that happened from the moment [an activity the child mentioned] to the moment [a subsequent activity].
> *Use a minimum of three time-segmenting invitations.*
>
> Thank you, [child's name], for telling me that. What you say is very clear, and that helps me understand what you mean.
>
> D.4 Tell me more about [an activity, object, thought, feeling].
> *Or*
> Earlier you spoke of [an activity, object, thought, feeling]. Tell me all about that.
> *Use a minimum of three cued invitations, including references to emotional and internal contents if the child has mentioned them.*
>
> D.5 [Child's name], thank you for telling me about [title of the event]. When we talk today, it is very important that you tell me everything about things that have happened to you.
>
> D.6 [Child's name], how are you feeling so far in our conversation?

2 The substantive phase

The substantive phase includes two main steps, the second of which includes four sections:

1 Transitional statements exploring whether there is an allegation
2 Exploration of one or more incidents

    a   Open-ended questioning
    b   Directive questioning
    c   Pause and review of the forensic information
    d   Option-posing questions if necessary

2.1 *Transitional part*

The transition to the substantive phase of the interview is a delicate piece of the interview where manifestations of discomfort or reluctance are common. The revised version of the NICHD Protocol offers the interviewer several options to support the child and deal with his/her reluctance; the nature of this non-suggestive support varies depending on the dynamics of the interview. It includes statements aimed at welcoming the child (e.g., "I am glad to meet you today / to get to know you / to get to talk"), reinforcing their efforts and behaviors (e.g., "You are telling clearly / in detail, and that's important"), expressing appreciation (e.g., "I appreciate your effort to remember and tell"), presenting the interviewer as someone to disclose to (e.g., "You can trust me and tell me if something has happened"), offering emotional support (e.g., "I hear it is difficult for you to tell"; "You said you were sad/disgusted / wanted to run away. Tell me more about that"), encouraging the child (e.g., "It's OK to tell me about this kind of thing / to say these words/bad words"), and so on (see appendix 5).

Statements of support are expected at various times during this transitional period. The support is expressed in a very general way (a–c) or be related more specifically to the relationship with the child (d–f). If the child denies or does not make an allegation, the interviewer should take a break and consider stopping the interview. If the child is avoiding cooperation and the interviewer has a serious concern about the child's well-being, s/he might proceed with questions aimed at eliciting a disclosure. When there is independent evidence raising suspicions, empathy can be communicated in relation to the feelings expressed by the child or in relation to his/her difficulties participating in the interview (g–k). These supportive interventions would be considered suggestive if there was no independent evidence corroborating the suspicions. It is important to note that the Revised NICHD Protocol is designed to support the child and promote disclosure, but we need to respect the child's right not to disclose and should not put undue pressure on the child.

The transition to substantive content is accomplished using a series of open-ended questions that are sequenced according to their degree of suggestiveness, so the inter-viewer should use the questions in the order indicated in the NICHD Protocol. If the child makes an allegation, the interview should proceed to the open-ended questions in the next section (E). It is important to note that if the child shows verbal or nonver-bal signs of reluctance, the interviewer should stop asking the substantive questions and provide support.

> Now that I know you a little better, I want to talk about why [you are / I am] here today.

> 1   I understand that something may have happened to you. Tell me everything that happened from the beginning to the end.
> 2   As I told you before, my job is to talk to children about things that might have happened to them. It is very important that you tell me why you think [your mom/dad/grandmother brought you here today / I came to talk to you today].

It is particularly common for young children to answer these questions by reporting events that are not those under investigation. The interviewer can then use the follow-ing intervention before moving on to the next question.

> I hear what you are saying to me, [child's name]. If you want, we can talk about that later. Right now, though, I want to know about something else that may have happened to you.

3   *If the child doesn't make an allegation and looks avoidant or reluctant, it is recommended that the interviewer use one or more of the general supportive statements to modify interview dynamics.*

    a   [Child's name], my job is to listen to children about things that have happened to them.

    b   [Child's name], I really want to know when something happens to children. That's what I am here for.

    c   [Child's name], here, kids can talk about good things and bad things that have happened to them.

If the child expresses his/her thoughts or feelings about the disclosure in response to one of these supportive statements or in response to a transition question, the interviewer should provide support by monitoring and exploring the child's state (e.g., "You are telling me that you are shy to talk. Tell me more about that"). This exploration could continue with open-ended questions (e.g., "Tell me more about being afraid to use some words" [as mentioned by the child]). In other words, before using the next transitional question, when the interviewer has observed signs of reluctance or the child discloses his/her emotional or thinking states, the interviewer should take time to explore it with the child supportively.

The next transitional question is only used when the child has previously made a disclosure to a professional. The intention of this question is not to get a verbatim account of the discussion but to allow the child to make the allegation.

4   I've heard that you talked to [a doctor, teacher, social worker, other professional] at [location, time of the alleged incident]. Please tell me what you talked about.

The next question is only used when bruises or wounds are visible or the interviewer has been told that there are signs of injury. This question is useful in cases of physical abuse. However, the interviewer must be careful not to name the relevant body parts if the children do not do so.

5   I [saw, heard] that you have/had [documented injuries, bruises] on your [body part]. Tell me everything about [those, that].

Then the interviewer may name the location or presumed time of the incident. The challenge with this question, particularly in the context of intrafamilial sexual abuse, is to specify the location without naming the suspected perpetrator. For example, if the alleged abuse took place at the dad's home during a shared custody visit, the interviewer must avoid saying the name of the alleged perpetrator and restrict the question to naming the room in which the alleged event occurred.

6   [Child's name], has anything happened to you at [location/time of the alleged incident]?

At this point in the interview, if the child has still not made a disclosure and their behavior appears avoidant or reluctant, other statements of support that do not refer to the alleged incident are suggested in addition to those mentioned previously (a–c).

d   You told me a lot of things about yourself. I feel I know you better, and you can tell me more [about things, about both good things, and about bad things] that have happened to you.

e   You have told me a lot of things about yourself. Thank you for letting me know. When you talk to me today, please go on and tell me about other things that have happened to you.

f   [Child's name], if there is anything you want to tell me, [I want to know/ listen, it's important for me to know/ listen].

If the child denies that something has happened to him/her or does not make an allegation, the interviewer can take a break and decide whether to continue the interview, using his/her observation of the child's verbal and nonverbal reluctance to evaluate the situation. The interviewer may consider a second interview to try to create better rapport and a stronger bond of trust. Only if the interviewer thinks that the child does not understand the objective of the interview or has serious concerns about the child's welfare might the interviewer use the following transitional questions.

7   [Child's name], has anybody been bothering you?

8   [Child's name], did someone do something to you that you don't think was right?

9   [Child's name], did someone [briefly summarize the allegations or suspicions without specifying the name of the alleged perpetrator or providing too many details]?

Again, when the child appears to be avoiding or resisting, and there is independent evidence to raise suspicion, the interviewer can use the supportive statements (g–k), which aim to express that concern and explore the sources of the child's resistance before continuing with a final question.

g   [Child's name], [I am / people are] worried about you, and I want to know if something may have happened to you.

h   [Child's name], if something has happened to you and you want it to stop, can you tell me about it?

i-1   [Child's name], if it is hard for you to tell, what makes it so hard?

i-2   [Child's name], is there anything you are concerned about?

i-3   [Child's name], what would happen if you told me?

i-4   [Child's name], has someone told you not to tell?

j   Sometimes children think that if something happened to them, it's their fault, but children are not responsible if things happen to them.

k   It's your choice whether to tell, and I will go with your choice.

The last transitional question is used only when someone has made a disclosure about the alleged facts. It is important to formulate it precisely, including as few details as possible about the alleged actions. Under no circumstances should the name of the alleged perpetrator be mentioned.

10   [Child's name], I understand [you, someone] [reported, saw] [briefly summarize allegations or suspicions without specifying the name of the alleged

perpetrator or providing too much detail]. I want to find out if something may have happened to you.

When the child clearly says s/he does not want to speak, statements of support (l–q) are also suggested to show empathy for the child's difficulties, reassure and support him/her, or recognize his/her decision not to disclose.

l [Child's name], I understand you are [difficulties the child mentioned; e.g., embarrassed]. Let's start talking, and I'll try to help you with it.

m Many children are [difficulties the child mentioned], and I try to help them.

n I understand that you are [difficulties the child mentioned]. Tell me more about that.

o *If the child expressed a lack of confidence:* I'm sure you can talk to me about it well.

p *If the child said s/he was worried about something specific, and the reassurance you can give is true:* Don't worry, I will [not tell the other children / make sure you are not late for the bus].

q It's your choice whether or not to tell me, and I will accept what you decide.

2.2 Exploration of one or more incidents

As soon as a child indicates that s/he has witnessed the alleged event or that s/he has been subjected to maltreatment, the interviewer begins open-ended questioning. Here, three scenarios are possible:

1 The child is clearly referring to a single event.
2 The child indicates that more than one incident has occurred.
3 The child reports the allegation in a generic way, suggesting that more than one event has occurred.

If the interviewer is unsure whether the alleged event has happened more than once, s/he should ask the child if it has happened once or more than once. The interviewer's doubts could arise from clues in the use of verbs (e.g., "Daddy comes to my room and he touches me" instead of "Daddy came to my room and he touched me") or the use of adverbs, such as "always," "sometimes," or "often." Distinguishing events makes it possible to avoid script memory accounts, which, as we have already mentioned, amalgamate into a single general scenario several episodes of the incident under investigation, resulting in less detailed narratives. The interviewer should instead ask the child to describe the last event since his/her memory should be richer, then to talk about the first one (which should be well encoded since it was a special event) and, finally, to recount another episode that s/he remembers well. This way of proceeding also makes it possible to have some idea about how long the abuse has been ongoing, its nature, and the possible progression of its severity over time. It also makes it possible to obtain information about specific elements of the event that the child remembers well, such as the use of an object, the presence of a witness, or a different place where the incident(s) may have occurred.

If the child mentions a specific incident:

[Child's name], you told me that [briefly summarize the allegation the child has made]. Tell me everything from the beginning to the end, as best you can.

If the child mentions a number of incidents:

[Child's name], you told me that [briefly summarize the allegation the child has made]. Tell me everything about [the last/first time/at a place/a time/specific incident] from beginning to end.

If the child gives a generic description and you cannot determine the number of incidents:

[Child's name], you told me that [briefly summarize the allegation the child has made]. Did that happen one time or more than one time?

Depending on the answer, please invite a first narrative.

If the description remains generic, please say:

[Child's name], you told me that [briefly summarize the generic description]. Tell me everything from beginning to end.

And then what happened?

Repeat this question as often as needed until you have obtained a complete description of the alleged event.

You have told me many things and helped me understand what happened. Now, [child's name], I want to ask you more questions about [incident title].

Thus, the child is first invited to recount everything that happened in order to elicit a full account of the event. The interviewer will support the unfolding of this account ("and then what happened?") until the end of the event – that is, until the child is no longer with the perpetrator or witness at the crime scene. Before starting the open-ended questioning cued by the information provided by the child, reinforcement and an explanation of the course of the interview help promote better collaboration. The interviewer can then use time-segmenting invitations and cued invitations (see question section for more details) to elicit further important details. Thus, using the details provided by the child, the story is first explored using time segmentation to divide the account into short chronological segments. Then when important details remain undisclosed, shorter time segments can be explored and cued invitations can be used. These two types of questions should be favored in order to obtain as much information as possible about the actions, perpetrator, forensically important details, and the location before using other types of questions.

[Child's name], think back to the time [day, night], and please tell me everything that happened from the moment/when [an activity the child mentioned] to the moment/until [a subsequent activity the child mentioned].

Tell me more about [activity, object, feeling, thought].

[Child's name], you mentioned [activity, object, feeling, thought]. Tell me more about that.

After an exhaustive use of the different types of invitations, the interviewer can utilize directive questions if necessary to obtain important undisclosed details. These will help the child to better specify where and when the event occurred, to give some indications concerning the positions of the victim and the perpetrator or to specify some actions that occurred. It is important to follow the answers to these specific questions with invitations, in accordance with the pairing principle, to increase the quality and quantity of details given by the child.

> [Child's name], you said that/mentioned [activity, object, feeling, thought].
> [How, when, where, who, what, which, how many, what did you mean]?
> *Wait for an answer:* Tell me more about that.

When the interviewer believes s/he has elicited as many details as possible using open-ended and directive questions, s/he should take a break to consult a colleague or anyone else monitoring the interview (e.g., psychologist, social worker). When being alone, the interviewer can use the time to review his/her notes (see the note-taking section) to see if other open-ended questions are necessary to clarify some details in the child's account.

> [Child's name], now I want to make sure I have understood everything you said and see if there's anything else I need to ask. I will take a couple of minutes to think about what you told me / go over my notes / go check with [colleague's name].

If there is still important information to be obtained, the interviewer should resume after the break by first asking open-ended and directive questions, and then, only if the information is absolutely necessary, option-posing questions. The latter must be used minimally since the answers obtained using this type of question are less reliable than those provided following open-ended or directive questions. In addition, such questions involve the interviewer introducing new details or content that may contaminate the child's memory (see the chapter on memory and suggestibility). At this point in the interview, the interviewer may question the child about information available to the interviewer that the child has not mentioned. This may be information that the child has disclosed to someone else or information reported by a witness. Care should be taken with the formulation of these questions as they may contaminate the child's memory if it turns out that the child provided this information to someone else as a result of suggestive questions. Option-posing questions should always be paired with invitations.

> [Child's name], when you told me about [specific incident embedded in time and place], you mentioned [activity, object, feeling, thought]. Did/have/has/is/are [a detail for the child to confirm or deny]?
> *Whenever appropriate, follow up with an invitation:*
> Tell me everything about that [activity, object, feeling, thought].

When multiple events have taken place, the interviewer should take the time to elicit a complete account of each of the three events that will be detailed (last, first, another time that the child remembers or characterizes well) from beginning to end first using time-segmenting invitations, then cued invitations, and then directive questions. When the three events have been well described, the interviewer can take a break to review his/her notes or consult his/her colleagues. If necessary, after the break, the interviewer continues with open-ended questions and more specific questions, such as option-posing questions. To facilitate the child's memory retrieval, open-ended and directive questions should deal with the events separately unless a question applies to all three events. It is strategic to label the events clearly to distinguish them (e.g., the time in the living room, the time you screamed, the time he touched your butt, the time after school rather than the first or last time). Studies have shown that 66% of children themselves tend to label events and that this tendency increases with age; it is important to use the label offered by the child (Brubacher, Malloy, Lamb, & Roberts, 2013; Brubacher, Powell, & Roberts, 2014). When there have been a few distinct episodes (e.g., four or five), and the child is cooperative and is not tired, the interviewer can proceed to obtain information about more than three events.

2.3   Disclosure and closing phase

The final two steps in the Revised NICHD Protocol are designed to obtain information about the disclosure process and to close the interview. When all the information regarding the events has been obtained, the interviewer requests information regarding the disclosure itself. If, during the narrative phase, the child mentioned having told someone about it, the interviewer can use this information to open the discussion about disclosure. Otherwise, s/he will check to see if anyone else knows about the abuse. If so, the interviewer could ask who these people are and how they learned about what happened. Any other relevant information concerning the reactions of the child and those of the recipient following the disclosure may be requested.

> You've told me why you came to talk to me today. You've given me a [lot of] information, and that really helps me to understand what happened.
>
> *If the child mentioned telling someone about the incident(s), you may say:*
> Now I want to understand how other people found out about [last incident].
> *If the child has not mentioned telling anyone, probe about a possible disclosure by saying:*
>
> Does anybody else know what happened?

At this last step of the NICHD Protocol, the interviewer will introduce a neutral topic to be discussed, such as the activities.

> [Child's name], what are you going to do after we finish talking?

3   Questions

The NICHD Protocol favors open-ended questions called "invitations." However, interviewers usually also need to ask directive or option-posing questions to get specific details. In the following sections, we provide brief definitions and examples of these different types of questions so that NICHD Protocol users can clearly identify the type of questions they have asked when rereading or reviewing their interviews. Definitions and examples are taken from the Interview Quality Analysis Scoring Manual developed by Lamb and colleagues (Lamb et al., 1996). Additional information on the effect of different types of questions on memory and suggestibility,

Table 6.1 The quantity and accuracy of details as a function of the questions types used during interview

Quantity of details	Types of question	Details accuracy
↑	Invitation Directive Option-posing Suggestive	↑

depending on children's age and developmental status, is provided in chapters 2, 3, and 4 of this book.

The questions can be ranked in ascending order according to the amount of detail obtained and the likely accuracy of those details. As the information elicited from recall memory is often more accurate and the responses are longer and more detailed, invitations should be preferred. Some directive questions also yield accurate content. On the other hand, option-posing questions and suggestive interventions draw on recognition memory, which is less accurate. In addition, the answers to recognition questions are usually short. The accuracy of the information obtained is influenced by the nature of the memory that is called upon by the different types of questions, as we pointed out in Chapter 2.

3.1 Invitations

Invitations can be defined as open statements using either questions or imperative verbs to obtain freely recalled information from the child. In general, open-ended questions give the child more flexibility in choosing which aspects of the event s/he wants to describe. For example, "Tell me more about his eyes" is a more open question than "What color are his eyes?" In line with best practice recommendations, open-ended questions should be used to begin the interview and, if possible, throughout the interview. With a good grasp of open-ended questions on the part of the interviewer and with a school-age or older child who has good cognitive skills, it may be possible to obtain all of the required forensic information using only this type of question.

Invitations fall into four categories: general invitations, follow-up invitations, invitations that include time segmentation, and cued invitations. General invitations are used to ask the child to elaborate on something they just said (e.g., "Tell me everything you know about this"; "Tell me everything that happened from beginning to the end"). Follow-up invitations (e.g., "And then, what happened?") are used to help children, particularly young children, to develop their account to the end of the event. Because of the reduced attention span, young children often stop their reports before describing the end of the event.

Time-segmenting invitations allow the child to focus on a very short period of time within the event being described in order to give more information. The invitation submitted to the child may refer to a single moment and seek information about something that happened just before or just after that precise moment (e.g., "You said he hurt you, then what happened?" "What's was the first thing that happened before he touched you?"). These questions can also refer to two specific moments revealed by the child, which serve to delimit the period of interest to the interviewer (e.g., "Tell me everything that happened from the moment he entered your room to the moment he touched you"; "Tell me everything that happened from the moment he pulled his pants down to the moment your hand touched his penis"). It is important that these time segments do not cover too long a period so as not to exhaust the child's attention span. When the time segmentation covers a long period, children often repeat the same information. This type of invitation is more effective with school-age children who understand time concepts better than younger ones (Orbach & Lamb, 2007). However, some 4- or 5-year-olds are able to understand and respond to them appropriately (Gagnon & Cyr, 2017). These invitations are helpful when moving forward through the narrative without losing the chronology of events and are best used after an initial entire free narrative to continue exploring the alleged event.

Cued invitations draw the child's attention to previously mentioned information to help them focus on providing more details about that piece of information. The cues used can be of different types: visual, auditory, sensory, verbal, related to the physical context or to the mental state, and so on. However, it is crucial that the cue be provided by the child; otherwise, it becomes suggestive. Here are a few examples: "Earlier you mentioned cream. Tell me more about it," "Tell me more about his hands on your stomach," "Tell me more about the hugs," and "You said he looked weird. Tell me more about that." The invitations that relate to action verbs (e.g., "Tell me more about kissing you") elicit more details than those relating to other types of cues (Lamb et al., 2003; Hershkowitz, 2001a). So if the child has reported an action, it is better to refer to it again in the invitation (e.g., "Tell me more about his hand rubbing your belly" versus "Tell me about his hand on your belly"). Recent research has also shown the superiority of cued invitations over directive questions to obtain information (Ahern & Lyon, 2013) and in children as young as 3 to 5 years old (Gagnon & Cyr, 2017). These cued invitations should, therefore, be preferred to general invitations since the cues help children to better understand the questions (see Chapter 7). In addition to action verbs, the use of cues involving an emotion, especially a negative emotion, increases the amount of detail given by the child (e.g., "You told me that you were afraid, tell me more about that"). This is true for both central and peripheral details. In situations where the abuse has occurred several times, formulating invitations referring to the negative emotions reported by the child makes it possible to seek more information about a specific event rather than generic details (Karni-Visel, Hershkowitz, & Blasbalg, submitted). Thus, when the information has been given by the child, it is always better to pose an invitation rather than a specific question (e.g., "You say he touched your vagina, tell me more about that" should be used in place of riskier questions like "Did he put his finger in your vagina?").

3.2   Directive questions

Directive questions guide the child's attention to content s/he has disclosed and seek additional information by asking who, when, where, what, or what else (e.g., "Where did this happen?" "What color was his car?" or "Who is this man?"). Some directive questions are much more open-ended than others ("How did he touch you?" "What position were you in?"), while others target more specific details that may not have been stored in a child's memory, like "What color was his hair?" Such questions may reinforce, in some children, the habit of trying to guess and giving an answer that may seem plausible instead of telling the interviewer that they do not know the answer (Saywitz, Lyon, & Goodman, 2011). In addition, narrow directive questions may be rooted in the interviewer's preconceptions or beliefs about the event and may influence the child's account (e.g., the interviewer assumes that the suspect had hair when he could have been bald). It is, therefore, necessary to use judgment and to ask directive questions only after having exhausted open-ended questions – that is to say, just before the planned break, taking into account the age and the capacities of the child to provide specific information (see chapter on child development).

In addition, all directive questions do not have the same effect since the same word (e.g., how) can target different types of content, and children's abilities to provide details depend on the requested content. The content prompted by the directive questions can be related to

- what happened ("How did it happen?"),
- actions ("How did he touch you?" "What did he do?"),
- the context ("Who is it?" "When did it happen?" "Where were you when it happened?"),
- static elements ("What color was his T-shirt?"),
- subjective evaluation ("How do you feel about him?"), and
- causality ("What made you scared?").

A study of children aged 4 to 13 years old tells us that the most general questions about the event elicit more details than all others (Ahern, Andrews, Stolzenberg, & Lyon, 2015). Second, action questions help children, both younger and older, produce longer narratives, although older children give longer and more detailed accounts. Questions asking for information about causality, subjective assessments, or context are comparable in the amount of detail they generate; all of the answers are shorter. Although they produce few details, such questions are sometimes necessary for the investigative process to better understand the event. However, it is concerning that, according to one study, they represent 52% of all questions, whereas those focused on what is happening (11%) and on actions (28%) together constitute just over a third of the questions asked. Are interviewers sometimes asking for details that exceed children's mnemonic, attentional, and language capacities? Indeed, studies carried out in the laboratory, where it is possible to check for the accuracy of the answers, have shown that answers to directive questions relating to action are more accurate results than to those relating to the context (Goodman, Hirschman, Heeps, & Rudy, 1991; Peterson, Dowden, & Tobin, 1999). Moreover, it should be noted that in addition to referring to several types of content, "why" and "how" questions are cognitively demanding. They require cognitive, linguistic, and metacognitive operations, including remembering, reflecting, and reasoning backward about causality. On average, 8.5 such questions are asked of children aged 3 to 5, whereas children answer only 1 in 5 (Malloy, Orbach, Lamb, & Walker, 2016); "why" and "how" questions are thus beyond the developmental abilities of the majority of 3- and 4-year-olds, whereas some 5-year-olds understand them. This is why they should be used sparingly. If an invitation question can be formulated ("Tell me more about his hand that touches you"), it should be favored over a directive how question ("How did he touch you?").

Some authors (Stolzenberg, McWilliams, & Lyon, 2017) suggest using directive questions when talking about clothes during the assault (e.g., "Where were your clothes?") to explore content previously mentioned by the child instead of more specific yes-or-no questions ("Did you have your clothes on?") for two reasons. First, directive questions allow children to answer by considering the intermediate position of the clothes (pants pulled down at mid-height, shirt unbuttoned, but held at the cuffs), which option-posing questions do not allow. In addition, asking directive questions makes it possible to obtain both more and more accurate details. However, the best question to get this type of information is still an open-ended question, such as "Tell me more about your clothes while he touched your butt."

As with invitations, some directive questions may become suggestive when addressing content the child has never mentioned. In these cases, the option-posing questions (e.g., "Did he say something to you?") is preferable and less suggestive than the directive question, which assumes that the suspect has done something (e.g., "What did he say to you?") when he may not have spoken.

3.3   *Option-posing questions*

Option-posing questions introduce information that was not given by the child and ask him/her to choose from two or more options to see if this information is stored in his/her memory. Thus, questions that begin with "did," "have," "has," "is," or "are" are interventions proposing a choice. The choice can be between yes and no (e.g., "Did he hurt you?" "Did this happen in the living room?"). These questions can be problematic with young children since some of them have a response bias for yes or no (Poole & Lindsay, 2001; Walker, 2013). This is especially true for children with intellectual disabilities (Finlay & Lyons, 2002). Option-posing questions may also provide the child with two or more specific options (e.g., "Did he touch you on top of or under your clothes?" "Did it happen before or after Christmas?") A common problem that arises with these choices is that they are not always exhaustive – "Did this happen in the living room, bedroom or kitchen?" omits other rooms in the house, such as the bathroom. However, in order to clarify some important legal details, it may be necessary to ask some of these questions after the break (which will have allowed time to verify whether necessary information is missing). The missing information could concern the possible presence of other people at the scene of the incident, the words that the alleged perpetrator could have said, the threats s/he could have made, or the possibility that s/he took photos or recorded the event. It is important to limit questions of this type as much as possible since they risk contaminating the child's memory if the child answers a question when s/he has not encoded the information. In addition, we do not want to introduce these questions before the break because we do not want to make the child feel that the accuracy of his/her answers does not matter to us. In order to help the child give us the most accurate answer possible, it is beneficial, before asking option-posing questions, to remind the child that if s/he does not know the answer, s/he can tell the interviewer (e.g., "If you don't know the answer or if you don't remember, tell me you don't know. Did it happen in the morning, afternoon or evening?").

3.4 Suggestive prompts

Suggestive prompts can take different forms. They could involve pressure put on the child to confirm or deny the interviewer's hypothesis (e.g., "He forced you to do this, didn't he?" "Are you sure he didn't threaten you not to talk about it?"). The interviewer may also come to a suggestive conclusion or make a suggestive assumption (e.g., "What did he say?" "What did he do to you after that?" or "What else happened?" when the child did not indicate that the perpetrator said or did anything or that anything else had happened). Any intervention that provides information that has not been mentioned by the child concerning the actions or identity of the suspect, regardless of the type of question used, is a suggestive intervention. A summary is also considered to be suggestive if the interviewer modifies details provided by the child or introduces new information that the child has never mentioned, such as the name of the presumed suspect or the alleged acts. Finally, prompts are suggestive when the interviewer offers non-exhaustive options, such as "You say you were lying on the bed. Was he lying on top of you or were you lying on top of him?" ignoring the possibility that they could be lying side by side. Section 3.1 on children's questions and suggestibility also provides other examples.

3.5 Summaries

Summaries are statements that repeat information provided by the child, often with the aim of reviewing the details obtained. It is not recommended that interviewers summarize in this way because summaries tire the child and require a degree of attentiveness, which often exceeds his/her capacity for attention. Consequently, the child is not inclined to correct the interviewer if the latter makes a mistake (Evans et al., 2010). If the error is not remarked by the child, the summary is not entirely accurate, and the interviewer is then on the wrong track.

4 Note-taking and the organization of open-ended questioning

In order to be able to formulate invitations that include cues or time segmentation in the child's words, it is important that the interviewer take a minimum of notes to make it possible to follow a chronological order in the sequence of questions and to have a better idea of the forensic elements of the account. Hershkowitz (2001b) suggests proceeding in the following way. At first, in response to the invitation "Tell me everything that happened from the beginning to the end," the interviewer will note the sequence of actions to get an overview of the whole incident. These could be called the "natural" segments. The next step, according to Hershkowitz, is to encourage the child, using open-ended questions, to give a more detailed account of the event being investigated. Often, young children do not begin their account at the start of the incident, and they may stop when they have not yet reached the end of the event. It is, therefore, important to encourage children to continue recounting the event by using prompts, such as "And then what happened?" For the interviewer, the event begins as soon as the child is with the suspected perpetrator, even before the act is committed, and it continues until the moment when the child is no longer with the suspect. The account usually includes descriptions of events, explanations, associations, digressions, or other types of information that are not necessarily organized or relevant to the investigation but that the child considers appropriate to share. It is, therefore, up to the interviewer to focus on those elements that together make up the entire allegation.

Once the entire allegation has been outlined, time-segmenting invitations are used to help the child explain in detail what happened between two specific occurrences or natural segments. These time segments should be short since long segments require a wider memory scan and are, therefore, more demanding and tiring for children, who do not have the same mnemonic capacities as adults. In addition, when segments are long, children often repeat information they have already given without adding details. It is best to start from the beginning of the incident and use the cues and language that the child has used. The segments should be explored chronologically to reflect the unfolding of the event. Then cued invitations can be used to help the child specify the central details that allow the interviewer to better understand what happened.

Thus, by expanding the child's narrative by exploring short segments of time and using cued invitations, the interviewer focuses on the elements that allow the central actions and activities committed by the perpetrator and the victim to be fully described. Depending on the context, physical evidence (DNA, object, etc.) relevant to the abuse should be revealed in response to open-ended questions. Once the entire narrative has been elaborated using time segmentation and cues have been used to explore the action details, invitations or directive questions can be used to elicit other forensic details, such as the identity of the perpetrator (e.g., "Tell me more about him"), the location ("Where were you?"), and the time of the incident. This sequence is recommended for several reasons. First, it builds on children's abilities; they are better at reporting what happened (actions) than at describing contextual elements (place, person, time). Second, it helps interviewers elicit the central elements before the child gets tired and inattentive. Third, it helps maximize reliance on recall memory rather than recognition memory. In addition, it maintains the child's self-confidence and cooperativeness. The challenge here for the interviewer is to set aside his/her natural preferences (e.g., where, who, when, and what happens) and instead follow the child's lead.

This is the order in which the content should be investigated during the substantive phase:

1   Central actions and gestures
2   Positions
3   Pieces of evidence (objects, clothes, etc.)
4   Perpetrator identification
5   Location
6   Time of incident
7   After the break

    a   Words/threats from the suspect
    b   Presence of witnesses

Appendix 2 reproduces an interview verbatim and appendix 3 the notes taken during this interview about a sexually abusive incident. This note-taking is organized in successive columns to allow other details to be added to those already mentioned by the child without having to rewrite information already collected. In addition, while the child recounts the incident, it is important to note only the central details and to leave some space to be able to write down new elements that may be added over time as the account is elaborated. In order to maintain good eye contact with the child, only keywords, not sentences, should be noted. In addition, only clues that would allow us to elicit new details about the actions should be written down. What is written should, therefore, be a verb and some indication of what that action was about (e.g., "touched my hand," "pulled down my pants," "hit me on buttocks").

The difficulty for the interviewer involves noting enough clues to be able to formulate invitations without compromising the relationship with a child who needs to feel heard and understood. Also, since many children, and especially younger ones, often use gestures or mimic certain actions, interviewers may miss important details about the reported abuse if they are too focused on their notes. It may also be useful to indicate the child's name at the top of the note-taking sheet as the interviewer should use it throughout the interview to capture the child's attention and make the relationship more intimate and warm.

For the interviewer, indicating at the bottom of the sheet the main elements of the investigation that s/he should ideally collect – such as the nature and frequency of the acts committed, the identity of the perpetrator, the location and the time of the incident, the elements of evidence (object, possible DNA, etc.) that might be collected, and the presence of witnesses or words/threats – serves as a point of reference to ensure that the keys forensic details were obtained. Because children seldom provide information in response to invitations about the presence of witnesses or words exchanged during the abuse, the interviewer will often need to ask option-posing questions after the break. Thus, a reminder of the forensic details that should be sought allows the interviewer to take short breaks while consulting his/her notes to assess what s/he has been able to gather and what is still missing. Obviously, depending on the child's age and abilities, some of these details may not be obtained before or after the break. When it is no longer possible to obtain some specific details with invitations, the use of which did not give access to the information sought, the interviewer can use directive questions (e.g., where, when). In addition, the use of option-posing questions (e.g., "Did he tell you something?") is possible after the break if some necessary information is still missing. However, these questions should be asked sparingly because of the risks involved and should, wherever possible, be paired with open-ended questions.

This strategy to help the child make their narrative clear and the accompanying note-taking are also used during the episodic memory training portion of the interview (see the example in appendix 4). We have already stressed the crucial importance of this step in the NICHD Protocol, which allows the child to better understand the task expected of him/her. However, during the memory training stage, it is not useful to write down all the central details mentioned by the child since we especially want to focus on establishing a trusting relationship and making the child recognize our interest in what happened to him/her. On the other hand, to ensure that the child has sufficient practice with short time segments and relevant cues, it may be useful to use square brackets to indicate the use of time segmentation and to underline the cues used. These make it possible for the interviewer to check, with a glance, that s/he elicited the child's account from beginning to end and see the number of time-segmenting invitations and cued invitations used in the practice. When there is a poor narrative that barely describes the event (with only two or three "natural" segments to the story), an occurrence, particularly if it includes actions, can be used to formulate a time-segmenting prompt instead of a cued invitation (e.g., "We put some varnish on the nails" can become "Tell me everything that happens after you put varnish on the nails" or "Tell me everything that happened from the moment you started to put varnish on the nails until that ended"). Interviewers should also use time segmentation within an occurrence described by the child in order to help him/her understand the amount of detail that is desired ("Tell me everything that happened when you started to put polish on the nails until you put it on your first nail"). It is important to remember that this practice must follow the same procedure as in the substantive phase. However, when practicing memory, we do not want to explore all the central elements reported by the child so as not to tire him/her. Since the goal is to practice using different types of invitations, we should also not waste time asking directive or option-posing questions.

5   Preparation and location of the interview

It is important to plan the meeting with the child well. Several pieces of information should be known by the interviewer before meeting the child (see the grid in appendix 6; Lamb et al., 2018; Poole, 2016). It is good to know about the child and his/her environment, more specifically with whom the child lives, as well as the names of his/her parents, brothers and sisters. If the child lives in shared custody or a blended family, the names of stepparents and half-siblings are also useful, as are the names of any pets. The child's daily activities (kindergarten, school level) and schedule should also be known. Poole (2016) suggests obtaining information about developmental problems (e.g., developmental or language delay, hearing problems, mental health problems, medication) that could influence the course of the interview or affect its optimal timing. The interviewer should also be aware of cultural considerations, including the language spoken at home, the perception of people in authority, or the child's ease at talking about sexuality or body parts. The usual words utilized by the child to describe their body parts, recent sex education, and family practices regarding sexuality (e.g., nudity at home) are other relevant things to know before the interview. To facilitate the pre-substantive phase, being informed of the child's leisure activities is helpful in case a child refuses to cooperate during the rapport building and memory practice steps. It is also preferable to have identified with the parents or guardians a recent activity that has been enjoyable to initiate the practice of episodic memory.

For the substantive part, it is good to know the alleged facts (nature of the abuse, the alleged perpetrator, the frequency, the place, and the time), as well as the way in which these were obtained, namely whether the child himself/herself made a disclosure and, if so, to whom and what s/he said. It is also important to know if the child has been questioned beforehand by one or more people (formal and informal interviews) in order to understand how the disclosures were made. This information will also make it possible to use certain questions during the transition to the allegation phase (e.g., prompts referring to disclosure to a third party, injuries, or the location where the abuse allegedly occurred). However, it is important to keep multiple hypotheses about these facts and to remain open to the child not reporting some details s/he had confided in someone or bringing in new facts that s/he has not mentioned previously. Indeed, the reactions and questions of adults during the disclosure, often suggestive, may have given rise to information, which will not be reported again by the child. In addition, it is very difficult for parents to accurately report conversations they have had with their children, as well as the questions they have used; they typically overstate the child's free narrative and underestimate their own contributions (Bruck, Ceci, & Francoeur, 1999; Korkman, Juusola, & Santtila, 2014; Korkman, Laajasalo, Juusola, Uusivuori, & Santtila, 2015).

Several recommendations also relate to where the interview should take place (Poole, 2016). The interview room should be quiet, isolated from noise and other conversations, and containing a minimum of distraction both in the room (e.g., toys, decoration, electronic equipment) and on the interviewer (e.g., badge, gun, jewelry). If decorative material is present, it must be neutral so as to be inclusive and not offend certain cultures or religions. The waiting room may contain toys, but these should not be too novel or too attractive so as not to provoke resistance when it is time for the child to go with the interviewer. As stressed previously, it is preferable for the interviewer and child to be alone. If a support person is required (interpreter, educator, parent), this person should be seated slightly behind the child and, with the exception of an interpreter, this person should leave the room when the substantive phase starts. Interview rooms should allow video recording of the interview and for other people (interviewer's colleague, police officer, social worker, etc.) to view from behind a one-way mirror or in a replay room. The room should include two comfortable armchairs and a table attached to the armchair so that the interviewer can place the interview protocol and take notes comfortably.

6   How to adapt the protocol to teenagers and adults

The NICHD Protocol was developed to interview children under 14 years old. It was informed by Tulving's encoding specificity principle (Tulving & Thomson, 1973), as is the Cognitive Interview. However, the Cognitive Interview does not emphasize the open-ended formulation of questions as clearly as the NICHD Protocol does. Previous research (Johnson et al., 2015; Luther, Snook, Barron, & Lamb, 2015; Schreiber Compo, Hyman Gregory, & Fisher, 2012; Wolfman, Brown, & Jose, 2016) has shown that it is not enough to recommend that interviewers use broad, open-ended questions, because interviewers tend to ask many directive and option-posing questions. As mentioned earlier, for asking invitations to become natural and common, interviewers need to have experience asking them frequently. For all of these reasons, it seems appropriate to suggest applying techniques incorporated into the NICHD Protocol, such as the use of invitations, note-taking, and the structure designed to help witnesses provide elaborate narrative descriptions when following Cognitive Interview instructions.

When used with teenagers, the NICHD Protocol needs some small modifications, mostly when explaining the purpose of the interview. Rapport building could be begun by, for example, adding, "Before we get started, I would like to get to know you better and to introduce the types of questions that I will use during our interview." The ground rules should be explained without practice. In addition to these ground rules, because of the characteristics of adolescents, it could be useful to say clearly that "it is important to tell me everything that happened because I don't want to ask you about what I guess may have happened" Depending on the jurisdiction, specific instructions concerning certain legal issues may be added. A short memory practice can be conducted, explaining that this is to show the types of questions that will be asked and the amount of detail expected. For that reason and because of the cognitive and memory capacities of teenagers, it is best to focus on one natural segment provided by the teenager when practicing both time-segmenting and cued invitations. With older teenagers, Cognitive Interview instructions could also be used.

7   Training in the use of the NICHD Protocol

Investigative interviews of children pose complex demands, which remain even when a structured interview protocol is used. In addition, people seldom use the open formulations (invitations) included in the NICHD Protocol in everyday life. It is, therefore, recommended that interviewers undergo training to learn how to use it appropriately. Beyond the training period, it is necessary to use these novel formulations as often as possible so that they become habits (Poole, 2016). Until the wording of invitations feels natural, it is more difficult for an interviewer to feel fully at ease and to benefit from the mental space required to observe the ambiguities or hesitations of the child and to adjust the interview strategy accordingly. As these invitations should also be favored during interviews with adult witnesses or victims, this learning should be facilitated. The necessary training is based on best practices in the field and on solid empirical data (see Chapter 7).

Initially, training in the use of the NICHD Protocol was carried out in groups, and depending on the number of participants, subgroups were formed during the practice periods (Lamb, Sternberg, Orbach, Esplin, & Mitchell, 2002). Training began with an intensive week that included several phases: reviewing the research on children's memory, suggestibility, and developmental abilities; examining in detail the NICHD Protocol and the reasons for its structure and form; watching videos demonstrating its use; putting the NICHD Protocol into practice during role-plays using predetermined victim scenarios (single or multiple events, children from 4 to 14 years old with various attitudes [collaborative, reluctant, shy, verbal, etc.]); reviewing and analyzing a recording of the practice interview; and discussing any difficulties with the interviewer and the whole group. Feedback was focused on the structure – that is to say, on the sequence of stages, the wording and clarity of the questions and their timing, identifying open-ended questions that could have been used instead of narrow questions to elicit some details, and the interviewer's verbal, nonverbal, and supportive attitude. To this end, appendix 7 includes a protocol adherence grid that structures the feedback to be offered during training. Following this week of training, interviewers also receive feedback on interviews conducted using the NICHD Protocol (Lamb, 2016; La Rooy et al., 2015).

With the revised version of the NICHD Protocol, it is recommended that this training be spaced out over a period of eight months to a year, with at least one group session per month including explanations, exercises, coding, mock interviews, and analysis of actual interviews (Hershkowitz et al., 2017). Individual meetings with an expert for two hours each month explore recent interviews by the trainees that have been transcribed and analyzed. Each group session has specific objectives. The first serves to explain the rationale behind the recommended supportive interventions, illustrate the supportive statements, and explain the system of coding questions, interviewer support, and children's reluctance. The second session focuses on the creation, development, and maintenance of rapport during the pre-substantive phase by, for example, promoting eye contact and the expression of emotions during memory practice. The third session focuses on the use of different forms of supportive intervention during the transitional phase, and the fourth, on the support to be offered during the substantive phase. The fifth session deals with the planning required and the principles guiding repeated interviews when the child does not want to disclose despite strong suspicions that something has happened to him/her. The sixth session deals with repeated interviews when few details have been obtained during the first interview. The seventh session is devoted to identifying and analyzing nonverbal signs of reluctance, while the eighth session provides guidance on the integrated conduct of a full interview. To this can be added a session on conducting interviews with children with intellectual developmental delays or on questioning young suspects (Lamb et al., 2018; Hershkowitz et al., 2017).

Based on several recent discussions of the effectiveness of training (Benson & Powell, 2015; Lamb, 2016; Powell, Guadagno, & Benson, 2016; Rischke, Roberts, & Price, 2011), it is recommended that training sessions be spaced out so as to allow interviewers to practice aspects of the NICHD Protocol before integrating others, as well as for extended supervision (see Lamb et al., 2018, for a review). It is important that a feedback system be implemented in the form of peer supervision or with an expert. Indeed, our studies (Cyr, Dion, McDuff, & Trotier-Sylvain, 2012; Cyr, Dion, Gendron, Powell, & Brubacher, 2020) that were conducted using the NICHD Protocol and those of colleagues working with other non-suggestive approaches (see Lamb et al., 2018, for a review) conclude that interviewing skills often decline. Investigative interviews with witnesses and victims require a set of complex skills, which, to be acquired and maintained, require regular practice and critical but constructive feedback in order to improve. To this end, the time spent during training in the analysis and coding of interviews helps interviewers develop self-supervision skills to maintain their skills. This practice is based on research, which has shown that the ability to analyze one's own interview is associated with greater use of open-ended questions (Yii, Powell, & Guadagno, 2014).

8   Conclusion

The Revised NICHD Protocol provides the interviewer with a structure that is both well-defined and, at times, flexible to guide him/her when obtaining details about the alleged event. In addition to helping interviewers use short sentences and a vocabulary accessible to all children, the NICHD Protocol favors the use of questions that are as open-ended as possible from the beginning of the interview. The NICHD Protocol also structures the phases of the interview in order to promote the development of a trusting and collaborative relationship with the child and to concretely prepare him/her for the task expected during the substantive part of the interview. The note-taking and the strategies used to elicit all the facts relating to the event and then to segment them into small parts allow the interviewer to support the child in an effective way by adapting to his/her cognitive and memory capacities. In addition, in the Revised NICHD Protocol, the attention that is paid in all phases of the interview to the different forms of reluctance and the offers of supportive comments that accompany them are a further step forward. The Revised NICHD Protocol offers the interviewer tools to deal with the cognitive capacities of children and their relational capacities and motivations. This makes it possible to better account for the interactive and dynamic nature of the interview where the two participants influence each other through their questions and answers, their nonverbal behaviors, and their engagement. However, mastering this interview protocol requires solid training, including mock interviews and frequent interviews supervised by one or more third parties or, at least, interviews regularly reviewed by the interviewer himself/herself, in order to correct errors and increase the reliance on open-ended questioning with the help of invitations and the non-suggestive support offered to the child during the interview. Because this structure and the formulations of the questions do not emerge naturally, they require considerable and regular practice in order to develop fluency and broaden the repertoire of open-ended utterances while maintaining a supportive relationship with the child.

References

Ahern E. C., Andrews S. J., Stolzenberg S. N., Lyon T. D. (2015). "The productivity of wh-prompts in children forensic interviews", *Journal of Interpersonal Violence*, 1–9.

Ahern E. C., Lyon T. D. (2013). "Facilitating maltreated children's use of emotional language", *Journal of Forensic Social Work*, 3(2), 176–203.

Benson M. S., Powell M. B. (2015). "Evaluation of a comprehensive interactive training system for investigative interviewers of children", *Psychology, Public Policy and Law*, 21(3), 309–322.

Brown D. A., Lamb M. E. (2017). "A contextually and developmentally sensitive view of children's memory development: Between the laboratory and the field", in Dick A. S., Müller U. (Eds.), *Advancing developmental science: Philosophy, theory, and method*, New York, NY, Routledge, 119–132.

Brubacher S. P., Malloy L. C., Lamb M. E., Roberts K. P. (2013). "How do interviewers and children discuss individual occurrences of alleged repeated abuse in forensic interviews?" *Applied Cognitive Psychology*, 27(4), 443–450.

Brubacher S. P., Poole D. A., Dickinson J. J. (2015). "The use of ground rules in investigative interviews with children: A synthesis and call for research", *Developmental Review*, 36, 15–33.

Brubacher S. P., Powell M. B., Roberts K. P. (2014). "Recommendations for interviewing children about repeated experiences", *Psychology, Public Policy, and Law*, 20(3), 325–335.

Bruck M., Ceci S. J., Francoeur E. (1999). "The accuracy of mothers' memories of conversations with their preschool children", *Journal of Experimental Psychology: Applied*, 5(1), 89–106.

Castelli P., Goodman G. S. (2014). "Children's perceived emotional behavior at disclosure and prosecutors' evaluations", *Child Abuse & Neglect*, 38(9), 1521–1532.

Cyr M., Dion J., Gendron A., Powell M., Brubacher S. (2020). "Test of three refresher modalities on child forensic interviewers' post-training performance", *Psychology, Public Policy, and Law*, 27(2), 221–230.

Cyr M., Dion J., McDuff P., Trotier-Sylain K. (2012). "Transfer of skills in the context of non-suggestive investigative interviews: Impact of structured interview protocol and feedback", *Applied Cognitive Psychology*, 26(4), 516–524.

Davies G. M., Westcott H. L., Horan N. (2000). "The impact of questioning style on the content of investigative interviews with suspected child sexual abuse victims", *Psychology, Crime & Law*, 6(2), 81–97.

Evans A. D., Roberts K. P., Price H. L., Stefek C. P. (2010). "The use of paraphrasing in investigative interviews", *Child Abuse & Neglect*, 34, 585–592.

Finlay W. M. L., Lyons E. (2002). "Acquiescence in interviews with people who have mental retardation", *Mental Retardation*, 40(1), 14–29.

Gagnon K., Cyr M. (2017). "Sexual abuse and preschoolers: Forensic details in regard of question types", *Child Abuse & Neglect*, 67, 109–118.

Goodman G. S., Hirschman J. E., Heeps D., Rudy L. (1991). "Children's memory for stressful events", *Merrill-Palmer Quarterly*, 37, 109–158.

Hershkowitz I. (2001a). "Children's responses to open-ended utterances in investigative interviews", *Law and Criminological Psychology*, 6(1), 49–63.

Hershkowitz I. (2001b). "Organizing the open-ended questioning in investigative interviews with children", Unpublished manuscript. Haïfa, University of Haifa.

Hershkowitz I. (2011). "Rapport building in investigative interviews of children", in Lamb M. E., La Rooy D. J., Malloy L. C., Katz K. (Eds.), *Children's testimony: A handbook of psychological research and forensic practice*, Malden, John Wiley & Sons, 109–128.

Hershkowitz I., Ahern E. C., Lamb M. E., Blasbalg U., Karni-Visel Y., Breitman M. (2017). "Changes in interviewers' use of supportive techniques during the revised protocol training", *Applied Cognitive Psychology*, 31, 340–350.

Johnson M., Magnussen S., Thoresen C., Lønnum K., Burrell L. V., Melinder A. (2015). "Best practice recommendations still fail to result in action: A national 10-year follow-up study of investigative interviews in CSA cases", *Applied Cognitive Psychology*, 29(5), 661–668.

Karni-Visel Y., Hershkowitz I., Blasbalg U. (2020). "Facilitating the expression of emotions by alleged victims of child abuse during investigative interviews using the revised NICHD protocol", *Child Maltreatment*, 24, 310–318.

Karni-Visel Y., Hershkowitz I., Blasbalg U. (submitted). "Emotion-enhanced recall in childhood: A developmental test in naturalistic contexts".

Katz C., Hershkowitz I., Malloy L. C., Lamb M. E., Atabaki A., Spinder S. (2012). "Nonverbal behavior of children who disclose or do not disclose child abuse in investigative interviews", *Child Abuse & Neglect*, 36(1), 12–20.

Korkman J., Juusola A., Santtila P. (2014). "Who made the disclosure? Recorded discussions between children and caretakers suspecting child abuse", *Psychology, Crime & Law*, 20(10), 994–1004.

Korkman J., Laajasalo T., Juusola A., Uusivuori L., Santtila P. (2015). "What did the child tell? The accuracy of parents' reports of a child's statements when suspecting child sexual abuse", *Journal of Forensic Psychology Practice*, 15(2), 93–113.

Lamb M. E. (2016). "Difficulties translating research on forensic interview practices to practitioners: Finding water, leading horses, but can we get them to drink?" *American Psychology*, 71, 710–718.

Lamb M. E., Brown D. A., Hershkowitz I., Orbach Y., Esplin P. W. (2018). *Tell me what happened: Questioning children about abuse* (2nd ed.), Hoboken, NJ, John Wiley & Sons Inc.

Lamb M. E., Sternberg K. J., Orbach Y., Esplin P. W., Mitchell, S. (2002). "Is ongoing feedback necessary to maintain the quality of investigative interviews with allegedly abused children?" *Applied Developmental Science*, 6(1), 35–41.

Lamb M. E., Sternberg K. J., Orbach Y., Esplin P. W., Stewart H. L., Mitchell S. (2003). "Age differences in young children's responses to open-ended invitations in the course of forensic interviews", *Journal of Consulting and Clinical Psychology*, 71(5), 926–934.

Lamb M. J., Hershkowitz H., Sternberg K. J., et al. (1996). *Quality of interview content analysis of investigative interviews codebook*, Washington, DC, National Institute of Child Health and Human Development.

La Rooy D., Brubacher S. P., Aromäki-Stratos A., Cyr M., Hershkowitz I., Korkman J., . . . Lamb M. E. (2015). "The NICHD Protocol: A review of an internationally-used evidence-based tool for training child forensic interviewers", *Journal of Criminological Research, Policy and Practice*, 1(2), 76–89.

Luther K., Snook B., Barron T., Lamb M. E. (2015). "Child interviewing practices in Canada: A box score from field observations", *Journal of Police and Criminal Psychology*, 30(3), 204–212.

Lyon T. D., Dorado J. S. (2008). "Truth induction in young maltreated children: The effects of oath-taking and reassurance on true and false disclosures", *Child Abuse & Neglect*, 32(7), 738–748.

Malloy L. C., Orbach Y., Lamb M. E., Walker A. G. (2016). "'How' and 'Why' prompts in forensic investigative interviews with preschool children", *Applied Developmental Science*, 21(1), 58–66.

Orbach Y., Lamb M. E. (2007). "Young children's references to temporal attributes of allegedly experienced events in the course of forensic interviews", *Child Development*, 78(4), 1100–1120.

Peterson C., Dowden C., Tobin J. (1999). "Interviewing preschoolers: Comparisons of yes/no and wh-questions", *Law and Human Behavior*, 23, 539–555.

Poole D. A. (2016). *Interviews of children: The science of conversation in forensic contexts*, Washington, DC, American Psychological Association.

Poole D. A., Lamb M. E. (1998). *Investigative interviews of children: A guide for helping professionals*, Washington, DC, American Psychological Association.

Poole D. A., Lindsay D. S. (2001). "Children's eyewitness reports after exposure to misinformation from parents", *Journal of Experimental Psychology: Applied*, 7, 27–50.

Powell M. B., Guadagno B., Benson M. (2016). "Improving child investigative interviewer performance through computer-based learning activities", *Policing and Society: An International Journal of Research and Policy*, 26(4), 365–374.

Rischke A. E., Roberts K. P., Price H. L. (2011). "Using spaced learning principles to translate knowledge into behavior: Evidence from investigative interviews of alleged child abuse victims", *Journal of Police and Criminal Psychology*, 26(1), 58–67.

Roberts K. P., Lamb M. E. (1999). "Children's responses when interviewers distort details during investigative interviews", *Legal and Criminological Psychology*, 4, 23–31.

Sayfan L., Mitchell E. B., Goodman G. S., Eisen M. L., Qin J. (2008). "Children's expressed emotions when disclosing maltreatment", *Child Abuse & Neglect*, 32(11), 1026–1036.

Saywitz K. J., Lyon T. D., Goodman G. S. (2011). "Interviewing children", in Myers J. E. B. (Ed.), *The APSAC handbook on child maltreatment* (3rd ed.), Newbury Park, Sage, 337–360.

Schreiber Compo N., Hyman Gregory A., Fisher R. (2012). "Interviewing behaviors in police investigators: A field study of a current US sample", *Psychology, Crime & Law*, 18(4), 359–375.

Stolzenberg S. N., McWilliams K., Lyon T. D. (2017). "Spatial language, question type, and young children's ability to describe clothing: Legal and developmental implications", *Law and Human Behavior*, 41(4), 398–409.

Talwar V., Crossman A. M. (2012). "Children's lies and their detection: Implications for child witness testimony", *Developmental Review*, 32(4), 337–359.

Teoh Y.-S., Lamb M. E. (2010). "Preparing children for investigative interviews: Rapport-building, instruction, and evaluation", *Applied Developmental Science*, 14(3), 154–163.

Tulving E., Thomson D. M. (1973). "Encoding specificity and retrieval processes in episodic memory", *Psychological Review*, 80(5), 352–373.

Walker A. G. (2013). *Handbook on questioning children: A linguistic perspectives*, Washington, DC, ABA Center on Children and the Law.

Wolfman M., Brown D., Jose P. (2016). "Taking stock: Evaluating the conduct of forensic interviews with children in New Zealand", *Psychology, Crime & Law*, 22(6), 581–598.

Yii S.-L. B., Powell M. B., Guadagno B. (2014). "The association between investigative interviewers' knowledge of question type and adherence to best-practice interviewing", *Legal and Criminological Psychology*, 19(2), 270–281.

Chapter 7

Empirical studies on the NICHD Protocol and testimony in court

To date, the NICHD Protocol is the most studied interview protocol, and in the next paragraphs, the main results will be briefly reviewed. Data from various studies examining the effects of the NICHD Protocol use on disclosure, interviewer's questions, and the amount of detail obtained from the child are presented. Next, results of empirical studies about the effect of open-ended questions (invitations) and the accuracy of the details provided by children are examined. Then studies that have examined the effect of using the NICHD Protocol on the court process and on children with intellectual disabilities or other developmental difficulties are discussed. A review of the research addressing the importance of NICHD Protocol training and suggested supervision are presented. The final section discusses recent research on children's testimony in court, even though these are not directly related to the NICHD Protocol. This could be the subject of another book, given the interest that this question has driven among researchers in recent years. However, we limit this examination mainly to the questions and their effects on children's testimony in accordance with the focus of this book.

I   Effectiveness of the Revised NICHD Protocol on child disclosure and narrative

The previous version of the Standard NICHD Protocol (SP) emphasizes cognitive factors associated with children's memory capacities, but less attention is paid to social factors and emotional issues that are associated with reluctance in children (see Chapter 1). The results obtained to date using the Revised NICHD Protocol (RP) concern the disclosure rate, the effect of support during the pre-substantive, transitional, and substantive phases, the effect of the NICHD Protocol on the number of details elicited, and the coherence of the narratives elicited.

A team of researchers (Hershkowitz, Lamb, & Katz, 2014) compared the allegation rates obtained with the use of the RP to the rate obtained using the SP in a study of 426 4- to 13-year-old suspected victims of intrafamilial abuse (sexual or physical). The results indicate that the RP was associated with a significantly higher rate of disclosure (60%) of sexual and physical abuse than the SP (50%). This increase of 10% is quite high, considering that the disclosure of abuse is lower in situations where the parent or an immediate family member is the alleged perpetrator. With the 3- to 13-year-old children who were suspected of being physically abused, the use of the RP led interviewers to offer more support to children who, in turn, required fewer

DOI: 10.4324/9781003265351-7

interventions during the transition phase to reveal their abuse (Ahern, Hershkowitz, Lamb, Blasbalg, & Karni-Visel, 2018). With a sample of 14,874 suspected victims of sexual and physical abuse aged 4 to 14 years, Hershkowitz and Lamb (2020) observe a higher rate of disclosure with the RP (79.07%) than with the SP (76.77%) after controlling for the age of the child, relationship with the perpetrators, type of abuse and the interviewer identity. As expected, higher rates of disclosure were observed in older children (73.2%) compared to younger children (70.9%), suspected victims of sexual abuse (73.3%) compared to suspected victims of physical abuse (71.8%), and suspected perpetrators outside of the family (86.2%) compared to parents, relatives, or caretakers (68.9%). It is important to note that the identity of the interviewer accounted for 12% of the variance in disclosure rates. This study also looked at the credibility assessment made by investigators based on the child's statements and behaviors during the interview and the investigative information available. No judgment was possible for 34.1% of the cases, and no difference was observed according to the version of the NICHD Protocol used. The rate of credible judgments was higher for older children (44% vs. younger children 21.4%), girls (37% vs. boys 31.5%), sexual abuse (42% vs. physical abuse 31.6%), and allegations made about others (50.9% vs. parents, relatives, and caretakers 30.2%). Here, too, the interviewer's identity accounted for 12% of the variance observed in disclosure. After taking into account these variables, allegations obtained with the RP were 10% more likely to be deemed credible than those obtained using the SP. Therefore, these studies indicate that the RP yields a higher disclosure rate and decreases the difficulty obtaining them when the interviewer is supportive, particularly in the pre-substantive phase. In addition, the RP increases the perceived credibility of these children's statements.

One of the main objectives of the RP is to encourage interviewers to use more non-suggestive supportive interventions so as to increase the child's sense of control over his/her involvement and feelings and thus decrease the anxiety and distress experienced during investigative interviews. Indeed, studies had shown that when the child did not collaborate with the interviewer, the latter tended to become more coercive, using option-posing and suggestive questions instead of offering support to the child (Hershkowitz, Orbach, Lamb, Sternberg, & Horowitz, 2006). Other studies have also indicated that interviewers do not adapt their style to children's age or reluctance by offering more support (Lewy, Cyr, & Dion, 2017). Thus, the use of the SP was not associated with many supportive behaviors (Lewy, Cyr, & Dion, 2015), and the presence of non-supportive behaviors predicted the low number of details reported by the children. With the RP, part of the objective to promote cooperation is achieved during the pre-substantive phase since the interviewers gave more supportive interventions than when using the SP, regardless of whether the child had shown signs of reluctance; in other words, interviewers' support did not only occur in response to children's manifestations of reluctance (Ahern, Hershkowitz, Lamb, Blasbalg, & Winstanley, 2014). The support offered using an early version of the RP was present during the pre-substantive phase and the transitional more than in the substantive phase (Hershkowitz, Lamb, Katz, & Malloy, 2015). This had the effect of reducing the reluctance of children during the pre-substantive phase and the substantive phase, although reluctance remained during the transitional phase. Open-ended questioning (invitations and directive questions) promotes disclosure more than closed-ended and specific questions, and these open-ended questions were more frequently used with the RP. It should be noted that although the interviewers were more supportive during the pre-substantive and transition phase when using the RP, this pattern was not maintained during the substantive phase. However, children continued to show less reluctance during the substantive phase despite the absence of supportive comments provided such support was provided in the previous phases of the forensic interview.

Two studies were conducted after further revision of the NICHD Protocol and longer training in conducting interviews using the RP (at least four days) with a focus on detecting and responding supportively to reluctance (Blasbalg, Hershkowitz, & Karni-Visel, 2018; Blasbalg, Hershkowitz, Lamb, Karni-Visel, & Ahern, 2019). A more detailed examination of the sequence of the interactions between the interviewer and the child indicated a decrease in the reluctance of the child when the RP was used. This, in turn, allowed more forensic details to be obtained in both the transitional and substantive phases of the interview. Thus, offering support not only decreased the reluctance of the child but also increased the amount of detail obtained. This could be explained by a decrease in the child's anxiety, an increase in the child's sense of confidence and self-efficacy, or a decrease in the child's degree of distraction. Furthermore, Blasbalg and colleagues (Blasbalg et al., 2019) observe that girls received more supportive interventions and that interviewers used more open-ended utterances during both the transitional and substantive phases, increasing the overall quality of the interview. As suggested by the authors, providing support could replace repetitive questioning in the transitional phase when the child did not disclose the suspected abuse. In addition, a review of forensic interviews with 200 6- to 14-year-old suspected victims of physical abuse perpetrated by a family member indicated that children's reluctance was associated with less coherent narratives (Blasbalg, Hershkowitz, Lamb, & Karni-Visel, submitted). The provision of support when using the RP thus decreased reluctance and increased the coherence (information about spatial and temporal location, chronology, narrative structure, etc.) of the children's narratives. So when the interviewer offers support, it allows reluctant or unwilling children to provide narratives that are better structured, thus making it easier to investigate events and assess the children's credibility.

Finally, the RP was also designed to support children with their emotions and to better use these as cues to elicit more details. This objective is based on recent studies that have shown that emotional content, particularly negative emotions, is better encoded and retained longer in memory (see Karni-Visel, Hershkowitz, Lamb, & Blasbalg, 2019). As expected, the expression of emotions (especially negative emotions) was associated with an increase in informativeness. Negative emotions were also associated with more central and peripherical details. Although children express few emotions (Katz, Paddon, & Barnetz, 2016), the use of the RP allows interviewers to facilitate more varied and frequent expression of emotions than the SP. Specifically, the RP was associated with the expression of more different emotions, more expression of abuse-related emotions, and more expression of emotions related to the interview context than the SP was (Karni-Visel et al., 2019).

In summary, compared to the SP, the RP helps

1   interviewers to

   a   offer more supportive interventions about positive behaviors and fewer negative or non-supportive statements;

b   refer more often to children's emotions, which allows them to obtain more details;

c   in the transitional phase, use more open-ended questions and fewer questions probing recognition memory (option-posing, suggestive questions); and

d   to use more open-ended questions and fewer closed-ended questions during the substantive phase; and

2   children to

a   be less reluctant in the pre-substantive, transitional, and substantive phases and, therefore, make fewer omissions in their answers (e.g., "I don't know," "I'm not sure," no answer, unclear answer), despite the lack of support during the substantive phase; and

b   provide increased numbers of details about the alleged events.

These results also indicate that the main objective pursued in the creation of the NICHD Protocol, which was to encourage the interviewer to use more frequent invitations, was also achieved when using the RP. The results of studies carried out using the SP in Israel (Orbach et al., 2000), in the United States (Sternberg, Lamb, Orbach, Esplin, & Mitchell, 2001), Canada (Cyr & Lamb, 2009; Cyr, Dion, McDuff, & Trotier-Sylvain, 2012) England (Lamb, Orbach, Sternberg et al., 2009), Sweden (Cederborg, Alm, Da Silva Nises, & Lamb, 2013), Japan (Naka, 2011), and Korea (Yi, Jo, & Lamb, 2016) are very convincing about its effectiveness (see also Lamb, Brown, Hershkowitz, Orbach, & Esplin, 2018, La Rooy et al., 2015; Benia, Hauck-Filho, Dillenburg, & Stein, 2015). This research was conducted either with police officers or social workers as interviewers, all of whom were already interviewing children before their training in the use of the NICHD Protocol. Thus, the forensic interviews carried out using the NICHD Protocol could be compared with those carried out by the same investigators in the months/years preceding their training. The results of these studies indicate that interviewers trained in the use of the NICHD Protocol used more invitations and fewer specific questions (directive, option-posing, and suggestive) than they did before the training. Contrary to what was expected, in some studies, the children gave an equal number of total details and central details in the interviews conducted with or without the NICHD Protocol. However, there was one important and consistent difference: more details were obtained in response to invitations and were thus more likely to be accurate. Since children gave much longer answers when interviewed with open-ended questions, investigators used fewer specific questions to get the forensic details they needed. Finally, a greater number of central details (that is to say, those making it possible to document the actions and the context of the abuse) were also obtained in response to the open-ended questions in interviews carried out using the NICHD Protocol.

2   Empirical support for pre-substantive activities

The usefulness of giving instructions to the child about the conversational rules (ground rules) of the interview has been verified in several analog and field studies (see Brubacher, Poole, & Dickinson, 2015, for a review). Thus, to indicate to the child that s/he must correct the interviewer, that s/he can say that s/he does not know the answer, that s/he does not understand the question, that the interviewer does not know what happened, and that it is important to tell the truth all have a positive effect on the child's behavior. The usefulness of these ground rules varies according to the age of the child. Although preschoolers are able to understand and use some of these rules, it is noteworthy that after the age of 7, children are more likely to apply them. Research has also shown the importance of taking the time to practice the ground rule with the child, which increases the likelihood that children will use them (Roberts, Brubacher, Powell, & Price, 2011; Danby, Brubacher, Sharman, & Powell, 2015; Dickinson, Brubacher, & Poole, 2015). In addition, it is important for the interviewer to respect the child's answers, especially when the child indicates that s/he does not know the answer. Indeed, in forensic interviews, research shows that children rarely say "I don't know" in response to questions (on average seven times per interview). But when children do, 30% of the time, the interviewer may not take this answer into account and continue asking other closed-ended questions (Earhart, La Rooy, Brubacher, & Lamb, 2014). Here is an example: I: "Do you remember when it happened?" E: "I don't know." I: "I will help you. Did this happen before or after school?" Although there are still several research questions that need to be investigated on how best to present the ground rules depending on the age of the child, it is currently recommended to communicate these ground rules since it only takes an average of between two and four minutes to do something from which many children may benefit (Lamb et al., 2018).

When creating the NICHD Protocol, its developers verified the effect that episodic memory training could have on children's performance during the substantive phase (Sternberg et al., 1997). Other studies have since been conducted: one examined forensic interviews (Price, Roberts, & Collins, 2013), including memory practice with open-ended questions or not, and two others carried out in an analog context (Brown, Lamb, Lewis, Pipe, Orbach, & Wolfman, 2013; Roberts, Lamb, & Sternberg, 2004). All these studies converge toward the same conclusion, namely that when the practice of episodic memory retrieval regarding a recent and pleasant event includes open-ended invitations, the children give much longer answers during the substantive phase than children who had not had any training or whose training included only specific questions (directive, option-posing). This effect is observed from the first response, in which children provide two and a half times more details than children trained using narrow questions. Moreover, examination of the interviews indicated that the answers to the first question provided important forensic details, such as describing some actions committed and the identity of the perpetrator. In a similar context, the researchers noted that children trained using open-ended questions added a few erroneous details in their first response, but overall they provided more accurate answers than children who were trained using specific questions. In addition, trained children are more efficient since they take less time to provide detailed narratives. This has a double effect: first, on the total number of questions (that decreases as the interviewer continues to use open questioning in the substantive phase) and, second, on the shorter duration of the substantive phase of the interview. It, therefore, seems that rapport building and episodic memory practice allow the child to give a more coherent and detailed account of any abuse experienced. These results confirm that it is possible to shape children's behavior during forensic interviews and thus improve their performance.

Finally, Brubacher and colleagues (Brubacher, Roberts, & Powell, 2011) observe in an analog study that when multiple events are to be reported, training the child's episodic memory by focusing on a specific instance of an event that occurred frequently (e.g., "Tell me more about your last piano lesson?") benefited 5- and 6-year-old children more than 7- and 8-year-olds. These children reported more relevant details and showed awareness of the repeated nature of the activity sessions. These children also continued providing an episodic description of the event, while those whose episodic memory training focused on generic memory ("Tell me more about your piano lessons") were more likely to provide generic narratives not linked to a specific episode in the substantive phase of the interview.

Another aspect that is part of the NICHD Protocol and that has been empirically tested is how to elicit information when the child has been repeatedly abused. Thus, Hershkowitz (2001) observes that when several events have occurred, separating them into distinct events results in the elicitation of a greater number of details. Focusing on a precise event helps the child to describe elements specific to each episode, which is essential for the purposes of the investigation. In addition, this avoids collecting information from script memory (see Chapter 2), which is known to be poorer since it only concerns the shared and repetitive elements of the events experienced.

It is noteworthy that two field studies (Sternberg et al., 2001; Yi et al., 2016) have shown that in NICHD Protocol interviews, interviewers were more likely to introduce themselves, outline the ground rules, and provide the children with episodic memory practice opportunities.

3   Effect of invitations and children's capacities

One may wonder about the ability of young children to respond in detail to invitations. Several studies conducted using the NICHD Protocol (Cyr & Lamb, 2009; Gagnon & Cyr, 2017; Hershkowitz, 2001; Hershkowitz, Lamb, Orbach, Katz, & Horowitz, 2012; Lamb et al., 1996; Lamb et al., 2003; Orbach et al., 2000; Sternberg et al., 2001, to name a few) have shown that children gave more detailed and lengthy answers to open-ended questions (invitations) than to more specific questions like directive or option-posing questions. The majority of the field studies conducted using the NICHD Protocol were carried out with children aged between 4 and 13 or 14 years. When the studies have looked closely at the degree to which younger children (4- to 6-year-olds and 7- to 8-years-olds) could provide informative details in response to invitations, results consistently showed that they could (Orbach & Lamb, 2000; Sternberg et al., 2001). With a larger group of young children aged 4 to 8 years, Lamb et al. (2003) confirmed again the superiority of all types of invitations over more specific questions to elicit forensically relevant details from children of all ages, although older children gave more detailed accounts. In addition, invitations including action cues elicited more details than time segmentation did. Invitations involving time segmentation are effective from the age of 4 but are much more effective from the age of 8; children of this age have a greater cognitive capacity and a better mastery of temporal concepts. Hershkowitz (2001) observes with children aged 4 to 13 years that the main invitation, which initiated the children's narratives, elicited the longest and most detailed responses. In preschoolers, another study (Gagnon & Cyr, 2017) observes that invitations or open-ended directive questions ("How did he touch your buttocks?") that include cues were more effective than simple invitations ("Tell me more about that"). Hershkowitz and colleagues (Hershkowitz et al., 2012) also report the superiority of invitations with respect to the amount of detail obtained from children aged 3 to 6, although children aged 3 and 4 gave as many details in response to directive questions and invitations, which is explained by the fact that their answers are always relatively short. In a similar study with a staged event in school "to meet the photographer," Brown and colleagues (2013) observe that cued invitations and time-segmenting invitations help to collect more details than general invitations ("Tell me more about that") and directive or option-posing questions from children aged 5 to 7. Additionally, cued invitations were the most effective at eliciting central event details.

Also, Hershkowitz (2001) observes that the first invitation that leads the child to talk about abuse is the one that provides the most details, with an average of 13% of the total information provided. According to her, this is explained by the fact that the child came to understand his/her important role as an informant during the episodic memory training exercise. It should also be noted that the use of invitations supported by facilitators (e.g., "hum-hum," "yes," "OK," repeating the child's sentence) allows for more details (Lamb et al., 1996). This also sends the child a clear signal that the interviewer is listening to his/her response and is interested in knowing more.

With a slightly different purpose, a study has examined and compared the accounts provided by victims and witnesses (Lamb Sternberg, Orbach, Hershkowitz, & Horowitz, 2003). They compared the NICHD interviews with 26 witnesses of 5 to 14 years and 26 victims matched with respect to their age, relationships with the alleged perpetrator, and seriousness of the alleged offenses. Results revealed that, overall, witnesses and victims provided the same amount of information, but the amount of detail differed with respect to age, with children under 9 giving less detailed accounts. Invitations elicited longer descriptions from witnesses (38%) than victims (22%), and the opposite was true for option-posing questions (11% vs. 22%, respectively). The researchers also noted that interviewers were more suggestive with the victims, of whom they asked more option-posing questions to victims, whereas they addressed more invitations to witnesses. These results confirmed that the NICHD Protocol is suitable for witnesses and suspected victims. The difference in the number of details observed could be attributed to many factors, such as the victims having been more stressed by their abusive experience (thereby affecting the amount of detail encoded), victims having been more ashamed or embarrassed describing the event, or that the lower use of invitations with the victims did not allow them to describe their experience in as much detail.

In summary, children of all ages give longer and more detailed answers to open-ended questions than to other types of questions, whether they are directive questions, yes-or-no questions, or suggestive questions. The length and depth of their response, however, is directly related to the child's age. Young children provide more information when the open-ended questions include a cue that they themselves provided in their narratives. In addition, cued invitations that include an action verb prompt the child to provide more details. Although the results of these studies do not all agree on the effectiveness of time-segmenting invitations according to age, their possible utility should be tested during the episodic memory training exercise since some children of 4 and 5 years old do manage to respond informatively.

4 The accuracy of details obtained

An important problem facing the interviewer to whom children disclose abuse is the inability to check the accuracy of the accounts obtained since, generally, there are no witnesses of the abuse reported. This is especially true in the case of sexual abuse. In the analog study by Brown and colleagues (2013) carried out using the NICHD Protocol with children aged 5 to 7 years, the answers given in response to invitations were generally accurate. However, they noted that the details obtained were sometimes wrong and that these inaccuracies more often concerned the peripheral details (secondary details) than the central details (details relating to the actions and the course of the event). The mistakes mostly occurred when using cued invitations aimed at specific details, such as the description of the pirate costume, for instance. So like all other types of questions, repetition or insistent focus on specific details can lead children to provide incorrect information, even in response to invitations.

Orbach and Lamb (1999) reported on a case study of a 13-year-old girl who was abused numerous times by her grandfather and who had audio-recorded the last event. The content revealed during the interview could be compared with the information contained in the audio recording, as well as the report made by a sister, who was in the presence of the victim when the grandfather entered the bathroom, and finally to the details provided by the grandfather when he was questioned. The results indicate that 50.8% of the details reported by the victim were corroborated by the audio recording; 97.9% of these were central details. The majority of the unsubstantiated details were action descriptions (e.g., "He tried to take my pants off"), which could not be verified or contradicted by the audio recording. Only 7% of the central details that could theoretically have been verified using the audio recording could not be corroborated. In addition, 36% of the details reported by the victim were also confirmed by questioning the suspect, and 75% were confirmed by the victim's sister. No detail reported by the victim was contradicted by any witness or the recording. It is important to note that 93.6% of the details obtained from the victim were obtained in response to invitations.

In another study by Lamb and colleagues (Lamb, Orbach, Hershkowitz, Horowitz, & Abbott, 2007), accounts provided by 52 young suspects who confessed to having committed sexual abuse were compared to those of the 43 victims. Seventy-one percent of the details reported by suspects confirmed the information provided by the victims in response to invitations, while only 28.7% of the details provided by suspects contradicted the information reported by victims. The low rate of contradiction between the accounts of the victims and that of the suspects can be explained by the fact that only cooperating suspects (i.e., those who partially or fully admitted the allegations) were included in this study.

The results of these three studies converge on the fact that the use of invitations in NICHD Protocol interviews elicits information that is accurate even though informants never provide 100% of the possible information because events are never fully encoded, and some details are almost always forgotten (see Chapter 2). Accuracy for children with intellectual disabilities is reported in the subsequent sections.

5   The effect of the protocol on credibility and the judicial process

Assessing the credibility of a child's testimony poses many challenges for which we still have few answers. In this context, Hershkowitz and colleagues (Hershkowitz, Fisher, Lamb, & Horowitz, 2007) examined the extent to which the use of the NICHD Protocol facilitated the judgment of stakeholders as to the credibility of children who had participated in forensic interviews. The researchers compared evaluations of twelve interviews made using the NICHD Protocol and twelve others made without the protocol. Half of these interviews had been classified as plausible cases by three independent experts on the basis of "ground truth" information, such as external evidence, including suspect admissions, witness statements, medical findings, and material evidence. Half of the cases were considered implausible allegations because such evidence was weak or nonexistent. Forty-two experienced interviewers were then asked to classify the statements provided as plausible or implausible using a 5-point scale. For implausible allegations, the rate of agreement between the evaluators' judgments was higher for interviews conducted using the NICHD Protocol than for those conducted without the NICHD Protocol ($\alpha = 0.64$ versus $\alpha = 0.34$). This significant difference was not apparent in the assessment of plausible interviews ($\alpha = 0.81$ versus $\alpha = 0.89$). Only 16.7% of the interviews conducted using the NICHD Protocol could not be classified as plausible or implausible, while this percentage was 52.4% for the other interviews. In addition, 60% of the ratings of the interviews made by the evaluators were accurate when the NICHD Protocol had been used compared with less than a third (29.6%) for the interviews conducted without the NICHD Protocol. These results, therefore, indicate that experienced investigators were twice as likely to accurately judge children's credibility when forensic interviews were performed using the NICHD Protocol, indicating that the use of the NICHD Protocol not only improves the quality of children's narratives but also facilitates the assessment of children's credibility; this is particularly impressive given the lack of other tools to assess credibility.

Pipe and colleagues (Pipe, Orbach, Lamb, Abbott, & Stewart, 2013) examined the impact of using the NICHD Protocol on prosecution decisions and court proceedings. To do this, they analyzed cases with children aged 3 to 14 years who had been interviewed using (N = 350) and not using (N = 410) the NICHD Protocol by the same police department. In total, 47.9% of cases resulted in filed charges. Regression analyzes indicate that the use of the NICHD Protocol was the primary factor predicting whether charges would be filed in these cases (52.9% versus 42%). Thus, an interview performed using the NICHD Protocol is 1.46 times more likely to lead to a charge, presumably indicating that the child's account was more comprehensive and more credible. The other factors associated with a charge being filed were the suspect's age (juvenile suspects rather than adults; 58.9% versus 43.6%;), the suspect's gender (95% were male), victims being over the age of 5 (2–4 years: 31.1%; 5–6 years: 42.8%; 7–9 years: 54.9%; 10–13 years: 50.8%), abuse that involved penetration (60.3% versus 41% for exposure and 34.8% for touch/fondling), and suspects who are not members of the immediate family (56.2% for extended family versus 44.1% for immediate family). In addition, the use of the NICHD Protocol was associated with decreases in the number of cases that were declined for prosecution (17.6% with the protocol and 28% without). Finally, although few cases involved trials, which is consistent with what typically happens in cases of child sexual abuse (Cross, Walsh, Simone, & Jones, 2003), guilty verdicts were obtained in 10 of the 11 cases that included an interview using the NICHD Protocol, while only 6 of the 12 trials resulted in such a verdict when the interview was not conducted using the NICHD Protocol.

In a study of the factors that influence prosecutors' decisions to proceed with charges that have been filed in Canada (Alonzo-Proulx & Cyr, 2017), the use of the NICHD Protocol in the forensic interviews led to a six times greater probability that the case would proceed to trial. Regression analyses also revealed that the amount of evidence corroborated by the suspect and by a witness, the presence of maternal protection, adherence to the NICHD Protocol guidance, and the length of the substantive part of the interviews predicted increases in the likelihood that the case would lead to criminal charges, while the young age of the child reduced this probability.

This research, therefore, provides important support for the use of the NICHD Protocol when interviewing children. Because of the length and quality of the accounts obtained, these forensic interviews have an effect on the other stages of the criminal justice process. Indeed, more charges are filed against suspects, and many of these cases are settled by plea agreement or by trial.

6   The NICHD Protocol and children with developmental disabilities

Several studies have been carried out to better understand the capacities of children with various developmental problems, including children with intellectual disabilities, those with autism spectrum disorder, and those with attention deficit hyperactivity disorder. A total of ten studies have focused on the effect of children's intellectual capacities on their performance during interviews using the NICHD Protocol, half in a forensic interview context and half in analog studies.

In an analog study (Brown et al., 2019) that compared children with mild and moderately severe intellectual disabilities with typically developing children matched for mental and chronological ages, researchers observed that level of development was directly related with the performance while learning the ground rules (telling the truth, saying "I don't know" when appropriate, and correcting the interviewer) and their use during the interview. Children with higher mental age and older children passed all rules, but a minority (44%), including more children with the lowest mental ages or with cognitive impairments, failed to implement at least one of the rules. Performance applying these rules was associated with accuracy during the interview, again as a function of developmental level. These results also underlined the importance of being careful with suggestive interventions since, even if children understand the rules, it is not certain that they will be able to use them at the appropriate time, and this is even more true for children with cognitive impairments.

Regarding the capacity to disclose abuse, children with minor and severe disabilities failed to disclose and delayed the disclosure of abuse more often than typically developing children, and this is true for both sexual and physical abuse (Hershkowitz, Horowitz, & Lamb, 2007). In another study, a graduated relationship between long-term memory capacities and disclosure has been noted: children who have better long-term memory make disclosures that are deemed to be well-founded, while children with weaker long-term memory capacities do not disclose or produce allegations that are deemed ambiguous (Cyr, Dion, & McDuff, submitted).

Although children with poor verbal skills provide fewer details than those with a normal verbal intelligence quotient (IQ) (Brown, Lewis, Lamb, & Stephens, 2012; Brown, Lewis, & Lamb, 2015; Dion & Cyr, 2008; Hershkowitz, 2018; Hershkowitz, Horowitz & Lamb, 2007), these children provided relevant information about the crucial elements of the abuse from the start of the interview (e.g., name of suspect, location, type of abuse) (Dion & Cyr, 2008). Children with mild disabilities provided more accurate details in response to open-ended questions than did children with severe disabilities (Brown et al., 2012; Brown et al., 2015). In addition, even in response to more focused questions, children with disabilities did not make more mistakes than those with typical development, although all were less accurate in their answers when questioned with focused (direct and option-posing) questions instead of invitations. For both children with mild and moderate intellectual disabilities and those without developmental delays, more errors were noted when the interviews took place after delays of six months rather than only one week. The level of accuracy was very high (89%) after a week and was lower (75%) at six months (Brown et al., 2012). Children with intellectual disabilities were able to answer open-ended questions, particularly cued invitations and directive questions, and children with mild intellectual disabilities performed at a level equivalent to children of the same mental age as them (Brown et al., 2012; Brown et al., 2015). Interviewers asked children with moderate or mild intellectual disabilities more questions than other children, which may be because the children with intellectual disabilities gave shorter answers (Brown, Lewis, Stephens, & Lamb, 2017; Hershkowitz, 2018). These children were also able to communicate key features of their experience in their narratives, offering a degree of coherence that allowed listeners to better appreciate their accounts (Brown, Brown, Lewis, & Lamb, 2018). More specifically, children with moderate intellectual disabilities reported fewer markers of chronology, content, and context than those with mild impairment or typically developing children of the same mental or chronological age. In summary, in children with mild intellectual disabilities, one should expect a performance similar to that of children of the same mental age, while those with a moderate intellectual disability may give less information.

Almeida, Lamb, and Weisblatt (2019) compared the abilities of children with autism to that of typically developing children of the same chronological age, two weeks and two months after an experienced event. The interview was conducted using an adaptation of the Revised NICHD Protocol. The results showed that autistic children recalled fewer correct details about the experience than children without autism. On the other hand, autistic children reported fewer details in response to invitations, cued invitations, and directive questions, but these details were as accurate as those provided by typically developing children. For both groups, cued invitations were particularly effective at eliciting details, even after a two-month delay (87% accuracy vs. 91% accuracy after two weeks). Therefore, autistic children are able to answer open-ended questions accurately, and cued invitations are a good tool to support them in this process because they allow the event to be divided into small units of time (time segmentation) or to focus on revealed actions (cued). Their performance after a delay is similar to that of typically developing children and, for all, reflects a drop in the amount of detail reported. It should be noted, however, that some inaccurate details may also appear in response to open-ended and directive questions, but significantly more incorrect details were reported in response to option-posing questions after two months. The interviewer should carefully plan his/her interview and obtain all relevant information about the child's functioning to guide him/her during the interview (see the grid in appendix 7). In addition, with autistic children, it may be useful to indicate on a sheet the different stages of the interview to give the child a visual reference and thus reduce his/her anxiety.

As for children with attention deficit and hyperactivity (ADHD) symptoms, two studies (Malloy, Mugno, Pelham, Hawk, & Lamb, 2016 and McLay, Brown, Palmer, Beaumont, cited in Lamb et al., 2018) were conducted to compare them with children without ADHD. In the first one, children were interviewed using the NICHD Protocol about a staged event that included an instance of wrongdoing by the experimenter. In the second study, the interview was about a health and safety event that took place at school. No group differences were noted in the overall amount of information, coherence, or suggestibility between, on the one hand, children with ADHD symptoms (as rated by parents and teachers) and, on the other hand, children without these symptoms. There were, however, subtle differences: children with ADHD were more likely to give irrelevant responses and to make ambiguous statements that required more questions. The answers provided by these children also provided less information about the social context surrounding the event, its outcome, or its consequences. Overall, the research on children with developmental difficulties consistently indicate that children with intellectual disabilities can perform well when interviewed using the NICHD Protocol.

7   Protocol training and supervision

An important question about the use of the NICHD Protocol concerns the development of interviewer competencies and their maintenance. As far as the Revised NICHD Protocol is concerned, four studies inform us about effective training and skills development. In one, a two-day training course was offered to seven interviewers who were already using the Standard NICHD Protocol in their interviewer duties. These two days focused on the peculiarities and reasons behind the modifications to the Standard NICHD Protocol and included practical applications. That training was sufficient to ensure that the interviewers offered more support to the children, especially in the pre-substantive part of the interview (Hershkowitz, Lamb, Katz, & Malloy, 2015), although this support was not adapted appropriately to the children's signals of reluctance (Ahern et al., 2014). Noting these results, the training was modified to add eight additional sessions using a train-the-trainer approach and encouraging interviewers to learn how to become their own trainers (i.e., showing them how to analyze and assess their own interviews). These eight sessions, delivered over a period of one year, included one group meeting per month, as well as two-hour individual supervision covering the interviews carried out during this period. The objective was to get the interviewers to better recognize the signs of active and passive reluctance and cooperation in children, to identify the support required for these different manifestations, and to detect the moments when support could have been offered during the interview. Halfway through this series of training sessions, the researchers

(Blasbalg et al., 2018) observe that in addition to providing more supportive behaviors during the transitional phase, they were also providing increased support during the substantive phase. Furthermore, the children's reluctant behaviors decreased, and interviewers used more open-ended questions and fewer closed-ended questions than when using the Standard NICHD Protocol. These results, therefore, demonstrate that among a sample of 4- to 14-year-old alleged victims of physical abuse, more extensive training accompanied by individual feedback not only made for better interview strategies but also increased cooperativeness and informativeness. In another study, results obtained from 321 interviews of children aged 3 to 14 years indicated that missed opportunities to offer support decreased between the second and third training session and that the support offered increased with each session. Also, inadequate support decreased gradually over the course of the training (Hershkowitz, Ahern, Lamb, Blasbalg, Karni-Visel, & Breitman, 2017).

The recommendation that post-training follow-up be offered following initial training is also supported by several studies carried out in the field and, more specifically, in those using the NICHD protocol (see Lamb, 2016; Lamb et al., 2018). Thus, three studies have shown that when interviewers receive a week of training and feedback on their interviews after the training, they use more invitation type questions and obtain more details using these questions when interviewing alleged victims (Cyr et al., 2012; Lamb et al., 2002; Price & Roberts, 2011). The results indicate that the absence of feedback is accompanied by a loss in skills and that the number of specific questions asked increases as the number of invitations declines utterances (Cyr et al., 2012; Lamb et al., 2002). Therefore, the findings indicate, as expected, that the number of invitations increases with the use of the NICHD Protocol, but this increase is greater when feedback is provided on real interviews after the classroom training. In addition, Price and Roberts (2011) observe that after initial NICHD Protocol training (two-day session followed weekly by written and oral feedback on interviews), the addition of a training refresher of an additional two days offered every two months made it possible to increase the quality of the interviews, thereby underlining the value of training spaced out over time. A recent study (Cyr, Dion, Gendron, Powell & Brubacher, 2021) aimed to compare the effectiveness of refresher training modalities (1) supervision with an expert, (2) peer group supervision, and (3) computer-assisted exercises on the maintenance of interviewing skills by interviewers using the Standard NICHD Protocol. Results show that the three modalities were effective at increasing adherence to the structure of the NICHD Protocol. With regards to the types of questions asked, all three training modalities helped interviewers to increase the number of invitations posed and to decrease the number of suggestive questions asked. These results thus demonstrated the value of offering post-training refresher interventions. The time devoted in this study to the refresher activities (three sessions of three hours over nine months) was probably not intensive enough to achieve more extensive changes.

Related to training is the choice of interviewers. Performing investigative interviews with children using the NICHD Protocol requires both cognitive skills to structure the interview and formulate appropriate open-ended questions, interpersonal skills to create a relationship of trust, and flexibility to adapt to the developmental capacities and reluctance of children. Lafontaine and Cyr (2016a) documented, with twenty-four investigators who attended a one-week training course on the NICHD Protocol, the effect of these variables on their performance during a simulated interview with an actor playing the role of a child victim of sexual abuse. Cognitive skills, the "openness to experience" personality trait, and being a woman were personal characteristics that were positively related to interview performance, while the number of years of experience and their stress management skills were negatively related to interview performance. In another study involving 114 interviews conducted with children by thirteen investigators trained to use the NICHD Protocol, the results differed slightly (Lafontaine & Cyr, 2016b). Results indicated that emotional intelligence and the personality traits of extraversion, conscientiousness, and agreeableness were personal characteristics positively associated with adherence to the NICHD Protocol structure and the use of open-ended questions, while the number of years of experience and the neuroticism personality trait were negatively associated with these two performance criteria. The level of cognitive skills of the investigators showed a positive association with the amount of information recounted by the child. It emerges from the two studies mentioned here that cognitive and relational skills are characteristics that allow better performance of investigators. Further studies are required in order to continue to better identify the personal characteristics that are related to better use of the NICHD Protocol.

8   Testimony in court

Over the past few years, research has increased on the abilities of children who testify in court. In the context of this book, we focus on studies that have focused on the questions asked, their complexity, the intended content, and repetition of questions, as well as their effect on children's responses and the children's ability to indicate their uncertainty and to deal with challenges to their credibility. The majority of these studies have been carried out either in England and New Zealand, where the videotaped forensic interviews are played in court, or in the United States, where the child gives testimony without regard to the existence of a filmed interview and is then cross-examined by the defense lawyer.

8.1   Questions

On the basis of all the research carried out on children's memory and suggestibility, it would appear that open-ended questions should be asked in court in order to obtain detailed and accurate testimony. Thus, the use of open-ended questions by prosecutors could increase the amount of detail reported in the child's testimony and increase their credibility. Contrary to these recommendations, several studies have shown that prosecutors, like defense lawyers, use more closed-ended than open-ended questions (Andrews, Lamb, & Lyon, 2015a, Hanna, Davies, Crothers, & Henderson, 2012; Klemfuss, Quas, & Lyon, 2014; Powell, Westera, Goodman-Delahunty, & Pichler, 2016; Stolzenberg & Lyon, 2014; Zajac & Cannan, 2009). However, prosecutors use significantly more invitations and directive and option-posing questions than defense lawyers, who use significantly more suggestive questions. For example, Andrews, Lamb, and Lyon (2015a) observe, when examining the testimonies of children under the age of 12, that the proportion of invitations was almost zero, both for prosecutors (3%) and for defense (0%). Option-posing questions (prosecutor 52% and defense 46%) were the most frequent. Prosecutors used more directive questions (29%) and fewer suggestive questions (16%) than defense lawyers, who asked more suggestive questions (42%) than directive questions (13%).

A careful examination of directive questions asked in court (Andrews, Ahern, Stolzenberg, & Lyon, 2016) tells us that prosecutors ask more directive questions ("how," "what") about what happened, about the dynamic ("How did it affect you?"), and about the child's evaluation ("How do you feel about him?"), whereas defense lawyers ask more questions about static elements that refer to the context (place, time, object: "What color was his shirt?"). This is in line with their motivation for questioning since by focusing on more peripheral details, it is more likely that the children will not respond, not know the answer, or contradict themselves. Children's memory for actions is better than that for contextual descriptions or their subjective or cognitive assessments of the event. Interestingly, children's responses to questions about causality ("How do you remember that?" "Why did he come?") were more developed when prosecutors rather than defense lawyers asked these questions, indicating that children were able to provide explanations when they feel they trust the person asking the question.

So the difficulties that children face when testifying do not arise only in cross-examination since prosecutors use more closed-ended than open-ended questions. The results for age are more inconsistent given the small samples in some studies and the large age differences. Some studies have reported more option-posing questions addressed to the youngest (Klemfuss et al., 2014; Stolzenberg and Lyon, 2014) and an increase in suggestive questions among the oldest (Klemfuss et al., 2014), while other studies have not found differences associated with the age of the children and adolescents involved (Andrews, Lamb, and Lyon, 2015a; Powell et al., 2016; Zajac, Gross, and Hayne, 2003).

According to Andrews et al. (2016), the explanation for these results lies in the fact that prosecutors deliberately avoid using invitations for two reasons. First, they carefully structure their examination, based on the child's previous revelations, around the charges in the file and any legal submissions informing the jury of what the child is going to talk about so they do not want new details popping up, which may happen if they ask invitations. Second, it is a common belief that asking for a free account is likely to raise an objection, knowing that anything the child can report about interactions with the accused is admissible in court. As for defense lawyers who want to limit the focus of their argument and limit the witness's report, invitations are not the right tool. They are encouraged to ask closed suggestive questions. Thus, directive questions are also little used because, like invitations, they create the opposite effect of closed-ended questions by prompting unconstrained, less predictable, and perhaps unwanted responses.

The complexity of the questions asked – whether defined by the vocabulary used, the number of questions or the number of clauses in the question, the number of words, the length of the words, false starts, or the length of the question – is another factor that affects the type and quality of responses obtained. For example, Andrews and Lamb (2017a) note that defense lawyers tend to ask more complex questions than prosecutors, confirming the results of other research (Powell et al., 2016; see Zajac, O'Neill, & Hayne, 2012, for a review). On average, simple questions are characterized by interventions that include a question consisting of a single sentence of 14 relatively short words, with few false starts or hesitations. Complex questions contain an average of 4 sentences per intervention and 2.5 propositions. Lawyers do not modify their questions according to the age of the child, and thus, younger ones tend to be asked as many complex questions as older ones. During their testimony, as the complexity of the questions increases, children become less likely to answer, express incomprehension, or contradict themselves. This, too, may influence the way in which children's testimonies are judged.

Klemfuss et al. (2014) also observe that defense lawyers, though not prosecutors, tend to abandon option-posing questions as children get older in order to ask more suggestive questions. This may be explained by the fact that suggestive questions allow both prosecutors and defense lawyers to include their interpretation of how the event unfolded in the question, and their confidence in the witness's tendency to respond in an expected way increases with age. Another observation from this research, which needs to be replicated in further studies, is that if one lawyer increases their suggestive question rate more than the other lawyer, the case is more likely to end favorably, either an acquittal for the defense lawyers or a conviction for the prosecutors. When both lawyers use a similar proportion of suggestive questions, it has no impact on the case outcome.

Another category of closed-ended questions (i.e., those worded like "Do you know?" or "Do you remember?") are also difficult questions for children who tend to answer them literally instead of answering the implicit content of the question. Often these questions lead to short yes-or-no answers to which it is difficult to identify which part of the question the child is addressing. For example, when "Do you know what alcohol smells like?" is asked, a yes answer could mean either "Yes, I know" or "Yes, I smelled it." Likewise, when "Do you remember if it was at home?" is asked, a yes answer can mean "Yes, I remember, but it may not have happened at home," just as it can mean "Yes, it happened at home." These questions are very common in the context of the court. A review of the testimony of children aged 4 to 9 (Evans, Stolzenberg, & Lyon, 2017) indicated that all children were asked to answer these types of questions, on average, 21 times. Both prosecutors (49%) and defense lawyers (50%) frequently used these questions. Ambiguous yes-or-no responses are observed between 26% (when they include directive questions [where, when, what, how, what; for example, "Do you remember where it happened?"]) and 48% (when they involve a question offering a choice, like "Do you remember going into the house?") of the time. A third of the time (22% to 37%), lawyers did not ask further questions to clarify the ambiguity caused by a yes-or-no response. With directive questions, older children tend to respond with a more elaborate response, while no effect of age is noted for yes-or-no questions, suggesting that at age 9, children are still not aware of the ambiguity of their responses.

8.2 The effect of questions on the quality of testimony

Children give less appropriate and less lengthy accounts in response to defense lawyers than to prosecutors (Andrews et al., 2015a; Andrews & Lamb, 2016; Klemfuss et al., 2014). There is little difference by age regarding the appropriateness of answers, although young children tend to give prosecutors shorter answers. However, with regard to suggestive questions, it should be noted that 70% of the time, children tend to answer affirmatively, more often when they are asked by defense lawyers than by prosecutors (Andrews & Lamb, 2016). Powell et al. (2016) report compliance rates of 74% and 75% for those under 12 and between 13 and 17, respectively, which is significantly higher than for adults (56%). They also observe that children under 12 asked for clarification less often (1.1%) than adolescents (2.1%) or adults (2.7%), although this behavior was infrequent. In addition, suggestive questions that ask for confirmation or approval with respect to what has just been stated ("You are not telling the truth, are you?") and those that affirm a content ("But you remember that he didn't speak?") are particularly difficult for children because they are highly persuasive. In court, suggestive questions seeking approval accounted for 6% of questions from prosecutors and 25% of questions from defense lawyers (Andrews & Lamb, 2016), and suggestive questions affirming content amounted to 12% for prosecutors and 29% for defense lawyers. Children provide fewer new details in response to these questions and are more likely to nod. Given the context, however, it is difficult to determine what percentage of these nods are inaccurate.

Part of this answer, however, is suggested by examining the number of contradictions. The way questions are formulated also affects the number of contradictions on the part of children in court. Although the total number of contradictions was low in their study, Andrews and Lamb (2016) note that 95% of the children contradicted themselves at least once in court, with 85.8% contradicting themselves in response to prosecutors and 90.8% in response to defense lawyers. However, this percentage can reach 100% of children when the suggestive question rate is higher (Andrews & Lamb, 2016; Andrews et al., 2015a; Powell et al., 2016; Zajac et al., 2003; Zajac & Cannan, 2009). The number of contradictions also varies depending on which lawyer is involved: between 0 and 2.7% of responses during the interaction with the prosecutors and from 3.6% to 6.5% with the defense lawyers. Suggestive questions lead to more contradictions than any other type of question, and option-posing questions lead to more contradictions than directive questions. It is important to stress that adolescents are not immune to contradictions since, in response to suggestive questions, children between the ages of 13 and 15 years old contradict themselves more often than younger or older children.

We have already pointed out (see chapter on suggestibility) that repeating a question is often interpreted by children, especially by younger children, as an indication that they have given a wrong answer or that their answer does not satisfy the interview and, consequently, this may lead them to modify it. In the court setting, questions are often repeated, and one may wonder what effect these repetitions have on the children's testimony. Studies carried out in the United States (Andrews et al., 2015b), in Scotland (Andrews & Lamb, 2017b), and in Australia (Powell et al., 2016) indicate that a significant percentage of questions are repeated by prosecutors (from 17.8% to 30.6% of questions) and by defense lawyers (from 33.6% to 39.6% of questions). The study by Powell and her colleagues find much lower rates with an average of 5% of questions repeated by prosecutors and 14% by defense lawyers. The questions were repeated only once in 30.8% to 38.5% of cases, while 61.5% to 69.2% were repeated more than once. Contrary to what has been observed in laboratory studies, younger children did not change their response more often than older children, even when they were asked more repeated questions. In fact, children repeated the same answer 60% to 74% of the time, elaborated 14% to 31% of the time, and contradicted themselves only between 10% and 11% of the time (Andrews et al., 2015b; Andrews & Lamb,

2017b). In addition, defense lawyers repeated more questions and these repetitions more often involved suggestive questions (52% versus 18% for prosecutors), and this causes more contradictions than in response to questions asked by prosecutors who use more option-posing questions and directive questions (Andrews & Lamb, 2017b). Finally, the interval between repeated questions is an important factor since the contradictions are more numerous when there is an interval between the questions than when the same question is repeated twice in a row (Andrews & Lamb, 2017b). It is surprising, given the high number of repeated questions, that few objections are made by prosecutors. In their study, Andrew and her colleagues (Andrews et al., 2015b) observe that an objection was raised by prosecutors only in 28 of the 118 trials examined while, on 61 occasions, a question was repeated more than nine times. The judge dismissed the objection more than half of the time (27/47), even though more than half of these questions had been repeated more than once.

8.3   Children's ability to express their uncertainty

In court, the accuracy and completeness of a child's account are important, especially in sexual abuse cases since the child is often the only source of evidence. The ability of children to signify their uncertainty is important since, in this way, they avoid inventing or choosing an answer when they do not know, either because the information is wrong, because it was not saved in memory, or because they do not remember the answer. In their study, Andrews and colleagues (Andrews, Ahern, & Lamb, 2017) observe that, during the entire duration of their testimony, only 38% of children were told that they could say they did not know the answer to a question. When offered, this warning was not accompanied by an increase in the amount of uncertainty expressed by children. Surprisingly, only 15% of children admitted uncertainty because the questions were often very specific, complex, and related to events that happened sometime before. They also noted that children between the ages of 13 and 15 were the ones who expressed the least uncertainty, particularly in response to invitations and directive questions. Adolescents may be more concerned about their perceived credibility (maturity and confidence) and may not fully understand the importance of stating when they do not know the answer. Moreover, since adults (jury members or lawyers) tend to overestimate the cognitive and linguistic abilities of adolescents, it is not surprising that they conform to these expectations. As for content, children were more likely to express uncertainty in response to questions from defense lawyers about central aspects of their testimony, perhaps because these questions were intended to discredit their testimony by confronting important aspects of their account. It is important to observe that there is no necessary association between the admission of uncertainty by children and the amount of detail provided or other manifestations of reluctance. So it seems that when children are allowed to exercise full control over their memory and their narrative, they are able to acknowledge flaws in their memory without this implying less cooperation.

8.4   Confrontations and challenges

Other studies have focused mainly on defense lawyers' questions designed to cast doubt on the child witnesses' credibility (Szojka, Andrews, Lamb, Stolzenberg, &

Lyon, 2017; Powell et al., 2016; Zajac et al., 2003; see Zajac et al., 2012, for a review). While the purpose of cross-examination is to test the witness, some questions directly address his/her reliability. These questions can be of a general nature and cast doubt on the honesty, the quality of the memory that would be incomplete or inconsistent, the victim's motivations, behavioral problems, good relations with the alleged perpetrators, lack of reluctance during the abuse, late disclosure of the facts, and the possible influence of adults on his/her testimony (parent, investigator, etc.). The questions can also be specific and highlight inconsistencies by omitting or add-ing information during testimony and cross-examination or between the videotaped interview and interventions in court. Studies tell us that the credibility of the victim will be called into question for the majority, if not all, of the trials examined; the percentage (85% to 100%) varies according to the strategy used (Powell et al., 2016; Szojka et al., 2017). Of all the questions asked by defense lawyers, studies indicate that from 12% (Zajac et al., 2003) to 15% (Szojka et al., 2017) raise doubts about the child's credibility: 78% are general and 23% relate to specific information. The possibility of the child lying is mentioned in 40% of these questions, contradictions are highlighted in 17% of the cases, and the influence of other people on the child's account is mentioned in 14% of the questions. Although there is a tendency for older children (under 17) to be asked questions about their credibility more often, this age difference is not significant since younger children (under 11) also often have to face these questions. Children are more likely to accept statements in questions about peripheral rather than central details. Likewise, children of all ages tend to recognize as true statements that the parents or the investigator influenced them, that they have behavioral problems, that they also have a good relationship with the suspect, or that their memory is not very good because they do not understand that these assertions on the part of the defense lawyer are intended to undermine their credibility.

9   Conclusion

The added value of the NICHD Protocol comes from the fact that several research teams are working to better understand its effects and, therefore, to improve its con-tent, such as by creating the Revised NICHD Protocol. The research conducted allows us to conclude that the revision of the NICHD Protocol has allowed interviewers who use it to improve the quality of their interviews. This version takes into account the relational and motivational factors affecting children's behavior and guides the interviewer to adapt his/her behavior in accordance with the child's needs. More-over, as in the first version of the NICHD Protocol, the Revised NICHD Protocol encourages a substantial use of the open-ended questions that engage the child's recall memory, allowing the child to recount a greater number of details with high accu-racy. Interviews conducted using the NICHD Protocol also facilitate the assessment of interviews as to the credibility of children's testimony and are associated with the prosecution of more cases; it can, therefore, be said that the use of the NICHD Pro-tocol improves the judicial process. Obviously, other studies should be carried out to confirm these very encouraging results. Studies of training and follow-up also tell us that forensic interviewing is a complex task and that continued feedback on inter-views conducted in real-world contexts are required to enhance and maintain inter-viewer performance. Overall, the recent research conducted on the NICHD Protocol enriches its use and optimizes its effectiveness in relation to children of different ages and with various characteristics or developmental delays. As research in this area continues, it is expected that, in the coming years, our knowledge of the NICHD Protocol will continue to evolve and improve.

In connection with the research on children's abilities that have guided the development of the NICHD Protocol, the increased interest of researchers in children's abilities during testimony opens up a new area for knowledge transfer. Research indicates that court practices are moving away from recommendations derived from knowledge developed on children's capacities, mainly with regard to the questions of prosecutors and defense lawyers. Many research questions still need to be investigated rigorously, but the high number of publications in recent years indicates an interest in better understanding how and under what conditions children can accurately contribute to the criminal justice process. Cross-examination is an essential part of the adversarial court process, but this should not come at the expense of seeking the truth (Myers, 2017). In order to help children, various tools or strategies have been developed such as books or programs to inform and prepare children for the court context, while other reforms include the presence of support persons, the use of recordings of forensic interviews to avoid forcing children to testify in open court, the pre-recording of cross-examination, and in-court closed-circuit television (Henderson & Andrews, 2018). In the coming years, clearer guidelines, based on empirical results, will be necessary to better design the questions admissible in court and thus allow children to maximize their competence as witnesses.

References

Ahern E. C., Hershkowitz I., Lamb M. E., Blasbalg U., Karni-Visel Y. (2018). "Examining reluctance and emotional support in forensic interviews with child victims of substantiated physical abuse", *Applied Developmental Science*, 1–12.

Ahern E. C., Hershkowitz I., Lamb M. E., Blasbalg U., Winstanley A. (2014). "Support and reluctance in the pre-substantive phase of alleged child abuse victim investigative interviews: Revised versus standard NICHD Protocols", *Behavioral Sciences & the Law*, 32(6), 762–774.

Almeida T. S., Lamb M. E., Weisblatt E. J. (2019). "Effects of delay, question type, and socio-emotional support on episodic memory retrieval by children with autism spectrum disorder", *Journal of Autism and Developmental Disorders*, 49(3), 1111–1130.

Alonzo-Proulx A., Cyr M. (2017). "Traitement des plaintes d'agression sexuelle envers les enfants dans le système de justice criminelle québécoise [Treatment of complaints of sexual abuse against children in the Quebec criminal justice system]", *Canadian Journal of Criminology and Criminal Justice*, 59(3), 397–424.

Andrews S. J., Ahern E. C., Lamb M. E. (2017). "Children's expressions of uncertainty when testifying about alleged sexual abuse in Scottish courts", *Behavioural Sciences & the Law*, 35, 204–224.

Andrews S. J., Ahern E. C., Stolzenberg S. N., Lyon T. D. (2016). "The productivity of wh-prompts when children testify", *Applied Cognitive Psychology*, 30(3), 341–349.

Andrews S. J., Lamb M. E. (2016). "How do lawyers examine and cross-examine children in Scotland?" *Applied Cognitive Psychology*, 30(6), 953–971.

Andrews S. J., Lamb M. E. (2017a). "The structural linguistic complexity of lawyers' questions and children's responses in Scottish criminal courts", *Child Abuse & Neglect*, 65, 182–193.

Andrews S. J., Lamb M. E. (2017b). "Lawyers' question repetition and children's responses in Scottish criminal courts", *Journal of Interpersonal Violence*, Advance online publication.

Andrews S. J., Lamb M. E., Lyon T. D. (2015a). "Question types, responsiveness and self-contradictions when prosecutors and defense attorneys question alleged victims of child sexual abuse", *Applied Cognitive Psychology*, 29, 253–261.

Andrews S. J., Lamb M. E., Lyon T. D. (2015b). "The effects of question repetition on responses when prosecutors and defense attorneys question children alleging sexual abuse in court", *Law and Human Behavior*, 39(6), 559–570.

Benia L. R., Hauck-Filho N., Dillenburg M., Milnitsly Stein L. (2015). "The NICHD investigative interview protocol: A meta-analytic review", *Journal of Child Sexual Abuse*, 24(3), 259–279.

Blasbalg U., Hershkowitz I., Karni-Visel Y. (2018). "Support, reluctance and production in child abuse investigations", *Psychology, Public Policy and Law*, 24(4), 518–527.

Blasbalg U., Hershkowitz I., Lamb M. E., Karni-Visel Y. (submitted). "The effects of support on the coherence of children's forensic statements".

Blasbalg U., Hershkowitz I., Lamb M. E., Karni-Visel Y., Ahern E. C. (2019). "Is interviewer support associated with the reduced reluctance and enhanced informativeness of alleged child abuse victims?" *Law & Human Behavior*, 43(2), 156–165.

Brown D. A., Brown E.-J., Lewis C. N., Lamb M. E. (2018). "Narrative skill and testimonial accuracy in typically developing children and those with intellectual disabilities", *Applied Cognitive Psychology*. Publié en ligne le 27 juin 2018.

Brown D. A., Lamb M. E., Lewis C., Pipe M.-E., Orbach Y., Wolfman M. (2013). "The NICHD Investigative Interview Protocol: An analogue study", *Journal of Experimental Psychology Applied*, 19(4), 367–382.

Brown D. A., Lewis C. N., Lamb M. E. (2015). "Preserving the past: An early interview improves delayed event memory in children with intellectual disabilities", *Child Development*, 86(4), 1031–1047.

Brown D. A., Lewis C. N., Lamb M. E., Gwynne J., Kitto O., Stairmand M. (2019). "Developmental differences in children's learning and use of forensic ground rules during an interview about an experienced event", *Developmental Psychology*, 55(8), 1626–1639.

Brown D. A., Lewis C. N., Lamb M. E., Stephens E. (2012). "The influences of delay and severity of intellectual disability on event memory in children", *Journal of Consulting and Clinical Psychology*, 80(5), 829–841.

Brown D. A., Lewis C. N., Stephens E., Lamb M. E. (2017). "Interviewers' approaches to questioning vulnerable child witnesses: The influences of developmental level versus intellectual disability status", *Legal and Criminological Psychology*, 22(2), 332–349.

Brubacher S. P., Poole D. A., Dickinson J. J. (2015). "The use of ground rules in investigative interviews with children: A synthesis and call for research", *Developmental Review*, 36, 15–33.

Brubacher S. P., Roberts K. P., Powell M. (2011). "Effects of practicing episodic versus scripted recall on children's subsequent narratives of a repeated event", *Psychology, Public Policy, and Law*, 17(2), 286–314.

Cederborg A.-C., Alm C., Lima da Silva Nises D., Lamb M. E. (2013). "Investigative interviewing of alleged child abuse victims: An evaluation of a new training programme for investigative interviewers", *Police Practice and Research*, 14(3), 242–254.

Cross T. P., Walsh W. A., Simone M., Jones L. M. (2003). "Prosecution of child abuse: A meta-analysis of rates of criminal justice decisions", *Trauma, Violence and Abuse*, 4, 323–340.

Cyr M., Dion J., Gendron A., Powell M. B., Brubacher S. P. (2021). "A test of three refresher modalities on child forensic interviewers' post-training performance", *Psychology, Public Policy and Law*, 27(2), 221–230.

Cyr M., Dion J., McDuff P. (submitted). "Child and abuse characteristics related to child disclosure during investigative interview of suspected sexual abuse".

Cyr M., Dion J., McDuff P., Trotier-Sylvain K. (2012). "Transfer of skills in the context of non-suggestive investigative interviews: Impact of structured interview protocol and feedback", *Applied Cognitive Psychology*, 26(4), 516–524.

Cyr M., Lamb M. E. (2009). "Assessing the effectiveness of the NICHD investigative interview protocol when interviewing French-speaking alleged victims of child sexual abuse in Quebec", *Child Abuse & Neglect*, 33(5), 257–268.

Danby M. C., Brubacher S. P., Sharman S. J., Powell M. B. (2015). "The effects of practice on children's ability to apply ground rules in a narrative interview", *Behavioral Science and Law*, 33, 446–458.

Dickinson J. J., Brubacher S. P., Poole D. A. (2015). "Children's performance on ground rules questions: Implications for forensic interviewing", *Law and Human Behavior*, 39(1), 87–97.

Dion J., Cyr M. (2008). "The use of the NICHD protocol to enhance the quantity of details obtained from children with low verbal abilities in investigative interviews: A pilot study", *Journal of Child Sexual Abuse*, 17(2), 144–162.

Earhart B., La Rooy D. J., Brubacher S. P., Lamb M. E. (2014). "An examination of 'don't know' responses in forensic interviews with children", *Behavioral Sciences & the Law*, 32(6), 746–761.

Evans A. D., Stolzenberg S. N., Lyon T. D. (2017). "Pragmatic failure and referential ambiguity when attorneys ask child witnesses 'do you know/remember' questions", *Psychology, Public Policy and Law*, 23(2), 191–199.

Gagnon K., Cyr M. (2017). "Sexual abuse and preschoolers: Forensic details in regard of question types", *Child Abuse & Neglect*, 67, 109–118.

Hanna K. M., Davies E., Crothers C., Henderson E. (2012). "Questioning child witnesses in New Zealand's criminal justice system: Is cross-examination fair?" *Psychiatry Psychology and Law Psychology and Law*, 4, 530–546.

Henderson H. M., Andrews S. J. (2018). "Assessing the veracity of children's forensic interviews", in Otgaar H., Howe M. L. (Eds.), *Finding the truth in the courtroom: Dealing with deception, lies and memories*, New York, Oxford University Press, 103–135.

Hershkowitz I. (2001). "Children's responses to open-ended utterances in investigative interviews", *Law and Criminological Psychology*, 6(1), 49–63.

Hershkowitz I. (2018). "NICHD-protocol investigations of individuals with intellectual disability: A descriptive analysis", *Psychology, Public Policy, and Law*, 24(3), 393–403.

Hershkowitz I., Ahern E. C., Lamb M. E., Blasbalg U., Karni-Visel Y., Breitman M. (2017). "Changes in interviewers' use of supportive techniques during the revised protocol training", *Applied Cognitive Psychology*, 31, 340–350.

Hershkowitz I., Fisher S., Lamb M. E., Horowitz D. (2007). "Improving credibility assessment in child sexual abuse allegations: The role of the NICHD investigative interview protocol", *Child Abuse & Neglect*, 31(2), 99–110.

Hershkowitz I., Horowitz D., Lamb M. E. (2007). "Individual and family variables associated with disclosure and nondisclosure of child abuse in Israel", in Pipe M.-E., Lamb M. E., Orbach Y., Cederborg A.-C. (Eds.), *Child sexual abuse: Disclosure, delay, and denial*, Mahwah, Lawrence Erlbaum Associates Publishers, 65–75.

Hershkowitz I., Lamb M. E. (2020). "Allegation rates and credibility assessment in forensic interviews of alleged child abuse victims: Comparing the revised and standard NICHD protocols", *Psychology, Public Policy, and Law*, 26, 176–184.

Hershkowitz I., Lamb M. E., Katz C. (2014). "Allegation rates in forensic child abuse investigations: Comparing the revised and standard NICHD protocols", *Psychology, Public Policy, and Law*, 20(3), 336–344.

Hershkowitz I., Lamb M. E., Katz C., Malloy L. C. (2015). "Does enhanced rapport-building alter the dynamics of investigative interviews with suspected victims of intra-familial abuse?" *Journal of Police and Criminal Psychology*, 30(1), 6–14.

Hershkowitz I., Lamb M. E., Orbach Y., Katz C., Horowitz D. (2012). "The development of communicative and narrative skills among preschoolers: Lessons from forensic interviews about child abuse", *Child Development*, 83(2), 611–622.

Hershkowitz I., Orbach Y., Lamb M. E., Sternberg K. J., Horowitz D. (2006). "Dynamics of forensic interviews with suspected abuse victims who do not disclose abuse", *Child Abuse & Neglect*, 30(7), 753–769.

Karni-Visel Y., Hershkowitz I., Lamb M. E., Blasbalg U. (2019). "Facilitating the expression of emotions by alleged victims of child abuse during investigative interviews using the revised NICHD protocol", *Child Maltreatment*, 24, 310–318.

Katz C., Paddon M. J., Barnetz Z. (2016). "Emotional language used by victims of alleged sexual abuse during forensic investigation", *Journal of Child Sexual Abuse*, 25(3), 243–261.

Klemfuss J. Z., Quas J. A., Lyon T. D. (2014). "Attorneys' questions and children's productivity in child sexual abuse criminal trials", *Applied Cognitive Psychology*, 28(5), 780–788.

Lafontaine J., Cyr M. (2016a). "A study of the relationship between investigators' personal characteristics and adherence to interview best practices in training", *Psychiatry, Psychology and Law*, 23(5), 782–792.

Lafontaine J., Cyr M. (2016b). "The relation between interviewers' personal characteristics and investigative interview performance in a child sexual abuse context", *Police Practice and Research*, 18(2), 106–118.

Lamb, M. E. (2016). "Difficulties translating research on forensic interview practices to practitioners: Finding water, leading horses, but can we get them to drink?" *American Psychology*, 71, 710–718.

Lamb M. E., Brown D. A., Hershkowitz I., Orbach Y., Esplin P. W. (2018). *Tell me what happened: Questioning children about abuse* (2nd ed.), Hoboken, NJ, John Wiley & Sons Inc.

Lamb M. E., Hershkowitz I., Sternberg K. J., Esplin P. W., et al. (1996). "Effects of investigative utterance types on Israeli children's responses", *International Journal of Behavioral Development*, 19(3), 627–637.

Lamb M. E., Orbach Y., Hershkowitz I., Horowitz D., Abbott C. B. (2007). "Does the type of prompt affect the accuracy of information provided by alleged victims of abuse in forensic interviews?" *Applied Cognitive Psychology*, 21(9), 1117–1130.

Lamb M. E., Orbach Y., Sternberg K. L., et al. (2009). "Use of a structured investigative protocol enhances the quality of investigative interviews with alleged victims of child sexual abuse in Britain", *Applied Cognitive Psychology*, 23(4), 449–467.

Lamb M. E., Sternberg K. J., Orbach Y., Esplin P. W., Mitchell S. (2002). "Is ongoing feedback necessary to maintain the quality of investigative interviews with allegedly abused children?" *Applied Developmental Science*, 6(1), 35–41.

Lamb M. E., Sternberg K. J., Orbach Y., Esplin P. W., Stewart H. L., Mitchell S. (2003). "Age differences in young children's responses to open-ended invitations in the course of forensic interviews", *Journal of Consulting and Clinical Psychology*, 71(5), 926–934.

Lamb M. E., Sternberg K. J., Orbach Y., Hershkowitz I., Horowitz D. (2003). "Differences between accounts provided by witnesses and alleged victims of child sexual abuse", *Child Abuse & Neglect*, 27(9), 1019–1031.

Lamb M. E., Sternberg K. J., Orbach Y., Hershkowitz I., Horowitz D., Esplin P. W. (2002). "The effects of intensive training and ongoing supervision on the quality of investigative interviews with alleged sex abuse victims", *Applied Developmental Science*, 6(3), 114–125.

La Rooy D., Brubacher S. P., Aromäki-Stratos A., Cyr M., Hershkowitz I., Korkman J., . . . Lamb M. E. (2015). "The NICHD Protocol: A review of an internationally-used evidence-based tool for training child forensic interviewers", *Journal of Criminological Research, Policy and Practice*, 1(2), 76–89.

Lewy J., Cyr M., Dion J. (2015). "Impact of interviewers' supportive comments and children's reluctance to cooperate during sexual abuse disclosure", *Child Abuse & Neglect*, 43, 112–122.

Lewy J., Cyr M., Dion J. (2017). "Soutien des intervieweurs et collaboration des enfants lors des entrevues d'enquête [Interviewer support and child collaboration in survey interviews]", *Criminologie*, 50(1), 11–33.

Malloy, L. C., Mugno, A. P., Pelham, W. E., Hawk, L. W., Lamb, M. E. (2016, June). "Memory and secret-keeping among children with Attention Deficit Hyperactivity Disorder", Paper presented at the 9th Annual Meeting of the International Investigative Interviewing Research Group. London, UK.

McLay L., Brown D. A., Palmer L., Beaumont S. (2016). "Event memory, coherence and suggestibility in children with ADHD symptoms", Manuscript in preparation.

Myers J. E. B. (2017). "Cross-examination: A defense", *Psychology, Public Policy and Law*, 23(4), 472–477.

Naka M. (2011). "The effect of forensic interview training based on the NICHD structured protocol", *Japanese Journal of Child Abuse and Neglect*, 13, 316–325.

Orbach Y., Hershkowitz I., Lamb M. E., Sternberg K. J., Esplin P. W., Horowitz D. (2000). "Assessing the value of structured protocols for forensic interviews of alleged child abuse victims", *Child Abuse & Neglect*, 24(6), 733–752.

Orbach Y., Lamb M. E. (1999). "Assessing the accuracy of a child's account of sexual abuse: A case study", *Child Abuse & Neglect*, 23(1), 91–98.

Orbach Y., Lamb M. E. (2000). "Enhancing children's narratives in investigative interviews", *Child Abuse & Neglect*, 24(12), 1631–1648

Pipe M.-E., Orbach Y., Lamb M., Abbott C. B., Stewart H. (2013). "Do case outcomes change when investigative interviewing practices change?" *Psychology, Public Policy, and Law*, 19(2), 179–190.

Powell M. B., Westera N., Goodman-Delahunty J., Pichler A. S. (2016). *An evaluation of how evidence is elicited from complainants of child sexual abuse.* www.childabuseroyalcommission.gov.au/research

Price H. L., Roberts K. P. (2011). "The effects of an intensive training and feedback program on police and social workers' investigative interviews of children", *Canadian Journal of Behavioral Science*, 43(3), 235–244.

Price H. L., Roberts K. P., Collins A. (2013). "The quality of children's allegations of abuse in investigative interviewers containing practice narrative", *Journal of Applied Research in Memory and Cognition*, 2, 1–6.

Roberts K. P., Brubacher S. P., Powell M. B., Price H. L. (2011). "Practice narratives", in Lamb M. E., La Rooy D. J., Malloy L. C., Katz C. (Eds.), *Children's testimony: A handbook of psychological research and forensic practice*, Malden, John Wiley & Sons, 129–145.

Roberts K. P., Lamb M. E., Sternberg J. (2004). "The effects of rapport-building style on children's reports of a staged event", *Applied Cognitive Psychology*, 18(4), 189–202.

Sternberg K. J., Lamb M. E., Hershkowitz I., Yudilevitch L., Orbach Y., Esplin P. W., Hovav M. (1997). "Effects of introductory style on children's abilities to describe experiences of sexual abuse", *Child Abuse & Neglect*, 21(11), 1133–1146.

Sternberg K. J., Lamb M. E., Orbach Y., Esplin P. W., Mitchell S. (2001). "Use of a structured investigative protocol enhances young children's responses to free-recall prompts in the course of forensic interviews", *Journal of Applied Psychology*, 86(5), 997–1005.

Stolzenberg S. N., Lyon T. D. (2014). "How attorneys question children about the dynamics of sexual abuse and disclosure in criminal trials", *Psychology, Public Policy, and Law*, 20(1), 19–30.

Szojka Z. A., Andrews S. J., Lamb M. E., Stolzenberg S. N., Lyon T. D. (2017). "Challenging the credibility of alleged victims of child sexual abuse in Scottish courts", *Psychology, Public Policy, and Law*, 23(2), 200–210.

Yi M., Jo, E., Lamb M. E. (2016). "Effects of the NICHD protocol training on child investigative interview quality in Korean police officers", *Journal of Police and Criminal Psychology*, 31, 155–163.

Zajac R., Cannan P. (2009). "Cross-examination of sexual assault complainants: A developmental comparison", *Psychiatry, Psychology and Law*, 16(sup1), S36–S54.

Zajac R., Gross J., Hayne H. (2003). "Asked and answered: Questioning children in the courtroom", *Psychiatry, Psychology and Law*, 10(1), 199–209.

Zajac R., O'Neill S., Hayne H. (2012). "Disorder in the courtroom? Child witnesses under cross-examination", *Developmental Review*, 32, 181–204.

Chapter 8

Conclusion

I Integration of theoretical, practical, and self-regulatory knowledge

Research carried out over the past thirty years, and summarized in this book, has allowed significant advances in the state of knowledge concerning children's memory and suggestibility. The *theoretical knowledge* acquired has demonstrated the ability of children, and even the very young, to provide true accounts of the experiences they may have had. Children's autobiographical memory can, therefore, be a reliable source of information. For example, 3- and 4-year-olds are able to identify and report in two or three sentences some of the actions that occurred during an incident of abuse. With age, there is a fairly rapid improvement in their ability to provide narratives that are coherent and that include evidence for police investigations, such as regarding the actions, a description of the suspect (in the case of an unknown perpetrator), and where and when the incident occurred. Disclosure of abuse, especially sexual abuse, is a difficult process and is often delayed; in such cases, we know that the recollection reported will be less comprehensive than if the disclosure had been immediate. However, research tells us that, under these circumstances, the most central details, namely those relating to the actions, should be better preserved than certain peripheral details (e.g., the clothes worn). The difficulty in disclosing the interpersonal violence experienced must also be taken into account since the victim needs support, time, and a reliable, credible, flexible, and sensitive person/interviewer to support him/her in this process. Like many adults, children are vulnerable to suggestions. Placed in front of a person in authority and willing to cooperate, children may, in order to meet the expectations of an interviewer, provide information that is not accurate, particularly if they perceive pressure from them. Research has also shown that formulating interview expectations and communication rules can help children resist suggestions.

This knowledge has also led to the formulation of precise recommendations regarding the conduct of investigative interviews and, therefore, to *practical knowledge*. Indeed, the quality of the information collected depends to a large extent on the quality of the questions asked of the child and on the support and flexibility shown during the interview by the interviewer. All aspects of the Revised NICHD Protocol were designed to provide interviewers with examples of concrete, non-suggestive support. The importance of using as many open-ended questions as possible to foster narratives based on recall memory is no longer controversial. Open-ended questions should

DOI: 10.4324/9781003265351-8

constitute the majority of the questions used during interviews. This ensures that the information obtained is accurate, although it may appear incomplete from a judicial point of view. Using simple, follow-up, cued, and time-segmenting invitations, as well as directives questions, is the best way to get the most detailed account possible from alleged victims of child abuse. Moreover, this way of proceeding better respects children's capacities because children, in response to open-ended questions, resort to free recall memories. However, even open-ended questions, especially some directives and cued invitations, could lead to inaccurate information being obtained when the same question is asked repeatedly or when the question seeks to obtain a very specific detail that may or may not have been encoded by the child. Respecting children's abilities to provide some type of detail depending on their age is another key requirement for eliciting accurate accounts. The difficulties faced by children under the age of 10 years in providing accurate information about the timing of the abuse or describing the people involved or the places where it occurred are not reliable indicators that nothing happened; rather, such difficulties testify to children's cognitive abilities. Thus, interviewers' questions should be adapted to children's capacities.

In order to help interviewers succeed at this complex task, interview protocols have been developed. In addition to placing open-ended questions at the heart of the questioning strategy, some of these protocols incorporate activities that foster the development of a comfortable working relationship between the child and the interviewer. The suggested activities also promote better cooperation with the child by familiarizing him/her from the beginning of the interview with the task expected of him/her. The Revised NICHD Protocol seems best suited to the needs of interviews with children, and the numerous studies devoted to it have demonstrated its effectiveness. Using the Revised NICHD Protocol, interviewers employ open-ended questions to obtain the majority of information. More importantly, the Revised NICHD Protocol focuses on the child's emotional states and offers the interviewer many ways to deal with the hesitations and reluctance of children during the interview. The use of the Revised NICHD Protocol does not, however, eliminate all the complexity of interviewing children and teenagers because each child brings his/her share of constraints and difficulties.

The interpersonal skills of the person who interacts with the child, *self-regulatory knowledge*, remain essential. These interpersonal skills include the ability to assess the child's overall level of development; to adapt flexibly to his/her cognitive, motivational, and emotional needs; and to establish a relaxed and facilitative climate while seeking to obtain the maximum amount of accurate information in a relatively short period. The flexible and supportive attitude of the interviewer is essential when attempting to accommodate a child who is often anxious or worried during this meeting. Adjusting his/her pace, tone of voice, gestures, and posture to the child's energy level; maintaining eye contact without intimidating the child; smiling; nodding in welcome; using minimal facilitators ("Hum-hum"); letting the child have time to think before asking another question; asking only one question at a time; and orienting toward the child in a relaxed way are all desirable behaviors. All this requires great sensitivity on the part of the interviewer and excellent interpersonal skills. Other behaviors, which are not discussed in the interview protocols, are nevertheless very important; for example, allowing a child with hyperactivity to move around the room without letting him/her become disorganized, being patient with a child who often digresses without losing track, encouraging and supporting a shy child who is hesitant to reveal anything. These behaviors are based on a human sense of relationships and a real desire to relate effectively to children whose revelations may prove overwhelming for the interviewer. This self-regulatory knowledge is also based on practical knowledge that needs to be well integrated. In other words, without complete mastery of the task to be performed and the technical and relational tools (question and support), it is difficult to interact with a child and to have the psychological space to manage both the relationship and the task of the interview with ease and efficiency. Thus, mastery of open-ended questions must be part of the interviewer's natural repertoire and be used in a reflexive fashion; this requires sustained and thoughtful practice (Poole, 2016). Even more difficult is the ability to observe and detect the many aspects of verbal and nonverbal reluctance and to be able to address it with sensitivity and in a way that is respectful of the legal context in which the investigative interview is conducted.

These interpersonal skills also require taking care of the psychological and emotional needs of the interviewer. Working daily with children and adults who are victims of interpersonal violence over long periods of time can promote the development of compassion fatigue or vicarious trauma syndrome (Mathieu, 2012). This professional burnout, which is not often addressed, tends to be interpreted by the professional concerned as a weakness instead of being recognized as a natural consequence of too much empathy toward the victims encountered. Recent neuropsychological research has made it possible to establish a link between repeated exposure to the traumatic narratives of victims and the recording by the brain of these emotions, among others, via mirror neurons. It is, therefore, important to be attentive to such signs as the following:

- physical: insomnia, extreme fatigue, somatization, headaches, etc.
- behavioral: increased consumption of alcohol, drugs, exaggerated sense of responsibility, absenteeism, etc.
- psychological: irritability, depression, negative self-image, self-blame, cynicism, decreased feeling of empathy, loss of hope, hypersensitivity or insensitivity to emotional material, changed belief systems about oneself, others, the world, or the future, etc.

In addition to repeated exposure to trauma, events in the workers' lives may increase their vulnerability to developing vicarious trauma, such as tense family situations, divorce, traumatic experiences as a child, overload at work, and working in isolation. The appearance of these signals should prompt people to seek the assistance required as soon as possible. This help can include individual psychotherapy, mindfulness meditation, a modification of the routine, and the integration of sports activities, as well as better diets and more frequent rest times. On the professional level, several elements can be considered as continuing education that offers a framework for identifying and naming one's experience, as well as tools for working differently. The organization of working time, working part-time, or even varying the nature of the workload are other factors that can protect workers from compassion fatigue. From an organizational standpoint, access to a process of group supervision and individual supervision and debriefing sessions on a regular basis are assets that allow interviewers to develop their expertise and continue using it for years.

2   Challenges for the coming years

Despite the significant advances of recent years, many challenges remain. The main ones involve assessing the credibility of children's narratives, identifying those who have been abused but who are not ready to disclose it, developing non-suggestive tools to help children who have developmental delays, training and post-training support for interviewers, integration of skills in work with other types of clients, and integrated multidisciplinary work.

2.1   Credibility assessments of children's narratives

The credibility of children's accounts can appear uncertain, particularly if the interviewer believes that children may enjoy fantasy and have difficulty distinguishing between the imagined and the real. The knowledge acquired over recent decades about children's memory and suggestibility has challenged this assumption and clarified the conditions in which children's accounts can prove to be accurate. In addition, recent phenomena, such as delayed disclosure of abuse by adults, have helped many to realize how widespread sexual abuse is and has made them more willing to consider disclosures to be credible. Nevertheless, determining whether the account provided by a child is true remains a complex task and, to date, few tools are available. The one that has been the most widely disseminated and used is an analysis grid based on Criterion-Based Content Analysis (CBCA) criteria (Raskin & Esplin, 1991; Steller & Koehnken, 1989; Yuille, 1988). The CBCA is one of the three components of the Statement Validity Analysis (SVA), and it should involve

- a high-quality interview,
- an analysis of this interview using the CBCA, and
- an overview of relevant elements using the validity checklist.

It was developed on the basis of Undeutsch's hypothesis, based on his courtroom experiences, that the description of true events is different from that of false allegations. The numerous studies carried out using this grid indicate acceptable inter-rater reliability for all but five of the nineteen criteria. Researchers have also shown that the results obtained using this grid were influenced by the child's age and by whether the event happened one or more times (Blandon-Gitlin, Pezdek, Rogers, & Brodie, 2005). A meta-analysis also revealed that the intensity of rater training, the type of rating scale used, the frequency of occurrence (base rate) for some CBCA criteria in the account are other factors that influence inter-rater reliability (Hauch, Sporer, Masip, & Blandon-Gitlin, 2017). Other studies (Steller & Koehnken, 1989; Yuille, 1989) have also observed that the CBCA has a bias that leads it to recognize as credible misleading statements (false positives), and several studies have led to the conclusion that twelve of the nineteen criteria should be revised. For example, when analyzing ninety-eight interviews, Lamb and colleagues (Lamb et al., 1997) observe that plausible cases include more CBCA criteria than implausible cases. However, the difference was small, and several of the criteria were not significantly more frequent in the implausible cases. In fact, only five of the fourteen criteria discriminated between plausible accounts and implausible ones, namely

- unstructured production,
- quantity of details,
- embedding of events in temporal and spatial context,
- reproductions of conversation (less frequent in improbable accounts than in plausible accounts), and
- descriptions of interactions.

In a review of studies conducted with adults and children in real contexts and in the laboratory, Vrij (2005) concludes that the first four criteria mentioned above are most often associated with truthful accounts. Some of the studies also indicated that people who are socially adept, monitor their behavior, are able to self-regulate, and have low social anxiety score higher. Since liars are less anxious and more socially skillful, they more often get a score indicating that their account is true. Other reviews of the scientific literature (Oberlader et al., 2016) also concluded that although the CBCA grid makes it possible to distinguish true accounts from those invented, this classification is only correct in 70% of cases. Given the weaknesses noted and false-positive rate of 30%, several researchers (Earhart, La Rooy, & Lamb, 2016; Hauch et al., 2017; Lamb et al., 1997; Pezdek et al., 2004; Vrij, 2005) recommend that the CBCA grid should not be used in court to determine the credibility of children's testimony. However, according to these researchers, this tool can helpfully draw attention to the complexity of the factors that must be taken into account when assessing children's allegations.

Among the other tools available, some are based on the theory of reality monitoring (RM) advanced by Johnson and Raye (Johnson & Raye, 1981; for a summary, see Masip, Spörer, Garrido, & Herrero, 2005). Reality monitoring theory assumes that two sources of information comprise an individual's memory: one external and based on sensory perceptions and one internal and based on imagination, extrapolation, reasoning, and other cognitive processes. According to this theory, the memory of an event is made up of three elements: information about context (where and when), information about perceived sensations (shapes, colors, smells, physical sensation), and information about emotions. It is, therefore, expected that the content of memories with an external origin (real events) will be richer in contextual, sensory, and affective details than are internally generated accounts of events (imagined events), which contain more information referring to cognitive processes, such as thoughts and reasoning at the time of encoding. This theory was also used to develop a grid to evaluate narratives (Sporer, 1997). Studies reveal problems similar to those seen with CBCA, such as a strong correlation between the number of criteria and the amount of detail, which puts young children's narratives at a disadvantage. In addition, children's truthful accounts included less visual and contextual detail than expected. For these reasons, it would be premature to use this set of criteria in expert assessments of children's credibility (Henderson & Andrews, 2018).

2.2   Identification of abused children

Another challenge for practitioners and researchers concerns the identification of abused children. We underlined in the first chapter of this book that the process of disclosure is often experienced in an ambivalent way by children and that, like adults, many of them are reluctant to reveal their abuse. What can be done when faced with a young alleged victim who is unable to disclose what has happened? The Revised NICHD Protocol (Lamb, Brown, Hershkowitz, Orbach, & Esplin, 2018) aims to better equip interviewers to deal with these difficulties and provide more non-suggestive support to children. It also offers interviewers the possibility of stopping the interview before starting the substantive part and of planning additional meetings with the child in order to develop better rapport. Following the Revised NICHD Protocol, in a recent research involving 202 suspected victims of abuse who did not make allegations during the first interview, they were seen again a few days later (Hershkowitz, Lamb, Blasbalg, & Karni-Visel, 2020). During this second interview, 104 children disclosed (51.5%). Higher support in the first interview was associated with improved rapport in the second and more spontaneous disclosures (fewer prompts in the transition). This study thus confirmed the importance of supportive interventions and the usefulness of the Revised NICHD Protocol when used to help reluctant children disclose abuse they have actually experienced. However, time intervals between sessions open the door to adult influence on alleged victims (Cross & Hershkowitz, 2017; Faller, Cordisco-Steele, & Nelson-Gardell, 2010). It is evident that continued research into the factors that facilitate or hinder disclosure is likely to help us develop better intervention strategies to employ with children.

We have emphasized that children with various developmental disabilities present particular challenges during interviews. Thus, children with moderate or severe intellectual disabilities have less ability to understand and cooperate in interviews. The research carried out with these children, as well as with children on the autism spectrum, suggests that the NICHD Protocol is a good tool to use with these children because it facilitates the elicitation of their accounts. The cognitive elaboration technique proposed by Saywitz and Snyder (1996) may help some of them, but more research is needed to better determine whether this strategy might become suggestive when used with children who have particular problems. It will also be necessary to be innovative and think of other tools to help these children (e.g., draw, write, manipulate objects) and make sure to evaluate these new practices before disseminating them.

2.3   Initial training and skills maintenance

Investigative interviews with children and the search for the truth are complex tasks that require the mastery of important practical knowledge and interpersonal skills. The issue of training and maintaining skills is particularly relevant since the training of forensic interviewers is expensive, the greater mobility of trained personnel increases the training needs of organizations, and the financial resources of organizations are often limited (Lamb, 2016). For the interviewer to become competent, the training must allow the acquisition not only of knowledge but also of technical skills and the personal and interpersonal attributes needed to perform interviews, even when employing a structured protocol, such as the Revised NICHD Protocol.

In addition, a significant number of studies (Cyr, Dion, McDuff, & Trotier-Sylvain, 2012; Johnson et al., 2015; Lamb et al., 2002; Yii, Powell, & Guadagno, 2014) have reported a deterioration of performance over time, thus suggesting the need to offer extended guidance and supervision following the initial training. Recent research on training has identified the necessary components of high-quality training (see also Powell, 2008): initial training that takes place over an extended period rather than being condensed (Cederborg, Lindholm, Lamb, & Norman, 2021; Rischke, Roberts, & Price, 2011), mastery of the codification of types of questions (Yii, Powell, & Guadagno, 2014), feedback on the type of questions asked (Pompedda, Antfolk, Zappalà, & Santtila, 2017), training and feedback on supportive interventions (Hershkowitz et al., 2017), and feedback on interviews conducted in real-world contexts (Cyr et al., 2012; Cyr, Dion, Gendron, Powell, & Brubacher, 2021). For example, Powell and her colleagues have developed an online computer-based program consisting of fifteen modules that are studied in a time-spaced fashion, which include video demonstrations, interview practices, and feedback. Their studies have shown how this distance training improves the course of interviews and increases the number of open-ended questions asked (Benson & Powell, 2015; Powell, Guadagno, & Benson, 2016). The use of avatars to allow remote practices is also another avenue that is being explored (Pompedda, Zappalà, & Santtila, 2015; Pompedda et al., 2017). Further research is needed to assess the effectiveness of different training and supervision modalities (e.g., intensive versus spaced training, immediate, deferred or written feedback, follow-up on difficult cases at regular intervals). With new technological tools (e.g., remote supervision, online practice manuals), new strategies can be developed and evaluated.

One way of facilitating the integration of this learning and the acquisition of new skills would be to promote the use of these interview techniques in different contexts. In fact, it is common for investigators who work with child witnesses or victims to be called upon to interview adults as well. Because the NICHD Protocol is based on the same principles as the Cognitive Interview often employed with adults, open-ended questioning based on invitations should also be used with adolescents and adults (see Chapter 6 for more details). In addition, the NICHD Protocol should be used when a child has to be interviewed regardless of the reason for the interview: child witnesses of marital violence, murder, school shootings, or some other disaster. In all these situations, the interviewer will have opportunities to use and continue to develop the skills discussed in this book.

2.4 Multidisciplinary teams

Finally, beyond the person who interviews the children, it is important that all professionals who are called upon to interact with children receive adequate training regarding children's abilities and limitations and about ways to interact with them without compromising their memory. This includes all those involved in the social and legal environment, such as the forensic interviewers (e.g., police, social workers), psychosocial professionals, child psychiatrists, pediatricians, forensic pathologists, lawyers, prosecutors, and judges. Too frequently, children are still questioned in a suggestive manner by multiple professionals before or after the investigative interview (Cross & Hershkowitz, 2017). It is still too often that the rather credible account of a young victim is not brought before the court because it is believed that the child will not be able to withstand a cross-examination that could be suggestive. It is also all too common for a child's testimony to be challenged because s/he cannot accurately indicate when or how many times events have occurred or elaborate on some peripheric details. It is, therefore, important that the knowledge that is summarized in this book and will be developed by researchers over the next few years be disseminated to all stakeholders involved in child maltreatment. In addition, several dimensions of the NICHD Protocol (establishment of rules, working relationship, practice of memory, open-ended questioning based on a free narrative) are elements that could be used when conducting psychological evaluations or interventions in nonjudicial contexts.

Because the investigative interview is just a piece, although an important one, of the investigation, this piece should be complemented by a multidisciplinary team working together. The Child Advocacy Model (National Children's Alliance, 2020) was developed in early 1980 to provide for children and their family members a coordinated response, based on empirically based evidence, of the different stakeholders, which include law enforcement, child protective services, prosecution, victim advocates, and medical and mental health professionals. The national core guidelines are produced by the National Children's Alliance (2020) to guide the development and activities in these Child Advocacy Centers. In a context where children and their families can receive all the services they need when sexual abuse is suspected or has been disclosed (forensic interview, medical exams, protective services, victim advocacy, mental health intervention) at the same location, we believe that it will be easier to disseminate the same knowledge about children's capacities and limitations to all the professionals involved. When a small number of professionals regularly work together, the efforts to implement continuous training and refresher activities that comprise empirically based practices should be facilitated. As suggested by Powell, Wright, and Clark (2010) such co-training could help to resolve some of the tensions or conflicts that may arise because of different organizational objectives (e.g., criminal vs. welfare). However, without good monitoring of effective practices, a multidisciplinary team can also hinder the use of best practices (Cross & Hershkowitz, 2017).

Multidisciplinary case review discussions should also enrich understanding of the child's situation from multiple points of view and allow better coordinated and efficient interventions. For example, forensic interviewers could brief the pediatricians and nurses about body parts touched or injuries incurred during the abuse described by the child during the interview, diminishing the number of suggestive questions the child is asked during the medical exam. In turn, medical staff may be privy to spontaneous disclosures by the child about his/her physical position during the abuse and other body parts involved. Meeting with non-offending caregivers, social workers, and psychologists may develop a better understanding of the family dynamics or mental, physical, and social problems faced by the child and his/her family and provide some hints about the child's attitudes during the investigative interview. Expanded understanding and shared responsibility for a particular case could also decrease high staff turnover and prevent burnout and vicarious trauma. More research (Westphaln et al., 2021) is required to evaluate the benefits of multidisciplinary teamwork and the factors that promoted their efficiency.

References

Benson M. S., Powell M. B. (2015). "Evaluation of a comprehensive interactive training system for investigative interviewers of children", *Psychology, Public Policy and Law*, 21(3), 309–322.

Blandon-Gitlin I., Pezdek K., Rogers M., Brodie L. (2005). "Detecting deception in children: An experimental study of the effect of event familiarity on CBCA ratings", *Law and Human Behavior*, 29, 185–197.

Cederborg A.-C., Lindholm T., Lamb M., Norman E. (2021). "Evaluating the quality of investigative interviews conducted after the completion of training program", *Investigative Interviewing: Research and Practice*, 11(1), 40–52.

Cross T. P., Hershkowitz I. (2017). "Psychology and child protection: Promoting widespread improvement in practice", *Psychology, Public Policy and Law*, 23(4), 503–518.

Cyr M., Dion J., Gendron A., Powell Martine B., Brubacher S. P. (2021). "A test of three refresher modalities on child forensic interviewers' post-training performance", *Psychology, Public Policy and Law*, 27(2), 221–230.

Cyr M., Dion J., McDuff P., Trotier Sylvain K. (2012). "Transfer of skills in the context of non-suggestive investigative interviews: Impact of structured interview protocol and feedback", *Applied Cognitive Psychology*, 26(4), 516–524.

Earhart B., La Rooy D., Lamb M. E. (2016). "Assessing the quality of forensic interviews with child witnesses", in O'Donohue W. T., Fanetti M. (Eds.), *Forensic interviews regarding child sexual abuse*, Cham, Springer International Publishing, 317–335.

Faller K. C., Cordisco-Steele L., Nelson-Gardell D. (2010). "Allegations of sexual abuse of a child: What to do when a single forensic interview isn't enough", *Journal of Child Sexual Abuse: Research, Treatment, & Program Innovations for Victims, Survivors, & Offenders*, 19(5), 572–589.

Hauch V., Sporer S. L., Masip J., Blandon-Gitlin I. (2017). "Can credibility criteria be assessed reliably? A meta-analysis of criteria-based content analysis", *Psychological Assessment*, 29(6), 819–834.

Henderson H. M., Andrews S. J. (2018). "Assessing the veracity of children's forensic interviews", in Otgaar H., Howe M. L. (Eds.), *Finding the truth in the courtroom: Dealing with deception, lies and memories*, New York, Oxford University Press, 103–135.

Hershkowitz I., Ahern E. C., Lamb M. E., Blasbalg U., Karni-Visel Y., Breitman M. (2017). "Changes in interviewers' use of supportive techniques during the revised protocol training", *Applied Cognitive Psychology*, 31, 340–350.

Hershkowitz I., Lamb M. E., Blasbalg U., Karni-Visel Y. (2020). "The dynamics of two-session interviews with suspected victims of abuse who are reluctant to make allegations", *Development and Psychopathology*, online publication, 1–9.

Johnson M. K., Magnussen S., Thoresen C., Lønnum K., Burrell L. V., Melinder A. (2015). "Best practice recommendations still fail to result in action: A national 10-year follow-up study of investigative interviews in CSA cases", *Applied Cognitive Psychology*, 29(5), 661–668. doi:10.1002/acp.3147

Johnson M. K., Raye C. L. (1981). "Reality monitoring", *Psychological Review*, 88, 67–85.

Lamb M. E. (2016). "Difficulties translating research on forensic interview practices to practitioners: Finding water, leading horses, but can we get them to drink?" *American Psychology*, 71, 710–718.

Lamb M. E., Brown D. A., Hershkowitz I., Orbach Y., Esplin P. W. (2018). *Tell me what happened: Questionning children about abuse* (2nd ed.), Hoboken, NJ: John Wiley & Sons Inc.

Lamb M. E., Sternberg K. J., Esplin P. W., Hershkowitz I., Orbach Y., Hovav M. (1997). "Criterion-based content analysis: A field validation study", *Child Abuse & Neglect*, 21(3), 255–264.

Lamb M. E., Sternberg K. J., Orbach Y., Hershkowitz I., Horowitz D., Esplin P. W. (2002). "The effects of intensive training and ongoing supervision on the quality of investigative interviews with alleged sex abuse victims", *Applied Developmental Science*, 6(3), 114–125.

Masip J., Spörer S. L., Garrido E., Herrero C. (2005). "The detection of deception with the reality monitoring approach: A review of the empirical evidence", *Psychology, Crime & Law*, 11, 99–122.

Mathieu F. (2012). *The compassion fatigue workbook: Creative tools for transforming compassion fatigue and vicarious traumatization*, New York, Routledge.

National Children's Alliance. (2020). *Standards for accredited chapter members*. www.nationalchildrensalliance.org/our-story/

Oberlader V. A., Naefgen C., Koppehele-Gossel J., Quinten L., Banse R., Schmidt A. F. (2016). "Validity of content-based techniques to distinguish true and fabricated statements: A meta-analysis", *Law and Human Behavior*, 40(4), 440–457.

Pezdek K., Morrow A., Blandon-Gitlin I., et al. (2004). "Detecting deception in children: Event familiarity affects criterion-based content analysis ratings", *Journal of Applied Psychology*, 89, 119–126.

Pompedda F., Antfolk J., Zappalà A., Santtila P. (2017). "A combination of outcome and process feedback enhances performance in simulations of child sexual abuse interviews using avatars", *Frontiers in Psychology*, 8, 1474–1474.

Pompedda F., Zappalà A., Santtila P. (2015). "Simulations of child sexual abuse interviews using avatars paired with feedback improves interview quality", *Psychology, Crime & Law*, 21(1), 28–52.

Poole D. A. (2016). *Interviewing children: The science of conversation in forensic contexts*, Washington, DC, American Psychological Association.

Powell M. B. (2008). "Designing effective training program for investigative interviewers of children", *Current Issues in Criminal Justice*, 20(8), 189–208.

Powell M. B., Guadagno B., Benson M. (2016). "Improving child investigative interviewer performance through computer-based learning activities", *Policing and Society: An International Journal of Research and Policy*, 26(4), 365–374.

Powell M. B., Wright R., Clark S. (2010). "Improving the competency of police officers in conducting investigative interviews with children", *Police Practice & Research: An International Journal*, 11(3), 211–226.

Raskin D. C., Esplin P. W. (1991). "Statement Validity assessment: Interview procedures and content analysis of children's statements of sexual abuse", *Behavioral Assessment*, 13, 265–291.

Rischke A. E., Roberts K. P., Price H. L. (2011). "Using spaced learning principles to translate knowledge into behavior: Evidence from investigative interviews of alleged child abuse victims", *Journal of Police and Criminal Psychology*, 26(1), 58–67.

Saywitz K. J., Snyder L. (1996). "Narrative elaboration: Test of a new procedure for interviewing children", *Journal of Consulting and Clinical Psychology*, 64(6), 1347–1357.

Sporer S. L. (1997). "The less travelled road to truth: Verbal cues in deception detection in accounts of fabricated and self-experienced events", *Applied and Preventive Psychology*, 11(5), 373–397.

Steller M., Koehnken G. (1989). "Criteria-based statement analysis", in Raskin D. C. (Ed.), *Psychological methods in criminal investigation and evidence*, New York, Springer-Verlag, 217–245.

Vrij A. (2005). "Criteria-based content analysis: A qualitative review of the first 37 studies", *Psychology, Public Policy, and Law*, 11, 3–41.

Westphaln K. K., Regoeczi W., Masotya M., Vazquez-Westphaln B., Lounsbury K., McDavid L., . . . Walsh W. (2021). "Outcomes and outputs affiliated with Children's Advocacy Centers in the United States: A scoping review", *Child Abuse & Neglect*, 111, on line 104828.

Yii S.-L. B., Powell M. B., Guadagno B. (2014). "The association between investigative inter-viewers' knowledge of question type and adherence to best-practice interviewing", *Legal and Criminological Psychology*, 19(2), 270–281.

Yuille J. C. (1988). "The systematic assessment of children's testimony", *Canadian Psychology*, 29, 247–262.

Yuille J. C. (Ed.). (1989). *Credibility assessment*, Dordrecht, The Netherlands, Kluwer.

Appendices

Appendix I

NICHD revised investigative interview: version 2021

A. Introduction

My name is [name]. Today's date is [date], and it is now [time]. I'm interviewing [child's name] at [location].
Verify that the recorder is on.
Hello, [child's name]. I am glad to meet you today. How are you?
My name is _____, and my job is to talk to children about things that have happened to them. As you can see, we have a video camera here. It will record us talking so I can remember everything you tell me.
In the introduction, gestures of goodwill are appropriate:
Are you comfortable?
Can I do anything to make you more comfortable?

B. Rapport building and narrative training

B.1 Now, [child's name], I want to get to know you better. Tell me about the things you like to do.
Wait for the child to respond.

If the child responds, express appreciation and reinforcement:
Thank you for sharing that with me. It helps me get to know you.
I'm glad I am starting to get to know more about you.
Then skip to B.3 if you think the child should go directly into narrative training from here.

If the child does not answer, gives a short answer, or gets stuck, you can say:
I know this is the first time we have met and I really want to know about you.
I am glad I can talk to you today, [child's name].
Skip to B.2 if you think more rapport building is necessary.

If the child displays nonverbal cues of avoidance or resistance (e.g., gaze aversion), address it right away:
[Child's name], let me see your eyes.

[Child's name], go ahead and sit closer to me.
[Child's name], I can see you're [crying, quiet], tell me what is happening so I can help.
[Child's name], thanks for letting me listen to you today. Please tell me about what you're going through.

B.2 I really want to know you better, [child's name]. I would like you to tell me about things you like to do at school, during recess, or after school.

Wait for an answer.
If the child continues showing avoidance or resistance:

Invite him/her to talk about a neutral topic chosen before the interview began (e.g., the child's caregiver may have been asked to report about activities the child enjoys):
I heard you like [activity, hobby]. Tell me about [activity, hobby].

Ask about distinctive items (e.g., clothing):
I can see you are wearing [a unique item, such as a soccer team T-shirt]. Tell me about [that item].

Offer the child the opportunity to draw:[1]
[Child's name], would you like to draw a picture or something [you like to do, something fun that happened]? Here are some crayons and paper for you.

B.3 Now, [child's name], tell me more about [activity the child already mentioned].
Avoid TV shows, videos, or fantasy.
Wait for an answer.

B.4 [Child's name], tell me about something fun that has happened to you [at school, at kindergarten].

B.5 Tell me about [something the child mentioned]. *Use various invitations to ask about different topics; one of those invitations should focus on internal contents: thoughts, feelings, sensations, or emotions.*

B.6 You told me about something [happy, pleasant, fun] that has happened to you. Now, tell me about something unpleasant that has happened to you [at school, at kindergarten].
Important: Do not mention the location in which the alleged abuse may have taken place.

B.7 Pleased tell me about [something the child mentioned]. *Ask various invitations to elicit richer information about a variety of topics; one invitation should focus on internal contents: thoughts, feelings, sensations, or emotions.*
If the child reveals distressing information, please explore that briefly while making supportive statements. You want to check whether the child has previously reported it. You told me about [the distressing incident]. Have you told an adult about that?
If the child says no, say: Would you like me to help you tell someone?

B.8 [Child's name], you told me about [pleasant event already described] and [unpleasant event already described], and you shared your [emotions, thoughts] with me [if s/he did]. Thanks for letting me know. It's important that you know you can talk to me about anything, both good things and bad things.

C.   Explaining and practicing ground rules

Adapt the questions according to the child's developmental level.

C.1 [Child's name], I'm interested in you, and I'll be asking you all kinds of questions today.

If I ask a question that you don't understand, just say "[interviewer's name], I don't understand." OK, [child's name]?

Pause.

C.2 If I ask a question, and you don't know the answer, just tell me, "I don't know." So, [child's name], if I ask you [e.g., "What did I have for breakfast today?"], what would you say?

Wait for an answer

If the child says, "I don't know," say: Right, you don't know, [child's name], do you?

If the child offers a guess, say:

No, [child's name], you don't know me and [e.g., "you weren't with me when I had my breakfast this morning"], so you don't know. When you don't know the answer, please don't guess. Just say that you don't know.

Pause.

But if you do know or do remember, it is very important that you tell me, OK, [child's name]?

C.3 And if I say things that are wrong, you should tell me. OK, [child's name]?

Wait for an answer.

So if I said that you are a 2-year-old girl [e.g., when interviewing a 5-year-old boy], what would you say?

If the child only denies and does not correct you, say: You're right, [child's name]. You're not a 2-year-old girl. What would be right?

Wait for an answer.

Reinforce the child if s/he gives the right answer: You are right, [child's name], you are not a 2-year-old girl. Now you know you should tell me if I make a mistake or say something that is not right.

Pause.

Correct a wrong answer: No, [child's name], you are not [wrong age]. You are [real age].

So if I say you were standing up, what would you say?

Wait for an answer.

OK.

[Child's name], now you understand that if I say something incorrect, you need to correct me and tell me what is right.

C.4 Part of my job is to talk to [children, teenagers] about things that have happened to them. I meet with lots of [children, teenagers] so that they can tell the truth about things that have happened to them. [Child's name], it is very important that you tell me the truth today about things that have happened to you. Do you promise to tell me the truth, [child's name]?

D.   Further rapport building and episodic memory training

Prior to the interview, please identify a recent, short, positive, and meaningful event in which the child actively participated. If possible, choose an event that took place at about the same time as the alleged or suspected abuse. If the alleged abuse took place during a specific day, event, or type of event, ask about a different event or type of event.

I'm glad to meet with you today, [child's name], and I would like to get to know you even better.

D.1 Main invitation
A few [days, weeks] ago was [a holiday, birthday party, other event]. Tell me everything that happened [during the event], from beginning to end, as best you can.

In case an event wasn't identified previously, ask: Did you do something special recently, like did you get to go somewhere or go to a birthday party?

If the child doesn't identify a suitable event, say: So I want you to tell me everything that happened [today/ yesterday], from the time you woke up.

D.2 Follow-up invitations:
Please repeat the first action that started the event. Then ask:
And then what happened, [child's name]?
Use this question as often as needed throughout this section until you have been given a full account of the event.
Thank you, [child's name]. You have told me many things [if s/he did]. I want to ask you some more questions about what you just told me.

D.3 Time-segmenting invitations
Try to use three time-segmenting invitations, although you may adjust the quantity and type of invitations to the child's capabilities and reactions.
[Child's name], I would like you to tell me everything about [the event]. Please tell me everything that happened from the moment [an activity the child mentioned] to the moment [a subsequent mentioned activity].

If the child has difficulty understanding delineated segments, say:
Please tell me everything that happened from the moment [an activity the child men-
tioned] began.

Thank you, [child's name], for telling me that. What you say is very clear, and that
helps me understand what you mean.

D.4 Cued invitations
*Try to use three cued invitations, but you may adjust the number depending on the
child's capabilities and reactions. Please focus on thoughts and feelings as well.*

Cued invitations can be used in one of two formats:
Tell me more about [an activity, object, thought, feeling].
Earlier, you spoke of [an activity, object, thought, feeling]. Tell me all about that.

D.5 [Child's name], thank you for telling me about [title of the event]. When we talk
today, it is very important that you tell me everything about things that have happened to you.

D.6 [Child's name], how are you feeling so far in our conversation?

---

*If, during the pre-substantive phase, the child is not cooperative and remains
reluctant, consider ending the interview now. Skip to section G in order to
end the interview, and schedule an additional interview for continued rapport
building.*

E. Substantive phase

E.1 *Transition to substantive issues*

*Important: If the child expresses explicit verbal resistance without denying the abuse
at any point, skip to section E.1.a, "support for managing overt refusals," and
deal with the resistance without using additional transitional prompts.*

Now that we know each other a little better, I want to talk about why [you are / I
am] here today.

At any stage, if the child makes an allegation, skip to section E.2.

If the child reports an irrelevant event, say: I hear what you are saying to me, [child's
name]. If you want, we can talk about that later. Right now, though, I want to
know about something else that may have happened to you.

1   I understand that something may have happened to you. Tell me everything about
that from the beginning to the end.

2   As I told you, my job is to talk to children about things that might have happened to them. It is very important that you tell me why you think [your mom/dad/grandmother brought you here today / I came to talk to you today].

3   *If the child doesn't make an allegation and looks avoidant or resistant, you may address him/her with general supportive statements which do not refer specifically to him/her, and do not mention abuse:*

---

a   [Child's name], my job is to listen to children about things that have happened to them.

b   [Child's name], I really want to know when something happens to children. That's what I am here for.

c   [Child's name], here, kids can talk about good things and bad things that have happened to them.

---

4   I've heard that you talked to [a doctor, teacher, social worker, other professional] at [time, location]. Please tell me what you talked about.

5   I [saw, heard] that you have/had [documented injuries, bruises] on your [body part]. Tell me everything about [those, that].

6   [Child's name], has anything happened to you at [location, time of alleged incident]?

If the child doesn't make an allegation and looks avoidant or resistant, you may use some of the supportive statements above (a–c) or one of the following statements, which refer specifically to the child, but still do not mention abuse.

---

d   You told me a lot of things about yourself. I feel I know you better, and you can tell me more [about things, about both good things and about bad things] that have happened to you.

e   You have told me a lot of things about yourself. Thank you for letting me know. When you talk to me today, please go on and tell me about other things that have happened to you.

f   [Child's name], if there is anything you want to tell me [I want to know/ listen, it's important for me to know/ listen].

If there is no allegation or a denial, evaluate and plan your next steps.

You may use the child's verbal and nonverbal indications of reluctance to evaluate the situation and decide whether or not to proceed. Consider ending the interview (skip to E.1.b) and planning an additional interview (appendix 2) if you believe that the child is resisting or avoiding cooperation and that an additional session of rapport building might be beneficial.

> *Proceed through the transitional prompts gradually when you suspect the following:*
>
> - *Abuse may not have occurred (because it may be important to understand why suspicions arose).*
> - *The child doesn't recognize the aim of the interview.*
> - *The child is resisting your efforts or avoiding cooperation, but there is serious concern about his/her welfare or the investigation, so delay might leave the child unsafe.*

7   [Child's name], has anybody been bothering you?

8   [Child's name], did someone do something to you that you don't think was right?

9   [Child's name], did someone [briefly summarize the allegations or suspicions without specifying the name of the alleged perpetrator or providing too many details]?

If the child doesn't make an allegation but looks avoidant or resistant and there is independent evidence arousing suspicion, you may use the above supportive statements (a–f) or one of the following:

> g   [Child's name], [I am, people] are worried about you, and I want to know if something may have happened to you.
>
> h   [Child's name], if something has happened to you and you want it to stop, you can tell me about it.
>
> i-1   [Child's name], if it is hard for you to tell, what makes it so hard?
>
> i-2   [Child's name], is there anything you are concerned about?
>
> i-3   [Child's name], what would happen if you told me?
>
> i-4   [Child's name], has someone told you not to tell?
>
> j   Sometimes children think that if something happened to them, it's their fault, but children are not responsible if things happen to them.
>
> k   It's your choice if you want to tell me, and it is my job to let you choose.

10   [Child's name], I understand [you, someone] [reported, saw] [briefly summarize allegations or suspicions without specifying the name of the alleged perpetrator or providing too much detail]. I want to find out if something may have happened to you.

E.1.a. Supportive statements to help manage overt refusals.

If the child has explicitly expressed difficulty or reluctance to disclose but hasn't denied the abuse, you may use the supportive statements above (a–k) and the following statements dealing with overt refusals to engage:

l   [Child's name], I understand you are [difficulties the child mentioned; e.g., embarrassed]. Let's start talking, and I'll try to help you with it.
m   Many children are [difficulties the child mentioned], and I try to help them.
n   I understand that you are [difficulties the child mentioned]. Tell me more about that.
o   *If the child expressed a lack of confidence:* I'm sure you can talk to me about it well.
p   *If the child said s/he was worried about something specific and the reassurance you can give is true:* Don't worry, I will [not tell the other children / make sure you are not late for the bus].
q   It's your choice whether or not to tell me, and I will accept what you decide.

E.1.b. Ending the interview without an allegation

If at any point while exploring whether abuse might have occurred you believe that the child is resistant or uncooperative and that rapport building will benefit from an additional meeting, end the interview and plan an additional one. Skip to section G if you want to end the interview.

E.2 Exploring the incidents

Throughout the entire substantive part, it is important to preserve and enhance the rapport established with the child, continue providing supportive statements, and address expressed inhibitions, distress, and conflicts.

E.2a Free recall invitations

11.a. Invitation for a first narrative about the incidents
If the child mentions a specific incident:
[Child's name], you told me that [briefly summarize the allegation the child has made].
  Tell me everything from the beginning to the end, as best you can.

If the child mentions a number of incidents:
[Child's name], you told me that [briefly summarize the allegation the child has made].
  Tell me everything about [the last/first time/at a place/a time/specific incident] from beginning to end.

If the child gives a generic description and you cannot determine the number of incidents:
[Child's name], you told me that [briefly summarize the allegation the child has made].
  Did that happen one time or more than one time?
Depending on the answer, please invite a first narrative (11.a).

If the description remains generic, please say:
[Child's name], you told me that [briefly summarize the generic description]. Tell me everything from beginning to end.

11.b. Follow-up invitations
Please repeat the child's description of the action/occurrence that started the event. Then ask:
And then what happened?
Use this question as often as needed until you have a complete description of the alleged incident.

11.c. Time-segmenting invitations
You have told me many things and helped me understand what happened. Now, [child's name], I want to ask you more questions about [incident title].
[Child's name], think back to that time [day, night] and please tell me everything that happened from the moment [an activity the child mentioned] to the moment [a subsequent activity the child mentioned].

11.d Cued invitations
Cued invitations can have two formats:

* Tell me more about [activity, object, feeling, thought].
* [Child's name], you mentioned [activity, object, feeling, thought]. Tell me more about that.

Use this question as often as needed throughout this section.
Important! Free-recall invitations should be exhausted before proceeding to directive questions.

E.2.b Directive questions
If some central details of the allegation are still missing or unclear after the exhaustive use of open-ended questions, use directive questions.

12. [Child's name], you said that/mentioned [activity, object, feeling, thought]. [How, when, where, who, what, which, how many, what did you mean]?
It is important to pair open-ended invitations with directive questions whenever possible:
Tell me more about that.

E.2.c Exploring multiple incidents
If, in reply to questions 1–10, the child mentions a single incident:

13. [Child's name], what you just told me, did that happen one time or more than one time?
If the child has said that such incidents happened more than one time, go back to question 11.a and explore additional incidents. It is often best to explore the last, first, or best remembered incident.

E.2.d Break

[Child's name], now I want to make sure I have understood everything you said and see if there's anything else I need to ask. I will take a couple of minutes to think about what you told me / go over my notes.

During the break time, review the information you have received, see if there is any missing information, and plan the rest of the interview. Be sure to formulate option-posing questions in writing and consider replacing them with open-ended or directive prompts.

E.2.e Option-posing questions – eliciting information that has not been mentioned by the child

You should ask these focused questions only if you have already tried other approaches and you realize that some forensically important information is still missing. It is very important to pair option-posing questions with open invitations ("Tell me all about that") whenever possible.

In case of multiple incidents, you should direct the child to the relevant incidents in his own words.

14. [Child's name], when you told me about [specific incident embedded in time and place], you mentioned [activity, object, feeling, thought]. Did/have/has/is/are [a detail for the child to confirm or deny]?
Example: Sarah, when you told me about being in the kitchen with Lewis, were other people there with you?

Whenever appropriate, follow with an invitation:
Tell me everything about that [activity, object, feeling, thought].

Before you move to the next incident, make sure you have obtained all the missing details about each specific incident.

F. Disclosure information

You've told me why you came to talk to me today. You've given me [lots of] information, and that really helps me to understand what happened.

If the child mentioned telling someone about the incident(s), you may say:

Now I want to understand how other people found out about [last incident].

If the child has not mentioned telling anyone, probe about a possible disclosure by saying:
Does anybody else know what happened?

Then explore the disclosure process, addressing the disclosure time, circumstances, recipients, potential discussions of the event, and reactions to disclosure by both the child and recipients. Use open-ended questions whenever possible.

G. Ending the interview

[Child's name], what are you going to do after we finish talking?
Talk to the child for a couple of minutes about a neutral topic.

Appendix I   Rapport building drawing supplement

If the child does not respond and looks distant, frightened, or disengaged during the rapport-building phase, you can use the following invitation:

[Child's name], would you like to draw something you like to do?
[Child's name], would you like to draw something fun that happened to you?

Offer the child blank paper and drawing tools and allow him/her to draw for several minutes. Sit next to the child, smile, and encourage him/her to talk while drawing.

Do not interpret the drawing. Ignore what the child has drawn and refer only to verbal information that the child mentions during or after drawing using open invitations.

If the child does not speak during or after drawing, use an open invitation:
Please tell me about the drawing you have made.
Once the child has finished drawing, offer praise:
Very nice, [child's name]. Thank you for drawing that.

Appendix 2   When you need an additional interview

An additional interview may be performed if the investigator believes that better rapport could be built in another meeting, allowing better insight into whether or not abuse has occurred (the transitional phase). Two or three interviews may sometimes be necessary.
   General guidelines for additional interviews:

1   *Collect personal information about the child from an external source in advance to help inform your rapport-building efforts (e.g., interests, positive events the child experienced, other relevant information)*
2   *Before the later interview, review the information obtained in the previous interview to refresh your memory about your conversation with the child*
3   *Depending on the child and the circumstances, the ground rules can be mentioned briefly at the beginning instead of being practiced in full*
4   *During the rapport-building phase, probe about friends, interests, significant events, or topics discussed in the previous meeting(s)*
5   *At any stage, if the child makes an allegation or mentions substantive information, proceed to the substantive part of the interview*

6   *Generally, an additional interview should follow the NICHD Protocol's structure, adjusted as needed to refer to the former interview in order to build on any rapport established earlier. For example:*

- As you may remember, [my name is . . .].
- Today, again, [I have a video camera with me].
- Last time we met you told me that [e.g., you like playing soccer].

7   *Progression and decision making about the interview flow and about the transitional phase should be guided by the criteria listed in the Protocol.*

Note

1 Note that this activity is designed to promote the child's comfort, not to learn about the abuse. Do not attempt to interpret what the child draws or ask the child to draw anything related to the suspicions that led to the interview (see appendix 1: Rapport building drawing supplement).

Appendix 2

Transcript of Sophie Jackson's interview

I   My name is Roxane Perreault. Today's date is February the 16th, 2021, and it's now four o'clock. I'm interviewing Sophie Jackson at Nicolet . . . (7 seconds) . . . Hi, Sophie. You can follow me. You can have a seat just over there. OK?

V   . . . (4 seconds.) Here?

I   Yeah. (5 seconds.) Oh, you, you can put it (face mask against coronavirus) on the table. Right.

V   . . . (Puts her face mask on the table)

I   So, hi, Sophie, I'm glad to meet with you today. How are you?

V   Hmm . . . Good.

I   Good?

V   (Positive nod.)

I   My name is Roxane and part of my job is to talk to children about things that happened to them, and you can see we have a video camera here. It will record us talking so I can remember everything you tell me. Are you comfortable?

V   Hmm . . . I think, just, hmm, a little bit shy, I think.

I   OK, Sophie, I understand. Tell me more about being a little bit shy.

V   It is because I feel shy.

I   Is there anything I can do to make you feel better?

V   I don't know.

I   You don't know? If something comes up that I can do to help just let me know. OK, Sophie?

V   (Positive nod.)

I   OK. Hmm, now, Sophie, I want to get to know you better. Tell me about things you like to do.

V   Hmm, the things I like to do?

I   Yeah.

V   Hmm, well, I like hmm, I like to craft, I like to make crafts, and I also like to talk about animals.

I   OK.

V   That, I really like. And I like to play outside with my friends.

I   OK. Thank you for sharing that with me, Sophie. Tell me more about making crafts.

V   Well, at school, we make crafts, and we have, like, special workshops, and we make different things at each workshop, and there's one with special scissors, the other one is, I think I remember it's painting.

I   Hum-hum.

V   And the last one is to build, build things.

I   OK. Tell me more about talking about animals.

V   Oh, I really like talking about animals. In my room I have like a map, a big, big map with all the countries, like of all over the world and I take my, it's like little animals.

I   Hum-hum.

V   And I have to pin them on the right country that they live in. And I really like to play that game.

I   Thank you, Sophie, for letting me know things you like to do.

V   And I even want, I even, I even have one right here (points her sweater).

I   Oh, I see that.

V   Yeah.

I   I really want to know you better, Sophie. I would like you to tell me about something fun that has happened to you at home.

V   Hmm, something fun . . . when my grandma, when she came at my house, and she taught me, she taught me about how to make fudge. I really liked that, that was really fun (positive nod).

I   Tell me more about "really fun."

V   It was really fun because we laughed a lot, I made her laugh a lot when we were making the fudge.

I   And tell me more about making her laugh, Sophie.

V   Hmm, I was making her laugh because you know when you do, when, when you do the fudge?

I   Hum-hum.

V   You have to take a spoon and mix it like that.

I   Hum-hum.

V   And when it's a little bit hard, you have to stop. Right away.

I   (Positive nod.)

V   But I didn't want it to stop, and my grandma, she was making jokes, and I made her laugh and I liked that.

I   Sophie, you told me about something fun that happened at home.

V   (Positive nod.)

I   Now tell me about something unpleasant that happened to you at home.

V   Unpleasant, like not fun?

I   Yeah.

V   Hmm . . . when my cousin, when he came at my house the other day, we went to play outside, and he pushed me from, from the top of the snow hill and I really didn't like that. I was really mad at him.

I   Hum. Tell me more about being really mad.

V   I was really mad because he always, he always does that. He always pushes, and he always steals my things, and this one time, there, this one time, he pushed me from the top of the hill. I was really on the top, and that's really high, and he pushed me from the top, and when I fell, I thought I was running out of air.

I   Hmmm. Tell me more about thinking you were running out of air?

V   It's like I couldn't breathe because my face, I fell down like that.

I   (Positive nod.)

V   Right in the snow. And I thought I couldn't breathe anymore.

I   Sophie, you told me about something fun that happened to you, making fudge with your grandma, and you told me something not fun when your cousin pushed you from the top of the hill.

V   Yeah, that's Henry. That's Henry.

I   Yeah.

V   Henry pushed me.

I   Henry. OK. Thank you for letting me know and for sharing your emotions with me. And it's important that you know that you can tell me here about anything, both good things and bad things.

V   (Positive nod.)

I   And I'm interested in you, Sophie, and I'll be asking you all kinds of questions today. If I ask a question that you don't understand, just tell me, "I don't understand." OK, Sophie?

V   (Positive nod.)

I   If I ask a question and you don't know the answer, just say, "I don't know." So, Sophie, if I ask you, "What did I have for breakfast today?" what would you say?

V   . . . Hmm, today?

I   Hum-hum.

V   Today, maybe you had cereals for breakfast?

I   No, Sophie. Well, you don't know because you weren't with me this morning, right? So when you don't know, don't guess the answer. Just say, "I don't know." OK?

V   (Positive nod.)

I   So if I ask you, "What's my son's name?" what would you say?

V   Hmm . . . I don't know because I don't, I've never seen him.

I   That's right, Sophie. If you don't know the answer or don't remember, it's very important that you tell me. OK?

V   (Positive nod.)

I   And if I say things that are wrong, you should tell me, OK, Sophie?

V   Yes.

I   So if I say, Sophie, that you are a 2-year-old girl, what would you say?

V   I would say, euh, that's not right, that's wrong.

I   . . . And what could you say to correct me?

V   I would say, "I'm a 10-year-old girl and not a 2-year-old."

I   That's right, exactly, Sophie! . . . So you know you should tell me if I'm making a mistake or if I say something that's not right.

V   (Positive nod.)

I   Part of my job is to talk to children about things that have happened to them. I meet with lots of children so they can tell me the truth about what happened to them. So, Sophie, it's important that you tell me the truth today about things that happened to you. OK?

V   Yes.

I   I'm glad to meet with you today, Sophie, and I would like to get to know you even better. I heard you had a pajama party lately.

V   Oh yes, that was fun!

I   I hear that you found it fun.

V   Yeah.

I   So think about the pajama party and tell me everything that happened from the beginning to the end as best you can.

V   Everything?

I   Yeah.

V   At the beginning, we, I arrived at my friend's house, at Kelly's house and . . . Hmm . . . We putted on our pajamas.

I   Hum-hum.

V   . . . And after that, we played games.

I   (Positive nod.) And then, Sophie, what happened?

V   And then we watched a movie, that's for sure because that's what we do at pajama parties.

I   Hum-hum.

V   . . . And we went to bed, and it was really late, like at midnight maybe.

I   And then, what happened?

V   I don't know because I was sleeping.

I   OK, that's right. You don't know. So it's important that you tell me when you don't know things . . . So thanks, Sophie, for sharing all this with me. Now I want to ask you some more questions about what you just told me.

V   (Positive nod.)

I   Sophie, tell me everything that happened from the moment that you arrived at Kelly's house until you put on your pajamas.

V   I arrived at Kelly's house with my mom and then my mom, she left.

I   OK.

V   And she told me not to forget to brush my teeth, but I didn't, I forgot. And then I went, and we had to wait for the other friends to arrive too before to put on our pajamas.

I   OK.

V   And I got really excited when, when I was waiting for the other friends.

I   Now, Sophie, tell me everything that happened from the moment you put on your pajamas until you played games.

V   Hmm . . . We put on our pajamas, everybody, all the friends and then we went to Kelly's room, and we, we chose a game, and she has a lot of games in her room.

Really a lot, a lot of toys. I don't have that many toys in my room, my mom doesn't want to. And then we chose a game, and we sat down, and we played the game.

I   Thank you, Sophie, for letting me know. And tell everything that happened from the moment you put your pajamas on until the moment you chose the game.

V   Hmm, we put on our pajamas and then the pajamas, we had to, not the pajamas, the clothes, we had to make our clothes in our bags, put our clothes in our bags. Not to lose them in her room. And Kelly, she showed us everything in her room, her bed, and then we chose the game.

I   OK . . . Sophie, you told me you were very excited when waiting for the other friends.

V   (Positive nod.)

I   Tell me more about that.

V   I was really excited because I was with Kelly, and we were looking at the window, and every time there was a car in the yard or on the street, we were trying to guess if it was a friend and which friend it was and sometimes we had it right, but sometimes it was not a friend but just someone passing on the street.

I   Hum. Tell me more about choosing a game.

V   Well, she had like this in a closet. It is so big. It goes, like, up to there.

I   OK.

V   And it's full of games, like she has a lot, a lot, a lot of games and I chose the memory game.

I   OK . . . Sophie, you told me she has a funny dog.

V   Yes.

I   Tell me more about that the dog being "funny."

V   It's because, it's, it's a small dog, but it's a long dog too, and he has really short legs, and when he runs, his legs are like that (moves her arms quickly). It goes really fast, and then we laugh, and we call him the "running hot dog."

I   Sophie, tell me more about cleaning the toys.

V   Well, we had to clean the room, well, not clean, but we had to put the toys away.

I   Hum-hum.

V   Because there were so many toys on the floor, we couldn't even walk! That's what her mom told us.

I   OK . . . So, Sophie, thank you for telling me about your pajama party. When we talk today, it is very important that you tell me everything about things that have really happened to you. Sophie, how do you feel right now?

V   Hmm, I feel . . . Not shy.

I   Not shy. Tell me more about feeling not shy.

V   Not too shy, I feel OK to talk with you.

I   OK. Now that we know each other a little better, I want to talk about why you are here today.

V   . . . Hmm . . . I don't remember really well.

I   You don't remember really well.

V   No.

I   Tell me more about that.

V   Hmm . . . I just have to take my hairband and fix my hair. I thought I lost my hairband.

I   Hum.

V   . . . (Ties her hair for 7 seconds.)

I   Hum. I understand that something may have happened to you. Tell me everything about that.

V   Hmm . . . It's just that I, I can't tell you because . . . my mom got mad.

I   Mom got mad.

V   Yes.

I   Tell me more about that.

V   She, but . . . She went yelling at the phone because maybe I did something wrong.

I   Hum-hum.

V   She was yelling at the phone, and she got in a fight with the principal, and she said I will never, ever go back to school again, not at this school, and I thought I was grounded.

I   OK, I can see what you say, that your mom was mad. You know sometimes kids think that they're responsible for things that happened to them, but it's not their fault. I meet with lots of children so I can help them tell me about things that happened to them, and I'm really interested in what happened to you, and I really want to understand what has happened.

V   Hum.

I   Sophie, as I told you, my job is to talk to children about things that may have happened to them. It's really important that you tell me why you think your mom brought you here today.

V   . . . Hmm, it's because I, I told my mom that the substitute teacher, he, he showed me his penis.

I   Hum . . . (4 seconds.) Sophie, you say your substitute teacher showed you his penis.

V   Yes.

I   Tell me everything that happened from the beginning to the end.

V   Hmm . . . At the beginning, at, euh, the bell rang.

I   Hum-hum.

V   Because it was playtime.

I   OK.

V   And then he asked me to stay to help him.

I   . . . (5 seconds.) Hum-hum.

V   And then I stayed . . . And he, he showed me his penis.

I   . . . (6 seconds.) I, I was just writing down so I can make sure I don't forget what, euh, you tell me.

V   (Positive nod.)

I   So he showed you his penis, and then what happened?

V   And then it became really gross.

I   Oh yeah? . . . And then?

V   And then I left, I went with my friends outside.

I   . . . (4 seconds.) And then?

V   And then I played, I played with them, but there was not so much time left for the playtime.

I   (Positive nod.) OK . . . (5 seconds.) So thanks, Sophie, for sharing that with me. Now, I want to ask you more questions about what happened when your substitute teacher showed you his penis. Sophie, think really hard and tell me everything that happened from the moment the bell rang until the moment he asked you to stay.

V   The bell rang for the playtime, and then everybody stood up and went to the door. And I was the last one to go to the door, and then he came to see me, and he told, he asked me if I could help him.

I   (Positive nod.)

V   If I could help him to prepare the, like the class.

I   OK. And tell me, Sophie, everything that happened from the moment he asked you to stay to help until the moment you stayed.

V   Hmm . . . He, he closed the door and . . . Then he showed me some cardboard . . . that we had to put on the walls.

I   Hum-hum.

V   And he asked me if, he asked me, "Sophie, have you ever seen a penis?" And I said "no" because I don't have brothers, and I've never changed a diaper because I'm too young. And then he did like that, *zip* (mimics unzipping her pants). And he showed me his penis.

I   Sophie, can you say in words what you just showed me?

V   He has unzipped his pant.

I   . . . (5 seconds.) OK. I see what you say. Now Sophie, tell me everything that happened from the moment he showed you his penis until it became really gross.

V   He showed me his penis like all of it, like, like, he unzipped and lowered her pants. And then he asked me if I wanted to touch it and I said "no" because . . . I don't want to touch, I didn't want to touch it.

I   Hum-hum.

V   And then he, he took my hand, and he made me touch it.

I   (Positive nod.) I see.

V   But I, I didn't feel like doing it.

I   Tell me more that you didn't feel like doing it.

V   I don't want to touch his penis, it is him who put my hand on it, not me.

I   (Positive nod.) . . . (10 seconds.) Sophie, tell me everything that happened from the moment it became really gross until you left to join your friends.

V   Hmm, it became really gross and . . . And then he, and then . . . Then he whipped it and m-me too because the sticky stuff, it was on my hand. And then I got, I went to get dressed. I putted on my coat, and I went to see my friends outside to play with them.

I   OK . . . (4 seconds.) Sophie, tell me more about the sticky stuff.

V   It was a little bit like a glue, not sticky as a glue but a little sticky.

I   Sophie, you told me he closed the door. Tell me more about that.

V   Hmm, he closed the door when everybody went out. And then we went to his desk to prepare the game, the cardboard for the game.

I   (Positive nod.) OK.

V   But I didn't help him with the game.

I   (Positive nod.) . . . (5 seconds.) Sophie, tell me more about him when he asked if you have even seen a penis.

V   Hmm . . . He was at his desk and with the cardboard, and then he asked me if I have ever seen a penis before.

I   (Positive nod.) . . . You say you went to his desk. Tell me about you and him at his desk.

V   He was at his desk, and I was beside him.

I   Tell me more about "beside him."

V   Hmm, like, this is the desk, and he's there and I'm here.

I   OK.

V   Beside the desk.

I   OK. Sophie, you're speaking really clearly, and that really helps me understand. Thanks. Tell me everything that happened from the moment you said "no" until he showed you his penis.

V   . . . Hmm . . . He, he asked me, "Have you, ever seen?" I said "no" and then he did like that with his pants, *zip* (mimics unzipping her pants).

I   OK.

V   And he took his penis out, out of his pants. And he was even naked from there to there (shows from her waist to her feet).

I   From there to there.

V   From there to there. All of his pants down.

I   (Positive nod.) OK . . . Tell me more about his penis.

V   Hmm he show – he showed me, and then he, he made me touch it.

I   OK . . . Sophie, tell me more about making you touch it.

V   He asked me if I wanted to touch it, and I said "no."

I   Hum-hum.

V   And then he took my hand, and he putted it on, on his penis with, with his hands.

I   OK. Tell me everything that happened from the moment he put your hand on it until it wasn't on it anymore.

V   Hmm, he putted his, my hand on it and then he started moving it.

I   (Positive nod.) OK.

V   From the bottom to the top. And, and then it, it became gross. Like it peed on me.

I   OK.

V   Like a weird pee. And, and then he took his hands off and mine, mine too.

I   (Positive nod.) OK. Sophie, you've given me a lot of information, and that really helps. Hmm . . . Tell me more about his penis when he was moving from the bottom to the top.

V   Hmm, he, it was not like when he putted his pants down. It was not facing down, it was like facing up.

I   Hum-hum. Tell me more about it facing up.

V   I was, he was, he was holding his penis and his penis, he was, it was like holding himself, by itself. I don't really know how to say it but . . .

I   OK.

V   (Shakes her head no)

I   OK. That's OK. Sophie, tell me more about his penis when you say "it peed."

V   Yeah, it, it, that was gross. That was when it was gross. It, it was like a weird pee in, in my hand and . . . And then we, we wiped it off.

I   . . . OK. Tell me more about the weird pee.

V   It was sticky. It's that, the, it, it was like a stick – a sticky stuff on my hand.

I   OK. You said he wiped it. Tell me more about that.

V   Well, there's, there's Kleenex.

I   Hum-hum.

V   Because my real teacher, she always keeps a box of Kleenex on her desk and then he took, like many Kleenex and he, he wiped it off.

I   OK. And tell me more about the Kleenex afterward.

V   Hmm, he opened the bottom drawer, and he made a ball and he putted it in the drawer and he closed it.

I   OK. Sophie, you said you wiped it too.

V   Yes.

I   Tell me more about that.

V   When I went to get dressed, there was still sticky stuff in my hand, and then I did like that on my coat, on the bottom of my coat (mimics rubbing her hand on her pants).

I   OK. Tell me more about your coat.

V   Hmm, well, it's my winter coat.

I   OK.

V   And . . . I got it last Christmas.

I   OK. And tell me more about your winter coat today.

V   Hmm, I, it's not here but maybe there because I put it to, to come here.

I   OK.

V   Because every time it's winter, I put it on.

I   OK.

V   Every time I go out.

I   . . . Hmm tell me more about your substitute teacher.
V   His name is Michael Thomas.

I   (Positive nod.)
V   And he's really, really tall.

I   Hum.
V   And really old. But he's not my real teacher.

I   (Positive nod.)
V   My real teacher is Miss Eloïse.

I   OK.
V   But sometimes he comes, maybe she's sick or maybe she has an appointment, I don't know.

I   (Positive nod.) OK. Sophie, when did that happen?
V   It happened yesterday.

I   Yesterday. Tell me more about that, yesterday.
V   Yesterday because it was the first day of school after the weekend.

I   OK . . . (4 seconds.) Tell me more about Michael when he started moving, bottom to the top.
V   Hmm, he had trouble breathing, and he was holding my hand really hard.

I   Tell me more about trouble breathing.
V   Hmm, like he was running really fast.

I   OK.
V   Like he couldn't concentrate because he had trouble breathing.

I   Hum. And, Sophie, tell me more about him when he had the weird pee.
V   Hmm, he make, he made a strange sound like he was a little bit choking like he had trouble breathing more.

I   OK . . . (4 seconds.) Thank you, Sophie. I'm just going to look at my notes, make sure I don't need to ask you for more information.
V   (Positive nod.)

I   I'll just take a few seconds to do this . . . (9 seconds.) Sophie, tell me more about hmm Michael when you left to your friends.
V   Hmm . . . I left really fast because I was happy that he let me go.

I   Tell me more of you were happy that he let you go.
V   Because I didn't like to touch his penis, it was gross.

I   OK.
V   And I think he stayed in the class sitting on his, in, on his chair.

I   OK.
V   On the desk.

I   OK. Sophie what you told me that happened with your substitute teacher, did that happen one time or more than one time?
V   . . . Oh, it happened just at one time.

I   Just one time.
V   Yes.

I   Now, Sophie, I'm going to make sure I have understood everything you said and see if there is anything else I need to ask you. So I'll just take a couple of minutes to go and talk with my colleague. OK?
V   (Positive nod.)

I   It won't be long.
V   I wait here?

I   Yeah. You can wait here, and I'll be back.
V   OK.

Break

I   Sophie, thanks for waiting for me. And you really told me a lot of information, and that really helps me to understand what happened.
V   (Positive nod.)

I   Hmm . . . You told me that Michael asked you to touch his penis. Did he tell you anything else when it happened?
V   Hmm . . . No. He just asked me if I've seen a penis before and to touch it.

I   OK. Hmm. You told me you left to join your friends and that the playtime was soon over. Then what happened?
V   I went outside to play with my friends.

I   OK.
V   But I had less time because I came, I came out after because I was in the classroom.

I   Hum-hum.
V   And then we played, we played under the swings.

I   OK.
V   Like the swings, there are like swings in the yard, and that's where we play.

I   OK. And then what happened?
V   Hmm, the bell rang again to tell us to come back in, and then we went back in the class.

I   OK. And then?
V   And then I went, I went to sit at my desk and I took my coat off of course, and it was like normal. We finished the class, it was a normal class.

I   OK. Sophie, so you told me why you came to talk to me today. You've given me lots of information, and that really helps me understand what happened.
V   (Positive nod.)

I   Hmm. You told me that your mom knows what happened?
V   Yes, I've told my mom.

I   Does anyone else know about what's happened?
V   I also told Miss Eloïse.

I   OK. You told Miss Eloïse.

I   Hmm, anybody else besides your teacher and your mom?
V   I told you now.

I   That's right. OK. . . . You've told me lots of things today, so I really want to thank you. Sophie, what are you going to do after we finish talking?

V   My mom, she bought me coloring books and new pencils, and I can't wait to go and try them.

I   Thank you. We can go to see your mom now.

V   OK.

End of the interview

Appendix 3

Notes taken during the substantive part of the interview with Sophie

Child's name: Sophie   **Title of substantive event:** Substitute teacher showed penis

Bell rang playtime

    last one

Ask me to stay

    closed door
    showed me cardboard   at his desk   I beside
    ever seen penis?
    said no
    unzipped pants

Showed me his penis

    lowered pants   took his penis out
    say no
    took my hand made touch it   moved bottom – top
    didn't feel doing it

Became really gross   peed   weird pee   sticky

    wiped it
    stick stuff on my hand
    putted my coat

Went with friends played outside

Michael Thomas
Yesterday

    ___ Action/gesture
    ___ Position
    ___ DNA, pieces of evidence
    ___ Perpetrator identification
    ___ Time of incident
    After break
    ___ Words/threats from the suspect
    ___ Presence of witnesses

Appendix 4

Notes taken during the episodic memory practice with Sophie

Child's name: Sophie   **Special event:** Pajama party

Arrived at Kelly's house

Mom left
had waited other friends
<u>excited</u>

Put on pajamas

Kelly's room
<u>chose game</u>
set down

Played games

<u>clean toys</u>
went downstairs
special beds

Watch movies

2 bags popcorn
Played <u>funny</u> dog

Went to bed

Sleeping

Appendix 5
Supportive non-suggestive techniques and utterances

Supportive non-suggestive techniques and utterances[1]

A   Addressing the child in a personal way

Address the child in a personal way using the name s/he prefers. Avoid using terms of endearment (e.g., "sweety").

B   Establishing rapport

- *Welcoming the child*

  I am glad to meet you today / to get to know you / to get to talk.
  It's nice to meet you, my name is _____.1

- *Expressing personal interest in the child*

  I really want to get to know you / about things that happened to you.
  Today is the first time we've met, and it is important for me to know you better.

- *Making small gestures of goodwill*

  Are you warm enough?
  Let me show you the toilets.
  Here is a glass of water for you.
  Do you want to look at the video camera?
  Do you need a short break?

C   Reinforcement

- *Reinforcement during the interview*

  You are telling me clearly / in detail, and that's important.
  You're really helping me understand/ know you.
  You corrected me, and that's really important.
  I understand what you're saying.
  Avoid "grading" ("You're explaining things better than you did before") or associating reinforcement with specific content ("You told me that you ran away, which was good").

- *Expressing thanks and appreciation*

   I want to thank you for your help.
   I really appreciate that you are talking to me.
   I appreciate that you are trying to remember and tell me.
   Thank you for sharing with me.

- *Emphasizing the child's agency*

   It's up to you whether you talk to me or not. I will respect your choice.

D   Using rapport

- *Mentioning and building on trust*

   You told me a lot about yourself, and I feel I know you better.
   Now that we know each other better, you can share with me what happened.

- *Expression of care or worry*

   I'm here for you.
   I care about you.
   You are important to me.
   People are / I am worried that something may have happened to you. [You
      can specify the cause for concern (e.g., "The teacher said you were crying
      this morning").]

- *Presenting the interviewer as someone to disclose to*

   If something happened, I'm here to listen to you.
   You can trust me and tell me if something happened.
   It's OK to share secrets / problems with me.
   I talk to many kids who tell me about things that have happened to them.
   It's my job to listen to the children if they have problems.

E   Emotional support

- *Generalized comments about the child's perceived difficulties*

   Many children find it difficult to talk/feel ashamed at the beginning but then
   find it easier.
   Many children have secrets.

- *Empathy*

   I understand it is difficult for you to tell me.
   I know it's been a long interview.

- *Checking for the child's feeling*

   How are you feeling so far/now that we are done?
   How did you feel before we began/during our conversation?

- *Exploring emotions*

   Tell me more about your fears.
   Tell me what you're afraid of.

Tell me why you're crying.
Tell me why you don't want to tell me.
You said you cannot tell. Tell me more about that.

- *Open questioning about expressing feelings or thoughts*

  You said you were sad/disgusted / wanted to run away. Tell me more about that.

- *Echoing emotions*

  You said you were sad / you were crying.

- *Acknowledging/accepting/recognizing emotions*

  You say that it was very painful.
  I understand what you said.
  I see what you are saying.

- *Reassurance*

  Don't worry, I won't tell other children.
  You won't be late for the bus.
  Nobody is going to arrest you.
  Sometimes it's possible to help families/people who have been hurt.
  Sometimes it helps children when they speak and don't have to keep a secret.

- *Removing responsibility from the child*

  If something happens/someone hurt you, it is not your fault.
  You are not responsible for that. [Or in a generalized way: "When things happen to children, it's not their fault."]
  Children are not responsible when they are hurt.

- *Exploring unexpressed emotions and conflicts*

  If there is something you are worried about, please tell me.

F   Encouragement

- *Emphasizing the child is the source of knowledge*

  I'm asking you these questions because I was not there.

- *Legitimating expression*

  You can talk about bad things and good things.
  In this office, you can say everything.
  It is OK to tell me about this kind of thing / to say these words/bad words.
  Many children tell me what happened to them.

- *Expression of confidence/ optimism*

  I think you can explain it well.

- *Offering help*

  I want to make it easier for you. What would help you to talk?
  Would it make it easier if you wrote it down?
  You can start talking, and I'll help you by asking questions.
  I am here to help.

- *Encouraging nonverbal communication*

  Could you please turn toward me?
  Come on, look at me.
  I'd like to see your eyes!

- *Encouraging disclosure*

  It is really important that you tell me if something has happened to you.

G Counter-supportive

1   Suggestive support – Presuming content, selective reinforcement, mentioning abuse prematurely during the transitional phase.
2   Confrontation – Interviewer challenges the information given by the child by suggesting it's implausible, mentioning competing external information, or pointing to inconsistencies in the child's statements.
3   Causing discomfort – Interrupting or criticizing the child's statements or behavior, being coercive, using the wrong name for the child.
4   Ignoring or not recognizing:

  A Clarification requests or inquiries by the child.
  B Non-substantive descriptions of physical injury.
  C Resistance, omissions, denials, or references to internal content (including conflict, emotions [positive or negative], or physiological responses associated with emotions or pain).

5   Unfounded support – unrealistic promises or reassurance.

Note

1   Adapted from table 9.1 in Lamb, M. E., Brown, D. A., Hershkowitz, I., Orbach, Y., & Esplin, P. W. (2018). *Tell me what happened: Questioning children about abuse* (2nd ed.). Hoboken, NJ: John Wiley & Sons Inc.

Appendix 6
Information to prepare the interview

Information to prepare the interview

Name and first name of the child:
Age:
Child's developmental problems:
Medications:

Last name and first name of the father:
Last name and first name of the mother:
First name and age of the siblings from the oldest to the youngest:
If the child lives in shared custody:
First name of the stepfather or stepmother:
First name and age of the siblings from the oldest to the youngest:

Name of the domestic animal living with the child:
Child's daytime environment and identification:
Kindergarten: School:
Name of the educator(s) or teachers responsible for the child:
Child's leisure activities:
Recent and pleasant event for the child to describe:
Child's usual words to describe private body parts:

Alleged facts:

Name of alleged perpetrator:
His/her relationship to the child:
Did the child make the disclosure himself/herself: to whom:
Context of the disclosure:

Child's verbalization:

Appendix 7

NICHD-R protocol adherence coding scheme

NICHD-R protocol adherence coding scheme

Name, first name of the investigator: _____
Date of the interview: _____
Gender and age of the child: _____
Allegation: _____

Table A7.1 NICHD-R protocol adherence coding scheme

A- Introduction	Done	Comment
Presentation of investigators and recording		
B- Relationship building and narrative training		
Things you like to do (1 to 2 things)		
Pleasant activity (target emotion/thought/sensation)		
Unpleasant activity (target emotion/thought/sensation)		
Section carried out using invitations		
C- Explanation/practice of ground rules		
Don't understand		
Don't know		
Correct interviewer		
Tell the truth		
D- Episodic memory training		
Special event/Yesterday/Today		
Get the story from beginning to the end		
At least 3 time-segmenting invitations (Tell me everything that happened from. . . . until. . . .)		
Segments are about short periods, well worded, refer to specific periods of time		
At least 3 cued invitations (Tell me more about . . .)		
Invitations include an action verb when appropriate		
Choice of clues is relevant (action, location, emotion, thought, object)		
Duration of the practice is appropriate to the child's cooperativeness and level of development		

Table A7.2

E – Substantive phase		
Follow the chronological order of the transition questions		
Deal with reluctance to reassure the child if needed		
Obtain accounts from beginning to end		
Follows a logical/sequential structure of the questions (time segmentation, cued and directives)		
Did this happen once or more than once?		
If more than once: Tell me about [last, first, other time] something happened.		
Before the break, the majority of questions were invitations		
Obtains forensically relevant information using open-ended questions – action, DNA, position, who, where, when		
Segments are short, well-worded, refer to specific periods of time		
Invitations included action verbs when appropriate		
Uses good cues in sufficient numbers		
Pause and consult notes/colleague		
Uses invitation following a directive question or offering a choice when appropriate (pairing principle)		
F – Disclosure information		
Does anyone else know what happened?		
G – Ending the interview		
What are you going to do after		
General attitudes		
Centered on the well-being of the child while respecting the Protocol (good listening, available, supportive and warm throughout the interview)		
Captures the child's attention (first name, facilitator, look, interest)		
Adapts to the age and capacities of the child (short sentence, vocabulary, let's think)		
Organized note-taking, but not at the expense of contact and support of the child		

Total number of interventions in the substantive part: _____
Proportion of invitation utterances: _____
Proportion of directive questions: _____
Proportion of option posing or suggestive questions: _____
Other remark or comments:

Index

Page numbers in **bold** indicate a table on the corresponding page.

47–49; factors related to children 32–37; factors related to the questions and to the context of the interview 37–45; other suggestive strategies used by the interviewer 45–46; pre- and post-event information 46–47; suggestibility, definition 31–32
suggestive interviews, effects of 48–49
suggestive questions/prompts 21, 35, 37, 38, 39–41, 46–47, 61, 91, 117, 123, 135, 137, 140, 146, 166
summaries 38, 123
supervision 145–147
supportive interventions 45, 112, 129, 135–136, 164, 165
Sweden, Standard NICHD Protocol (SP) in 137
syntax 66–67

teenagers see adolescents/teenagers
temperament of children 69–70
temporal attributes 70–74
testimony in court 142–143, 147–152; see also NICHD Protocol, empirical studies on
time segmentation 125–126, 139

time-segmenting invitations 38, 119–120, 124, 140
training: episodic memory 108–111; initial 164–165; narrative 104–106; pre-interview training sessions 91; protocol 145–147; in the use of the NICHD Protocol 128–129
transitional statements 111–115
trisomy 21 75, 76
trust and rapport with the child 85

uncertainty, expression of 151
Undeutsch's hypothesis 162
United States, quality of testimony in 149
United States, Standard NICHD Protocol (SP) in 137

verbal cues 91
verbal intelligence quotient 59, 144
verbal intelligence skills 76
verbal memory 26
verbal reluctance 161
vicarious trauma syndrome 161
vocabulary 63–66

Wechsler intelligence test 76
Williams syndrome 75
working memory 33